BORISKA'S PROPHECY
A Story of Survival and Renewal
N E V E R   T O L D   B E F O R E *

---

*F*or 45 years Alice Adler surpressed
the horrors of her wartime experiences

"I stayed up all night to finish it...a real 'page turner'
beautifully written with tremendous emotional impact."
-David Sutcliffe,
Host/Producer, Storer Cable Channel 4

*"As a contemporary witness and equally affected, I was
deeply moved by this suspenseful book...told by a survivor
who is alive today and who speaks for the six million who
can't."*
-Richard Essex,
Former U.S. Consul, Innsbruck, Austria

"This book meets its responsibility to speak for the millions that couldn't, can't or won't, with power and grace."
-Paul P. Ohran, Kingsley's Book Emporium

*"...read it until 3AM this morning...it is powerful, sus-
penseful and GOOD...very compelling...an incredible story!"*
Sherril T. Estes, Author and Lecturer

"*B*ORISKA'S PROPHECY is a compelling and inspiring account of Ms. Adler's experience of the German invasion of Hungary during World War II and of her survival in spite of many atrocities. As a survivor of the terrible period "BORISKA'S PROPHECY is a compelling and inspiring account of Ms. Adler's experience of the German invasion of Hungary during World War II and of her survival in spite of many atrocities. As a survivor of the terrible period chronicled in this book, I appreciate its importance and found this very moving."

Tom Lantos (D-California)
United States Congress, Foreign Affairs Committee

"*Ms. Adler's thinking is of the Positive variety. And it has helped her survive experiences that bring shudders to those who hear her story.*"

Think & Grow Rich

"*Such a life! Such a life! Such a life! Captivating survival of the human spirit! ...Unforgettable!*"

Robert B. Levitt,
Charlie's News of Sunny Sarasota, Florida

I'm from Kuwait an
there's a big resemblance in both
situations. I wish I could deal
with Kuwait the way you handled
the holocaust. Thank you for talking
to us. Love,

Dear Mrs. Adler,
    Thank-you for coming in and telling the
class about your escape from the Concentration
Camp. I liked it when you told us how you
escaped. I thought it was neat when you were
talking about America being free. Since, I
was born here I don't notice it being very free.
I am glad you came to Brookside again. Sincerely,
                                        Brandon Holda

            you taught us more
            about life and history
            in that hour than
            we could even learn
            in a school book.
Dear Mrs. Adler,   Love, Robin Blackmer
    Thanks for coming to talk to us. I thought
it was a really neat experience. I told my
mom and she didn't even know some
things about it. She also thought it was
amazing. Lots of people don't have opportunity
to hear something like that. My parents
said that they never had somebody to talk
to them. I had a very good time listening
to you.
                              Wesley Holda

Boriska's Prophecy

A True Story of Survival and Renewal

NEVER TOLD BEFORE

Alice Dunn Adler

AN AUTOBIOGRAPHY

ACROPOLIS BOOKS LTD.

ACROPOLIS BOOKS, LTD.
In Metropolitan Washington since 1958
Editorial Office :
11741 Bowman Green Drive
Reston, VA 22090   (703-709-0006)

Printed in the United States of America

Attention: Schools and Corporations
ACROPOLIS books are available at quantity discounts with bulk purchase for educational, business, or sales promotional use.
For information, please write to:
SPECIAL SALES DEPARTMENT,
ACROPOLIS BOOKS, LTD.,
11741 Bowman Green Drive
Reston, VA 22090   (703-709-0006)

**Library of Congress
Cataloging-in-Publication Data**

Adler, Alice Dunn, 1913- Boriska's prophⁱ
a story of survival and renewal : an
autobiography / by Alice Dunn Adler.

ISBN 0-87491-962-2 : $19.95
1. Adler, Alice Dunn, 1913- .
2. Holocaust, Jewish (1939-1945)- -Hunⁱ
gary—Budapest—Personal narratives.
3. Holocaust survivors- -New York (N.Y.)
Biography.
4. Jews—Hungary—Budapest—Biograpⁱ
5. Jews—New York (N.Y.)—Biography.
6. Budapest (Hungary)- -Biography.
7. New York (N.Y.)—Biography.
I Title.
DS135.H93A352 1991
940.53'18'0943912 - dc20   90-2⁵
                                   Cⁱ

CONTENTS

I The Prophecy
• 1 •

II The Family Conference
• 5 •

III A Painful Parting
• 11 •

IV The Parisian Episode
• 17 •

V An Alternate Plan
• 23 •

VI The Volcano's Edge
• 30 •

VII The Encounter
• 38 •

VIII The New Regime
• 46 •

IX Murder
• 51 •

X Fear Comes to Stay
• 57 •

XI Baptism of Terror
• 61 •

XII Purgatory in Poland
• 73 •

XIII *Aufseherin* Margit
• 87 •

XIV The Factory at Tchopau
• 103 •

XV The Ouija Board's Message
• 112 •

XVI The Departure
• 123 •

XVII The Train to a *Vernichtungs Lager*
(Extermination Camp)
• 127 •

XVIII A Walk in the Woods
• 133 •

XIX An Unexpected Encounter
• 137 •

XX Among Friends
• 140 •

XXI The Americans
• 154 •

XXII The Patient
• 170 •

XXIII Welcome to France
• 182 •

XXIV A New Paris
• 194 •

XXV Cousin Erna
• 201 •

XXVI George
•221 •

XXVII Into Mother's Arms
• 236 •

XXVIII New York's Many Faces
• 244 •

XXIX Unexpected Discovery
• 250 •

XXX No A.135.00
• 261 •

XXXI Alice Dunn
• 277 •

XXXII Reborn Confidence
• 296 •

XXXIII Time-Tested Love Affair
• 314 •

XXXIV Growing Suspicion
• 318 •

XXXV The Revelation
• 327 •

XXXVI The Funeral
• 337 •

XXXVII A Prophecy Fulfilled
• 343 •

Epilogue
• 349 •

ACKNOWLEDGMENTS

*M*y heartfelt appreciation goes to Martha Friedmann, who early in my creative writing class gave me courage and confidence to put my experiences into a biography. My dear friend Carolyn Tuttle's participation was invaluable in the creation of the book.

Doug Lasswell led me by the hand through the labyrinth and complexity of thousands of thoughts, recollections, pain, and agony. His keen eye sifted through the shattered pieces, helping to create the real story. My gratitude to Juliet J. Mickey for her professionalism, giving strength to my work. Sincere gratitude to Erhard Dabringhaus, Alphons J. Hackl, Kathleen P. Hughes, Sandy Trupp, and Lynne Shaner. Without their participation, Boriska's Prophecy would never have seen the light.

My great friends, Doris Goldman, Lila Hillman and Janet Post helped bring *Boriska* into real life. Dear, wonderful cousins, Betty and Fred Egre, with their faultless, scholarly knowledge of the language, edited my chapters with the greatest sensitivity. Theirs was a labor of love. So many countless people just suddenly appeared in my life, carrying out some important role in furthering the birth of this book.

They know who they are and I love them all!

PROLOGUE

*T*his is my story, the story of a survivor. I have always felt that I was spared by a special fate to share my experiences . . . to speak out loud and clear and be heard. In so doing, I speak not only for myself, but for the millions of others who have been silenced forever. It is those victims of oppression, and the inarticulate, who cry out through me.

I am proud not only to be a survivor, but also to have become a productive, functioning member of society . . . a Jew, who against all odds, was destined to live. This privilege, shared by so few of my generation, created a debt for which this book serves as a partial settlement. It is my very own unique contribution to society, a story of the indomitable human spirit, of courage, and a supreme confidence in fate, none of which was ever lost throughout my ordeal.

This, then, is my story. I hope that you, the reader, will find it as compelling in its reading as it was for me to live and, subsequently, to perpetuate through the written word.

Alice Dunn Adler

FOREWORD

by Abraham H. Foxman*

*J*FIRMLY BELIEVE THAT ALL SURVIVORS of the Holocaust have unique stories to tell and that ways should be found to tell them. It is only in this manner that future generations will be able to grasp what Holocaust victims endured — those who survived as well as those who did not.

One can readily understand why those who survived the cruelty of the murderous death camps put the abusive horrors of their experiences behind them as they attempted to rebuild their lives. Undoubtedly telling the story means reliving the nightmare with all of its pain, suffering and humiliation.

We should be grateful therefore that Alice Dunn Adler has had the moral courage to endure once again that horrible — yet ultimately triumphant — period of her life in order "to speak out loud and clear" for herself as well as the other millions of Holocaust victims. And she does speak eloquently. What emerges from her autobiographical narrative is the clear voice of an intelligent, attractive and creative Hungarian Jewish woman, who survived the degradation of Auschwitz and other concentration camps to seize her one slim opportunity for escape and then overcame the trauma and rebuilt her life in her adopted country, the United States. To read this autobiography is to accompany her from the heights in her pleasant, fulfilling career as a couturier to the social aristocracy of Budapest to the depths of victimization by the Nazis and then the slow climb upwards toward rehabilitation.

Her ability to overcome the trauma is contrasted with the experience of a friend who, on the verge of a successful career as a concert pianist, commits suicide because of her Holocaust memories.

It is a heart-wrenching revelation of the continuing power of this atrocity even years after liberation. On the other hand, there are accounts which lift one's heart of the French partisans, righteous gentiles, who helped to save Mrs. Alder's life.

Boriska's Prophecy is a story that had to be told. I am glad Mrs. Adler did so.

Mr. Foxman is national director of the Anti-Defamation League

Alice's Odyssey
and
Route of Escape

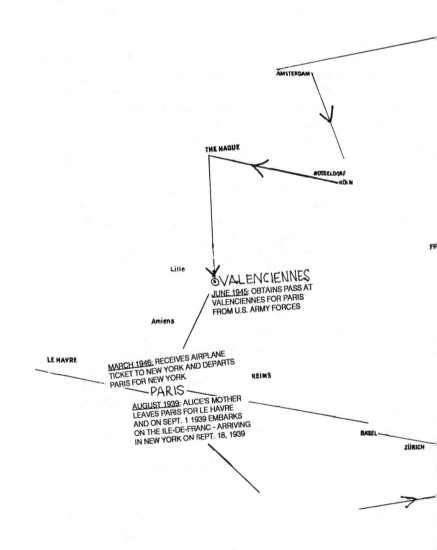

AMSTERDAM

THE HAGUE

DÜSSELDORF
KÖLN

Lille

⊙VALENCIENNES
JUNE 1945: OBTAINS PASS AT
VALENCIENNES FOR PARIS
FROM U.S. ARMY FORCES

Amiens

LE HAVRE

MARCH 1946: RECEIVES AIRPLANE
TICKET TO NEW YORK AND DEPARTS
PARIS FOR NEW YORK.

—PARIS—

REIMS

AUGUST 1939: ALICE'S MOTHER
LEAVES PARIS FOR LE HAVRE
AND ON SEPT. 1 1939 EMBARKS
ON THE ILE-DE-FRANC - ARRIVING
IN NEW YORK ON SEPT. 18, 1939

BASEL
ZÜRICH

Boriska's Prophecy

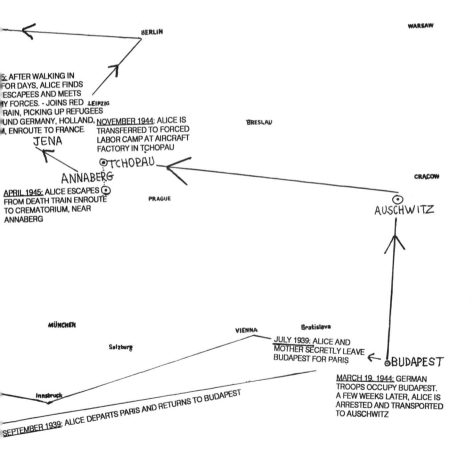

BERLIN

WARSAW

...URS

...: AFTER WALKING IN
...FOR DAYS, ALICE FINDS
...ESCAPEES AND MEETS
...Y FORCES. - JOINS RED   LEIPZIG
...RAIN, PICKING UP REFUGEES
...UND GERMANY, HOLLAND,   NOVEMBER 1944: ALICE IS   BRESLAU
...M, ENROUTE TO FRANCE.   TRANSFERRED TO FORCED
                            LABOR CAMP AT AIRCRAFT
JENA   FACTORY IN TCHOPAU

⊙TCHOPAU
ANNABERG   CRACOW

APRIL 1945: ALICE ESCAPES ⊙   PRAGUE   ⊙
FROM DEATH TRAIN ENROUTE   AUSCHWITZ
TO CREMATORIUM, NEAR
ANNABERG

MÜNCHEN

                                        VIENNA   Bratislava
        Salzburg   JULY 1939: ALICE AND
                                                   MOTHER SECRETLY LEAVE
                                                   BUDAPEST FOR PARIS   ← ⊙BUDAPEST

Innsbruck   MARCH 19, 1944: GERMAN
                                                   TROOPS OCCUPY BUDAPEST.
                                                   A FEW WEEKS LATER, ALICE IS
SEPTEMBER 1939: ALICE DEPARTS PARIS AND RETURNS TO BUDAPEST   ARRESTED AND TRANSPORTED
                                                   TO AUSCHWITZ

To Jerry, with enormous gratitude
for helping me put my shattered
life back together. Your support
and faith made my prodigious task
a proud one.

Chapter I

THE PROPHECY

Driven by youthful eagerness and curiosity, I swiftly climbed the steep cobblestone street up a hill in Old Budapest. It was a bright, chilly day, and I could see each breath as it escaped from my lungs. "What an unusually cool start of autumn," I mused. "Good for my fall line!"

Somewhere in the distant city below me a church carillon was chiming a familiar tune. For a moment I couldn't place it. "Why of course, it's Frère Jacques," I reassured myself. I had sung it many times as a child in my French class. That was only one of the three foreign languages I had studied. I was quite proud that I was now fluent in all of them. I couldn't have known it then, but my childhood diligence would pay big dividends in the days to come. The year was 1938.

I hurriedly glanced at my watch as my mind returned to the present. Was it ten o'clock yet? I did not want to be late for this appointment. It had taken nearly a year for Silbiger Boriska to grant me this meeting. Would this finally be the day when I would have my destiny revealed? Mme. Boriska's reputation was well known to me. She was recognized as Hungary's foremost clairvoyant. Her clientele was known to include many European heads of state and royalty, as well as the cream of Hungary's business and society set. Now I was about to benefit from her renowned psychic powers and insight. I desperately wanted her guidance at this crucial stage of my life, when my new-found professional success was being clouded over by the growing unrest in the world around me.

Finally, after what seemed like hours, I arrived at the street corner my friends had described. There, down the narrow alley at the dead end, I recognized the century-old building with the faded brick facade. "So, this is it," I thought to myself. My heart beat faster as I approached the narrow doorway and pulled on the ancient bell chain.

An obscure figure opened the door and motioned me to enter. I looked down at my watch nervously. It was precisely ten o'clock.

"I'm Alice Dunn. I have . . ." As I started to explain, the figure turned away without waiting for me to finish, and motioned me to follow her down a long, narrow hallway. To the left, an open doorway beckoned us. To my surprise I found myself in a very dark oblong room. The only light came from a half-burnt-down candle which was melting into its wrought iron holder. It stood on a massive desk located in the center of the room. Behind the desk and chair hung heavy, dark curtains which were drawn to shut out all of the bright morning sunlight. I had the distinct feeling of having entered a cave. Even the air in the room had a musty, cavelike odor, and I could feel myself gasping for breath.

"If that candle burns down," I mused worriedly, "we could be in total darkness." To reassure myself, I turned around to locate the door behind me, which was now closed.

Suddenly a door to the right opened and a diminutive but imposing figure in a black gown strode majestically into the room. As she sat down in the chair behind the desk, I could not help thinking to myself that this was surely the ugliest woman I had ever seen. Her face was a collage of leftovers, parts which in no way fit together. Her dark, deep set eyes peered out from under the bushiest of eyebrows. But, oh, how those eyes burned from that hideous face. I felt them now, fixed on me, piercing my skull, as though examining every thought in my brain. These were eyes that could truly see beyond . . . .

I was beginning to get frightened as I remembered what my friends had told me. Silbiger Boriska had a reputation for dismissing those clients whose future foretold disaster. What if she now decided to dismiss me? I was standing there, mesmerized, partly in awe, partly in fear. I could feel beads of perspiration forming on my forehead and I could hear my heart pounding. Then I noticed her hand, with the long, slender fingers of a noblewoman, pointing in the direction of a chair in front of her desk. I sat down with a feeling of relief. I was not to be dismissed after all.

"Let me have your ring," a hoarse voice whispered. Her ice-cold fingers touched mine as I placed the birthstone, a recent gift from my mother, into her hand. She closed her eyes and, seemingly oblivious to my presence now, began turning the ring over and over in the palm of her hand. I sat there, quite shaken and apprehensive, awaiting her verdict. It was turning out to be a very different experience from the one I had so eagerly anticipated just a short while ago.

Suddenly, I could see her lips begin to move, but I could not hear her words. She was murmuring to herself. Then, I began to hear her hoarse whisper. Her words came haltingly and I leaned forward in my chair so I would not miss a single pronouncement.

"I sense turmoil . . . much turmoil . . . yes, even chaos. Also the death of a loved one . . . a creature very close to you . . . a cruel death . . .

"I see your family . . . your two brothers . . . safe in a place far away. . .your beloved mother . . . on a voyage over water . . . on her way to join them . . .

"I perceive much hardship for you . . . a test of endurance . . . yes, even an attempt to end it all . . .

"I see crowds . . . naked bodies . . . confined together in many different places . . . horrible places . . . I see you there among them . . . clawing your way out . . . alone . . .

"I see you receiving help . . . guidance . . . from strange and unexpected sources . . . directing you to your liberation . . .

"I sense your survival . . . by means of difficult choices and decisions . . . your survival in both body and spirit . . .

"There is also a man . . . kind, wise, witty . . . yes, even handsome . . . A man who will play a significant role in your life . . .

"And, finally, I see you sharing your experiences with others

. . . young and old . . . even young children . . . ."

She stopped speaking. Her eyelids fluttered open. She shuddered, shaking her head as in disbelief. She looked straight at me. "Go now," she ordered. "You have much to do, many things to arrange. Get started quickly! And, above all, remember to rely on your intuition and inner strength to get you through your travails."

As she finished speaking, she rose from her chair and walked toward me, her right hand extended. I thought she meant to touch me or shake my hand. Instead, she dropped the ring into the palm of my hand and, without another word, disappeared through the door from which she had entered.

Chapter II

THE FAMILY CONFERENCE

My brief encounter with Silbiger Boriska had left me totally shaken. It had been one of the most unsettling experiences of my life. I had found myself completely unprepared to face the revelations I had come for. I left the room in a daze and was out the front door before realizing that I had forgotten to leave the expected gratuity. Reluctantly, I pulled the bell chain once more and apologetically handed the envelope to her assistant.

As I began to walk back up the alley to the corner, completely wrapped in thought, I almost bumped into a young couple walking happily, hand-in-hand, evidently on their way to Boriska's place. The man was wearing the uniform of a lieutenant in the German army, a swastika armband adorning his sleeve. His companion, I assumed her to be his girlfriend, wore a simple skirt and sweater, similar to those worn by most of Hungary's younger working class of that day.

"I'll bet they didn't have to wait a year for their appointment," I mused. "Even Silbiger Boriska's clientele seems to be on the decline!"

The sight of German soldiers on the streets of Budapest was not unusual. Since March, when Hitler's forces had annexed Austria by means of the *Anschluss*, the Nazi presence in Hungary had increased daily. But so far, we had been spared the hurt and shame of being overrun. Our government had cleverly prevented this fate by declaring Hungary an ally of the Nazi regime, and the strategy seemed to be working. Germans came over to Budapest as tourists, shopping and enjoying the many theaters and movies.

My mother, my brothers, and I, however, began to fear the worst. We had heard unsettling accounts from friends and members of our family living in Austria. Many of them who were born there, or had lived there since childhood, had been forced to flee or face imprisonment, or worse. Couldn't it happen here as well? It was a question begging for a solution, one that we would have to face sooner or later. And Boriska's stern admonition made a hasty decision seem even more imperative. The time was indeed ripe for a family conference. Accordingly, I decided to broach the subject at the dinner table that evening.

I arrived home a little later than usual, and found my mother and brothers already seated and eating. The Friday evening candles burned brightly in the ornate silver candelabras that had been in our family for generations.

"Where have you been?" asked Laszlo, my older brother, in a rather stern voice. "You know Mother likes to serve dinner as soon as she has blessed the candles at sundown. Is it too much to ask you to be on time one night a week?"

I was in no mood to be distracted by getting involved in an argument with Laszlo. We loved each other very much, but he had become somewhat overbearing after my father's death some eight years earlier. I felt he was taking his role as head of the household a little too seriously.

"I'm sorry to be late, Mother," I said, ignoring my brother's remarks. "Please continue eating, everyone. I'll fetch my own dinner from the kitchen."

When I had seated myself at the dining room table, I began to relate the day's events as I picked at the food on my plate. "You know I saw Silbiger Boriska this morning," I began.

"What did she have to say?" asked my younger brother, Erno, with noticeable excitement in his voice.

I could see them all stop eating now, their curiosity about my encounter with Mme. Boriska stronger than their appetites. Even Laszlo was staring at me from his position at the head of the long table, waiting for my report, his admonishment forgotten for the moment.

"Well, I must tell you that it was a very frightening experience. Her vision of my future is not all bright, but I won't go into that now. She mentioned all of you. I have no idea how she knew."

"What did she have to say about us?" Erno wanted to know.

I was glad that Erno was focusing on the subject I wanted to discuss with them. There was no need to relate the horrible things Boriska had foretold about me.

"She said you and Laszlo were both going to be safe in places far away from the turmoil, as she put it. And Mother was going on a great voyage over water to join you."

"What about you, Alice?" Mother wanted to know. "Were you on that voyage with me? Were you going to be safe also?"

"She didn't say, and I didn't have the opportunity to ask her. She disappeared from the room before I had a chance to question her. I had a million questions to ask, but I was so stunned I could hardly speak until I was out the door. It was quite an experience, I assure you."

Their curiosity had been fully aroused by now. I could see that. But I wanted to discuss only one topic tonight. There would be time for the rest another day.

"I think we should give serious consideration to leaving Budapest now, before the Nazis do to us what they did to Austria. Mme. Boriska was very direct in her caution to make all our arrangements as quickly as we could. I think she's correct about that."

Mother's reaction was predictably negative. "I can't leave Budapest, now or ever. You children go ahead with your plans. Do what you think is best for you, but please don't include me in them. I have too much tied up here: my life, my memories, my friends, my reputation, my business. It's all here in Budapest. I'm too old to start a new life in a new place. Please, go ahead without me. Besides, they won't harm an old lady. I'll give them whatever they want, so they should leave me in peace."

Mother was beginning to sob. My heart went out to her. I got up and put my arms around her shoulders, hugging her from behind.

"Mother, dear, I know how hard it must be for you to even

think of leaving all this behind. But you really cannot stay. You must be brave. We, your children, love you very much. We'll help you get started again, wherever we end up. And remember this, we'll all be together as a family. Isn't that what counts most?"

She was crying openly now. Huge sobs shook her entire body. I kissed and hugged her, wiping her tears with my handkerchief. My brothers remained in their chairs, looking on uncomfortably, saying nothing.

After a few minutes Mother stopped crying. She patted my hand, took out her own handkerchief, and blew her nose. "I know you are right, Alice. Please forgive my emotional outburst. I couldn't help it, really. There's so much here that is part of me that I can't face leaving it behind. But you're entirely right. We must choose to look ahead, not behind us. What do you propose? How do you think we should proceed?"

I was so proud of my mother. She was about to make the most difficult decision of her life, and here she was, apologizing for her emotions. It was going much better than I had anticipated. We were more than halfway there, already.

"What about you, Laszlo, Erno?" I asked, turning to my brothers, who had yet to say anything. "Are you in agreement with what I've told Mother?"

It was Laszlo who spoke first, with noticeable hesitancy. "Of course, you're quite right, Alice. All of us must leave Budapest as soon as possible. It's no longer safe here for any of us. The Nazis have no regard for age, or anything else. They're totally ruthless." He hesitated momentarily, then continued speaking in a low voice. "As for me, I haven't mentioned anything about my own plans to you yet, since I didn't want to upset you needlessly. But I just received an answer from the firm in Argentina to which I applied for a designer's position some time ago. Their letter arrived in the mail just this past Monday. They want me as soon as I can arrange for a passport, visa, and work permit. I judge to have all of that in my possession in a couple of months. I plan to book passage to Argentina sometime next spring."

We were stunned. Mother looked at her son as though she were seeing him for the first time.

"Are you telling me, Laszlo, that you were going to leave

without letting us know ahead of time? What kind of son are you, anyway? How could you be so self-centered?"

Laszlo was on the defensive for the first time I could remember since my father's death. "Of course, I was going to tell you, Mother. Erno and I were discussing this very thing only today. I just didn't know how to broach the subject with you. You know how emotional you tend to get."

"And perhaps you would deny me my emotions at a time like this? I'm truly surprised at you, Laszlo, and disappointed too. Is there anything else that someone hasn't told me? Now is the time. I'm totally unemotional." She turned to look at Erno. "Erno, you've been rather quiet throughout all this. Do you have something to tell me?"

"Yes, Mother," Erno answered sheepishly. "I, too, have made plans to leave Budapest. I've applied to the New York World's Fair Committee for a permit as an exhibitor. I am planning to display a new kind of fur, a mouton lamb, there. I'm still waiting for the permit to arrive, but I won't be leaving until some time in early spring, anyway. I thought I would have lots of time to discuss this with you and Alice."

I could see Mother was totally unprepared for this new revelation, but, somehow, it served to strengthen her resolve. "All right, Alice. Go ahead with your plans for us. I can see that if we want to keep this family together, we'd better move swiftly. Incidentally, Laszlo, are you planning to remain in Argentina?"

"No, Mother. As soon as I have some money saved, I plan to apply for a resident visa to the United States consulate there. With Argentine citizenship, I should be able to obtain a U.S. visa much more quickly. I originally hoped to go to America directly, but I was told that I would have to wait several years because of the immigration quota. This way, I'll be working and waiting in safety, and I also won't be too far from you. Alice, you and Mother are planning to go to America, aren't you?" he added, turning toward me.

"Of course, you know that has been my dream since childhood. I've always had a love affair with America. I love their movies, their language, the people who come from there, and the freedom they have. Also, it'll be the safest place to be in case of war. And, of course, Erno will be there ahead of us now. He'll make the necessary arrangements for our arrival. By then, perhaps, he'll have the contacts to make our visitor's visas permanent. In any case, I doubt that they would deport us back to Hungary, to the Nazis."

"Do you want me to help you with any of the arrangements for your departure?" Laszlo asked, thoughtfully.

"No, I've already spoken to Mr. Gilbert at the U.S. Steamship Lines office on the Vaczi-utca. That's why I was late for dinner tonight. He said he would be happy to obtain the necessary papers for us, like passports, visas, etc. When he knew they were on the way, he was going to book passage for us on one of the ships leaving for America. I guess having only two people to worry about should make things a lot easier. He's waiting to hear from me on Monday."

Mother stood up, straightened her dress, and began to collect the dishes from the table. "Well, no one can say that you children wait for your old mother to make the plans for this family. I'm totally dumbfounded by what you told me tonight. But I'm also proud. And I'm sure that your father, God bless him, if he were alive today, would be proud of you as well. You all have brains and initiative and, I hope, good sense. I'll go along with your plans. There's nothing I could say or do that would change your minds, anyway, not that I would want to. May God, in HIS infinite wisdom, bless your plans with success and may He see fit to bring us together as a family in the New World."

"Amen!" we all agreed.

Mother took the dishes into the kitchen. We could hear her heave a great sigh, then her voice called out to us, "Anyone for dessert?"

I followed her into the kitchen and kissed her on the cheek. She was a brave lady, there was no doubt of that in my mind. What I didn't know was whether I would succeed in pulling off my part of the plan. Only time would tell.

Chapter III

A PAINFUL PARTING

I mobilized our extensive connections to advance our departure with the greatest of secrecy. We both realized that we were running the risk of being arrested, and having our businesses and bank accounts forfeited by the Hungarian authorities, if our plan to leave Budapest permanently was discovered.

Finally, after months of waiting, I received the phone call I had so eagerly anticipated. It was from Mr. Gilbert, director of U.S. Steamship Lines, whose Hungarian wife, Mitzi, had become both a client and friend of mine over the years.

"Alice, your papers arrived in the mail today. I therefore took the liberty of booking you and your mother on the *Bremen*, the next ship scheduled to leave for the United States that has not been fully booked. Its national registry is German, but I'm assuming you won't have too great an objection about that. It's known to be a fast, clean ship with an excellent reputation for service and courtesy. Its departure is scheduled for August 29 from Le Havre, France. That gives you almost two weeks to make your personal and business preparations. If that's O.K. with you, you may pick up the papers from my office anytime this week. I'll be in after 10 A.M. daily."

You can imagine my excitement upon hearing this news. While I was not entirely thrilled about traveling on a German ship, especially under the present circumstances, just the thought of going to America took my breath away. That night, I flung open the door to our apartment, and greeted Mother with the great news. "Guess what, Mother!" I exclaimed, as soon as the door had closed behind me. "We're leaving for New York on the 29th. Our ship sails from Le Havre, which makes it even better. We'll tell everyone that we're attending the usual end-of-summer fashion shows in Paris, as we always have. It's a perfect cover, and no one will be suspicious of our leaving together."

Mother, understandably, failed to join me in my enthusiasm over our forthcoming trip. But neither did she show any signs of changing her mind. Since last September, we had both done everything in our power to prepare ourselves, both mentally and physically, for the inevitable shock of leaving behind a beautiful past replete with financial success, outstanding private and business reputations, and the splendid life we had forged for ourselves over the years in one of Europe's great cities. It had been a little easier for me than Mother, as I still had my youth and energy to rely on and, in addition, a great desire to experience the "American way of life" as it had been pictured for me in movies and magazines.

My brothers, meanwhile, had already departed Budapest some months earlier, in accordance with their own plans, so it remained only for Mother and me to prepare the last minute details before leaving. On the surface, everything proceeded normally in our fifty-year-old fashion business, run by Mother, as well as in my own boutique next door. I had every reason to be immensely proud of my specialty shop's first-class reputation throughout Hungary, one that was bolstered by the rave reviews it had received recently in the Budapest press. But that was all in the past, now. We were careful to avoid discussing the details of our departure near employees to avoid arousing their suspicion. Our actual plans were shared only with our most trusted friends, and then only when absolutely necessary.

Thus, after the usual goodbyes a few days later, Mother and I were finally standing in the doorway of our precious home, taking one last look at all the possessions that represented so many meaningful connections to our happy past, but none to our uncertain future. As I looked at the dining room table, I remembered the many wonderful meals presided over by my father. And the grand piano in the drawing room, a giant Bosendorfer, regal in design and always perfectly tuned, which produced the most magical sounds under the expert coaxing of my brother, Erno, who was such a truly talented musician. Would I ever hear that marvelous music again? I was beginning to get very sentimental when I noticed Mother had tears in her eyes. I quickly realized that all our plans were about to fall prey to a nostalgia trip, so I turned to her, and with all the assurance I could muster at that moment, gave her a hug and said, "Don't worry, Mother, we'll have all this and more when we get to America. I promise you!"

A small, whining noise suddenly brought me back to the present. It was Peggy, my seven-year-old cocker spaniel. She had been acting very moody of late, as if sensing that something out of the ordinary was about to take place. Ever since Mother and I had begun packing our bags, Peggy had refused to come out from under my bed while we were around. Now she stood in the living room, tail between her legs, looking at us with suspicious eyes.

"My goodness!" I exclaimed, happily changing the topic. "I had almost forgotten about Peggy. I haven't seen her for a day. I think she knows that we're about to leave her with Mr. Skenyi. I don't think she likes him very much."

"Oh, but he's such a nice man," interjected Mother. "And I think he likes Peggy, too. We're lucky to have him to take care of her while we're away. Incidentally, did you remember to ask Mitzi if she would take Peggy home with her?"

"Of course, Mother. Do you think I could forget? She'll be happy to keep Peggy for us until we write her. I gave her a note to show Mr. Skenyi when she comes to pick Peggy up in a few weeks. That way, everything will seem normal on the surface. Look, I'll bring Peggy down to Mr. Skenyi now while you go to hail a taxi for us. There should be plenty of them at the corner today, it being a Saturday. You can ask the driver to come upstairs and help us with those heavy bags."

I picked Peggy off the floor, took her in my arms, and kissed her on the neck. "Come, Peggy. We'll go visit that nice Mr. Skenyi, our superintendent. You like him, don't you? Remember the nice collar he bought you the last time you stayed with him?"

Peggy didn't answer, but she squirmed in my arms. She didn't seem too eager to visit with him. Perhaps she knew something we didn't.

When I handed Peggy over to Mr. Skenyi, I told him that we would be back to pick her up in two or three weeks, depending on what we found in Paris. I couldn't know then how accurate my projection would be. He shrugged his shoulders, took Peggy from me, and closed the door to his apartment. I could hear Peggy barking and growling. She didn't sound very happy.

Just then, the taxi driver arrived to pick up our luggage. "God, these sure are heavy! What have you packed in them, anyway? Gold? I'll have to make two trips. You ladies go wait in the taxi for me."

My heart almost stopped beating. His reference to the bags' contents had come closer to the truth than he had jokingly guessed. Actually, the four suitcases we had packed for our trip contained not only our everyday personal necessities and clothes, but also as much of our personal wealth, in the form of jewelry, as we could take along without arousing the suspicion of the French and Hungarian customs agents. But we anticipated few problems on that score, since, as successful professionals on a business trip, we would be expected to carry quite a bit of jewelry with us. Or, at least, so we hoped.

We arrived at the train station in plenty of time. As we had anticipated, our customs check was fairly routine, and soon we were seated in our private compartment as the train pulled out of the station. Presently, we were moving swiftly along, passing the all-too-familiar countryside that we had viewed on so many other trips to Paris. But something was different now. At every border crossing we could see soldiers and military equipment being moved into place. The apprehension of an impending breakout of hostilities surrounded us everywhere. We congratulated ourselves on having made our move in the nick of time.

As our train pulled into the station in Paris, some forty-eight hours later, we were warmly greeted by Mlle. Thomas, who had been our local business representative in Paris for many years. After helping us to obtain customs clearance for our luggage, she drove us to our hotel. There, over French confectioneries and coffee, we confided our plans to her. I noticed her unusually somber expression as Mother finished outlining the details.

"I'm most unhappy to inform you," she began, "that we too are fearful of an outbreak of war in our homeland. Although our famed Maginot Line is considered by our government as an invulnerable defense against the *Boche*, many here believe that our country's very existence is threatened by the aggressive Nazi war machine. You will soon notice the extraordinary measures we've had to take in recent days. Our government has ordered total mobilization and mandatory conscription for all males. Those too old to serve in the military are being used as air raid wardens. We now have air raid drills daily, and the city lights are dimmed at night all the time. We no longer deserve our famed reputation as Europe's famed City of Lights. And now, as of this week, food rationing has been instituted. We can only guess what will come next. But even more important to you, I read in the French press only yesterday that all ships of German registry anchored in French ports are canceling their scheduled trips to leave for Germany. It is, therefore, most unlikely that your ship, the *Bremen*, will ever sail to America. I urge you to consider exchanging your tickets for the *Île-de-France*. She is leaving for America in a few days. I know because my cousin is leaving on it."

Mother and I were totally stunned by the news. This was something we had not expected, not prepared for. Yet, we were hardly about to cancel our plans and return to Budapest. In fact, our resolve to leave the Continent and sail to America, a land that would hardly be touched by any war, became even firmer.

Yet, we were not prepared for Mlle. Thomas' report the next day at breakfast. She had been able to obtain only one berth on the *Île-de-France*. It seemed that many other Europeans with means, like ourselves, had flocked to their tourist agents to request passage to America in unprecedented numbers. Thus, it became clear that only one of us would be able to set sail at this time. The remaining one would be left to her own devices to escape at a later date, if at all. I tried hard not to remember Mme. Boriska's recent prophecy. But, I knew full well, in my heart, who would be the one leaving by ship to America. It was a very disquieting thought.

I tried very hard for several days to persuade Mother to leave on the *Île* without me, reassuring her that I would follow her on the very next ship for which I could book passage.

"Absolutely not! I won't hear of it!" Mother protested, indignant. "What kind of mother would leave her daughter behind at a time like this? What if war broke out before you were able to leave? No, we must stay together, no matter what, and that is my final decision."

But I did not take her no for a final answer. For the following two days, I pleaded, cajoled, and even threatened Mother in attempting to change her mind. I even told her that I would leave at night while she was asleep and return to Budapest by myself.

Finally, with the help of Mlle. Thomas, she began to weaken. We explained to her that it would be much easier to obtain a single ticket than passage for two on the next ship leaving.

With time running out on the *Île-de-France*'s scheduled departure, Mother finally relented, and on the morning of September 1, 1939, we accompanied her to Le Havre, where the ship was docked. It was a terribly tearful departure, needless to say. How do you bid farewell to a mother you loved so dearly, a mother you might never see again? Naturally, I had not confided my fears to her, realistic fears about my own survival. But we all put up a good front, and as the ship departed from the dock, I waved to that familiar figure on the deck until the *Île* disappeared over the horizon. It was then, and only then, that I gave way to my own emotions and collapsed into Mlle. Thomas's arms.

Chapter IV

THE PARISIAN EPISODE

The part of Silbiger Boriska's prophecy dealing with Mother was turning out to be right on target; there was no arguing with that. I had good reason to hope that certain other elements would prove somewhat less accurate.

Thus, with heavy hearts, albeit with a feeling of accomplishment, Mlle. Thomas and I decided to return to Paris. There was little else we could hope to accomplish in Le Havre. In a sincere effort to lessen my feeling of deprivation and loneliness, she graciously offered her home to me for the remainder of my stay.

We spent countless evenings in front of her fireplace talking about the world situation and our relationship when, unexpectedly, Mlle. Thomas said, "You know, Alice, I have represented your firm now for quite some time in business transactions, but I've never had a chance to know about you personally. Please tell me about your childhood, your background, what your interests are, something about the fascinating city you live in."

"It will be my pleasure," I replied. "Reflecting on the past will certainly help me temporarily forget the present."

In 1906, my parents, both designers, founded the *atelier* of ladies' high fashion. It occupied the first floor of what had been an old hotel that had housed the overflow of guests invited to see

Emperor Ferencz Jozsef. After his reign, it was converted to commercial use. The marble ballroom on the main floor had become an exclusive movie theater and the second floor served as our eight-room apartment.

It was there that I was born and raised.

The gray marble columns in the lobby which rose a dozen feet to the glass dome, were perfect for playing hide-and-seek with my friends. I grew up amid the bronze plaques on the walls, commemorating the Emperor's visits to the building. Sometimes I was allowed to operate the elevator at the end of the hall, a giant bird cage of interlaced wrought iron and bronze, glossed with sparkling cut glass.

I had also grown up with the caress of silk, the best of styles and fashion, music, good books, and a serious study of languages. When I was six, I scribbled a dress design on paper and begged my mother to have it made in our *atelier*.

"What color would you like your dress?" she wanted to know.

Just as I was encouraged to make my own choices, I was also trained to be meticulous. Even as a child I always wore gloves in public.

Though beautiful things and rich tradition were among my greatest fascinations, I came to have an entirely different obsession. My mother consented, after I finished homework, to my visiting matinee performances of the cinema downstairs--The Corso Mozi. It showed movies of Chaplin, Tom Mix, Clara Bow (my all-time favorite), Marion Davies, Harold Lloyd, and Milton Sills.

"Mother," I would shout when I got home, "when I grow up I want to live in America. I love everything I see in the movies. The people are so different from us."

Though the flame had varying degrees of brightness, I carried the torch for America through my early school years and kept it alive. My formal education of four years of elementary school at *Deak-Teri-Elemi* was followed by eight years of gymnasium at *Erzsebet-Kiralyne*. Instead of attending college, I enrolled in an academy of art and design led by Hungary's respected fine arts teacher, Jashik Almos, who also became famous for designing the country's currency. Away from school, I was taught the reality of business. The aspects of my training melded to become one and I came to learn that beautiful fabric is at the center of creating and it is what inspires the creation. I learned that less is more, and came to believe the simplicity of lines, quality of materials, and workmanship count the most. This belief became the trademark of my boutique and in the ever-changing climate of styles, it came to be appreciated by the most discriminating clientele of Budapest. The city was called the Paris of the East and its fashion-conscious women were faithful customers from the start.

"Mlle. Thomas, it is getting late and I have kept you up too long with my story. I hope I didn't bore you. I only trust that returning to Budapest will not be too dramatic, certainly so much going on in the world has had an impact on our small country, especially now that we have become allies of the Nazis. But I don't want to give up hope. Somehow, with your connections, you will get me passage to America."

In the ensuing days, she made countless futile attempts to secure my passage on another ship bound for an American port. But Paris, and indeed all of France, had more than my flight to contend with in those dark days. The newspaper headlines in the French press screamed the news that none had wanted to hear: Hitler, encouraged by the signing of a mutual nonaggression pact with Russia, had turned the full fury of his *Blitzkrieg* on the hapless Poles. Thus, France and Britain, reluctant guarantors of Polish independence, were about to be thrust into war against Nazi Germany, despite futile, last-minute attempts at appeasement.

So it was that Mlle. Thomas, together with the newspapers she delivered each morning, became the bearer of more and more bad tidings as each day passed. The final straw arrived one morning at breakfast. "Mlle. Dunn," she announced sadly, "I am distressed to have to report that under a new French law, all foreigners with visitor's visas, like yourself, are required to leave this country immediately, or face fines and deportation."

It became amply clear that under those circumstances I could no longer allow myself to impose upon her generous hospitality. Later that day, we said our tearful goodbyes as she drove me to a small, nearby hotel where Mother and I had stayed on the many prior occasions we had visited Paris. I planned to spend the next few days there, while deciding where to turn next for the assistance I would need to escape from the continent. Only a fool, or an ostrich, would have failed to realize the ever-increasing threat to my safety and freedom posed by the gathering storm clouds on the horizon. And, I hoped, I was neither.

But times had changed dramatically in the Paris I had loved and admired. The concierge at the hotel, who had become a personal friend of the family, was not at all happy to see me. Instead of welcoming me with an embrace, as was his custom, he now viewed me with open suspicion. Without mincing words, he coldly reminded me that all "foreigners," especially Hungarian nationals, who had ties to the hated Nazi regime, had been ordered forthwith to leave the country.

"What has this world come to?" I asked myself. "How ironic that I'm now to be considered an enemy alien by the French whose existence is being threatened by the very same Nazi regime that's threatening mine." But I made no attempt to explain this lack of logic to the concierge, choosing instead to reassure him that I had every intention of complying with the law. I would need a place to stay only until my exit visa had been processed. He reluctantly turned over a key to a room that turned out to be significantly smaller and less attractive than the ones I had been assigned on previous occasions. Even so, the room rate quoted was more than double. But I wisely decided to forgo any complaint. It would do fine for the short time I expected to occupy it.

There were other signs that Paris, in its imminent crisis, no longer welcomed its foreign visitors with the fervor it once had. Shopkeepers who had happily taken my money in the past were now much more reluctant to share their rapidly disappearing inventories with "foreigners." On several occasions I noticed, first in anger, then in resignation, that a significant discrepancy existed between prices charged native French and nonnatives. But I was content to obtain the few items I desired at any price, and without argument.

After suffering a second sleepless night in my hotel, I finally came to a decision while munching on a truly priceless breakfast brioche. It was, unfortunately, a decision I would regret for the rest of my life. I concluded that my only choice was to return to Budapest, as there seemed little to be accomplished by remaining in Paris, where I could conceivably be arrested and deported by the

French. "Over my dead body!" I thought to myself. If I was going back to Hungary, it would be as Mlle. Dunn, prominent citizen and proprietress, not as a deportee. Once there, I would discreetly tap every familiar resource that my family and I had cultivated over the years to help me find my way to America. Looking at it from my perspective at the time, the plan made good sense. After all, our contacts had been successful in getting my mother and brothers out. They would have to do the same for me now.

With this firm resolve in mind, I made my way to the Prefecture Offices to obtain an exit visa to Hungary. But I soon learned that this was no small feat in itself. There existed at the time a kind of Catch-22 for those wanting to comply with the recent French laws. Upon entering the huge anteroom, each person was asked to state his business, then given an application form to complete at one of the many tables that had been set up for this purpose. However, I quickly noticed that there was not one empty space available at any of the tables. Furthermore, as soon as someone had completed his form and left his place, several others dashed over and fought to take possession of it. Except for the seriousness of the times, one could laugh at the comic nature of the scene.

After a few minutes, I decided to take my form back to the hotel and fill it out in the privacy of my room. I could readily observe that the famed European code of gentlemanly conduct was not about to be practiced here.

The following day I returned to the Prefecture Offices with my completed form proudly in hand. I was directed to hand in my form at a window in the far corner of the anteroom where a huge line had already formed. I chastised myself for not getting there earlier, as I found myself subjected to another hour-long wait. But I soon discovered that my waiting had only just begun. After submitting my form to the window clerk, I was directed to another huge room where more long lines formed in front of several desks arranged alphabetically. Reluctantly, I took my place at the end of the A-E line, which was more than twice as long as the U-Z line. "Why couldn't I have been born into a family with another surname?" I reasoned with a growing frustration. Yet, I was about to face an even greater challenge. As my turn finally came, after another seemingly endless wait, the harried official at the desk looked up and asked my name. When I told him, he proceeded to shuffle through a huge pile of forms on his desk and announced in a gruff voice, "I don't see your name on any of these applications. Are you sure you handed it in?"

When I assured him that I had done so many hours ago, he mumbled something about its probably having gotten lost. "No wonder," he added sarcastically, "with all the damn foreigners ending up in Paris!" Before I could raise my voice in protest, he called, "next!" and I found myself being pushed unceremoniously from my place at the desk.

With tears of frustration in my eyes, I was instantly made aware of my shortcoming when I observed the next person in line surreptitiously slip a hundred franc note into the official's hand. I vowed to return the next day to play the "game" by the rules I had just learned the hard way.

But nothing was meant to come easy for me on this day. Upon my return to the hotel, I found my packed bags standing in a corner of the lobby. After inquiring, I was told that I had overstayed my time, and that a new party, with a prior reservation, had already been moved into my room. I was stunned. It was the first time in my life that I had ever been evicted. It was not a good feeling, especially coming after my earlier frustrating experience, but I made up my mind to bury my hurt and play the new French "game" I had just learned. It worked beautifully, and within minutes my bags and I were resting in another unoccupied room. It made me feel better, although I found myself a hundred francs poorer.

The next day, after a successful early trip to the Prefecture Offices, my exit visa, my bags, and I boarded a train for Budapest. To say that I was unhappy to leave Paris would be a lie. But then, I had no knowledge of what lay ahead.

Chapter V

AN ALTERNATE PLAN

Shattered dreams crowded my mind on the endless train ride back to Budapest. The magnitude of actually witnessing history in the making had a crushing effect on me. Millions like me were drifting, helplessly carried away by an unbeatable force.

It scared me to think about facing the world I had left behind, but I had to persevere. I would handle the past as I would my present and pretend nothing had happened.

The darkened train, loaded with passengers returning to their native countries, sped past the familiar countryside in a blur. The border crossings in France, Italy, and Yugoslavia bristled with military equipment and personnel awaiting orders to unleash their destructive power on an unseen enemy. I hoped I would be far away when those orders arrived!

As we crossed the French border, the train stopped briefly at a siding outside a small Italian village. The locals, in colorful costumes, stormed the train, hawking bowls of steaming pasta through the train windows. I had discovered before boarding that our train carried no food, so I took the opportunity to fill my stomach with this welcome treat. It would be the only real food I would have until my arrival in Budapest.

The remainder of the two-day journey found me alternating

between fitful sleep and thoughtful reflection on the decisions that
had brought me to this point in my life. I wondered about the
decisions that now awaited me upon my return from Paris. I fully
realized that every option required careful consideration in view of
Mme. Boriska's dire warnings, and I determined to undertake only
those that promised success in achieving my singular goal: joining my
mother in America. I had not reached any significant conclusions by
the time the train pulled into the familiar station. There was no rush
of happy anticipation on this homecoming, one I could hardly have
foreseen upon departing nearly three weeks earlier. So, burdened
with a heavy heart and two equally heavy bags in hand, I hailed a
taxi for the short ride home.

But Peggy quickly made me forget my troubled mood. As the
door to Mr. Skenyi's apartment opened, she was in the hall like a
flash, jumping on me and licking my face as I bent down to pet her.
I wondered what her reaction would have been had she known our
original plans for her.

"Did Peggy behave herself while I was gone?" I inquired of
the building superintendent.

"As always," he answered rather noncommittally. "How was
your trip?"

"Fine, but Mother had to remain in Paris to handle some
additional details. I don't expect her for at least another week," I
lied.

He nodded, then handed me my mail. "You have two overseas
airmail letters here. I hope they have good news."

I took the mail and my two bags and, after leaving him a nice
tip, proceeded up the stairs to our apartment, with Peggy following
close behind. "It's just you and me now, Peggy," I whispered in her
ear as I bent down to pick up the suitcases after opening the door.
She answered by licking my face over and over again to let me know
how happy she was to see me. Perhaps she had already forgiven me
for almost abandoning her. But what choice did I realistically have?
My past plans could not possibly have included her. And what about
my future plans? We would have to cross that bridge when we got to
it.

I took off my coat and hat and, after putting up some water for
tea, I turned my attention to the mail. I felt an inner excitement as

I quickly opened the envelope with the familiar handwriting of my brother, Laszlo. His letter, only the second we had received since his departure, related his success and promotion at the designer's studio in Buenos Aires, and how much he enjoyed his life there. He also inquired whether Mother and I had been successful in booking a trip to America.

"If only we had been!" I murmured. "What I wouldn't give to be with Mother on that ship right now!"

I opened the second letter, noting with an even greater rush of excitement that it had been mailed in the United States. The most beautiful American airmail stamp adorned the right-hand corner of the envelope.

"Soon I too will be using those lovely stamps," I told myself optimistically.

Calming myself, I fetched my cup of tea and some cookies from the kitchen, and settled down on the couch in the living room to read Erno's letter. Peggy jumped up next to me, as if wanting to share the news. But, instead, she settled for a stroking under her chin.

Erno, too, had been successful in finding not only an apartment in a resident hotel on Central Park West, but he also had opened a wholesale fur studio in the heart of New York's fur district. I repeated the address, 250 West 27th Street, over and over again, marveling at its beautiful, melodious sound. I envisioned him celebrating Mother's arrival, and wondered if my absence would dampen their enthusiasm. "But then, it won't be long before I join them," I fantasized. "What a great celebration that will be!"

I don't know why, but in the midst of my imaginary jubilation, I found myself examining the two envelopes more closely. The ink on the return addresses on the back of both envelopes was smudged, as though the letters had gotten wet in the rain. Yet, the writing on the front, bearing my mother's name and address, was perfectly clear. When I touched the edge of both flaps, I came to a chilling conclusion. There could be no doubt! Both envelopes had been steamed open and then reglued. "But who, and why?" I asked myself. I had little trouble determining the "who." It had to be Mr. Skenyi, and, if so, he also now had knowledge of my secret plans. I gritted my teeth in anger, realizing that my resolve to share my plans only with those in position to aid my flight had been compromised. I could only guess at the consequences of Mr. Skenyi's actions. They most certainly boded trouble, but there was little I could do about that now. I firmly resolved to redouble my efforts to find a way to get to America while continuing my normal activities in as casual a manner as possible. Any confrontation now would serve no useful purpose. But I made a mental note to write my family that evening, asking them to address any future letters to my shop. That would be the best way to thwart Mr. Skenyi's meddlesome curiosity.

Ignoring the remainder of my mail, I turned my attention to unpacking and settling down for the night. As I came upon the jewelry I had so thoughtfully taken along to Paris, I made the decision not to return it to the vault. After all, I couldn't know when I would be leaving again, and the jewelry would have to be available for packing at that time. However, I would need a place to hide it in my apartment. There was no need to take any chances of having it stolen. My life might depend on my having it with me. As I glanced around the apartment for a good hiding place, I remembered the letter we had received from our Austrian relatives, describing how they had been forced to hide their jewelry from the Nazis. "I think I remember them hiding it in the light fixture," I murmured to myself. "If it worked for them, it could work for me as well. After all, no one is going to search this apartment that carefully, anyway." So I unscrewed the light shade on the kitchen light, and after placing the various pieces in the shade, I screwed it back into place. "Very clever," I told myself smugly. "No one is ever going to find them now!"

I finished my unpacking, and after remembering to wind up the old grandfather clock in the living room, collapsed on my own sweet bed. I hadn't realized how tired I was from the long trip and lack of sleep the past few days. I would need a good night's rest so my mind and body would be fresh for the next day's challenges. But I need not have worried about getting to sleep, for as soon as my head hit the pillow, Morpheus gained control over me.

The next morning arrived all too soon, as I was awakened by Peggy's wet tongue on my face. The sun streamed through my bedroom window, as if to remind me that I needed to arrive at the studio on time to make everything seem as natural as possible. I finished dressing, ate a quick breakfast in the kitchen, and dutifully prepared Peggy's food and water dishes. As I bent down to say goodbye to her, I could hear the grandfather clock chiming, as if urging me to leave. I remembered having learned to tell time on that clock as a child, but that seemed so long ago. I had no time for the past now, I decided. What mattered most was what I would do today that would ensure my future well-being. I leaned down to kiss Peggy's head, reassuring her that I would return that night, before closing the door behind me on my remembrances.

I made my entrance into the studio that day as casually as I could manage. All the employees greeted me with their usual inquiries, which I answered quite naturally, if not altogether truthfully. "Were there any messages for me?" I inquired. I was told that among others, Mr. Gilbert of the U.S. Steamship Lines had called. I wondered what he had wanted to tell me, but decided that I had business with him that could not be discussed over my office phone. I planned to walk over to his office during the lunch hour when nobody would miss me. I could hardly finish my morning's work in anticipation of that visit.

When I finally found myself in his office a few hours later, I was so excited that I could hardly speak. It was he who started the conversation.

"I tried calling you at your studio and at home as soon as I found out that the *Bremen* was not going to sail, but you had already left for France. At least, that was what your staff led me to believe. What happened?"

"Well, Mother and I left a few days early to spend some time with our representative in Paris. It was Mlle. Thomas who told us that our ship's departure was going to be canceled, and it was she who got Mother a berth on the *Ile-de-France*, which sailed a few days later. Unfortunately, she was able to obtain only one ticket, so I'm still here. Do you think you can get me out? I want to join Mother in New York very badly. Please say you can help me!"

"Alice, dear, I know how badly you want to leave, but you must realize that you're only one of a million with that very desire. I, myself, have so far unsuccessfully tried to get Mitzi to my family in New York. I would like very much to see her as far away as possible from this political mess, before the whole thing blows. I must admit that I'm truly surprised that your contact in Paris was able to obtain passage for your mother. The *Île* had supposedly been totally booked for months. That was the ship I originally wanted for you, but we were too late. You should consider yourself very lucky to have gotten your mother out on it. I would have to assume that there was a last-minute cancellation."

I could see that things were not going the way I had planned. If he had been unable to find a berth for his own wife, there could be little hope for me. "What can you suggest then?" I inquired, still groping for an answer to my problem.

"Well, I have something that you might want to consider." He was speaking in a low tone now, almost whispering. "It's a little risky, and quite expensive. But if you need a safe place to weather the storm, this may be just the thing."

"What is it? Please tell me. I'll do anything to get to America. I'll pay anything you say!" I was beginning to raise my voice in my excitement. Mr. Gilbert put his finger to his lips, reminding me to keep my voice down.

"This is not altogether legal, you understand. I've been able to get several friends out already, though. We can get you a Swiss passport and visa. You would travel under an assumed name to Switzerland, which is probably the safest place on the continent. But you would be unable to get to America from there. As you know, it's a landlocked country."

I was beginning to lose some of my enthusiasm already. "How much would it cost?" I inquired, somewhat less eagerly.

"A thousand dollars. That's about five thousand pengo. These fellows aren't cheap, but they're good. Their papers are first quality. We've had 100 percent success with our people so far. If you're interested, Alice, please let me know by tomorrow. I don't know how much longer this project will last. It's quite risky for all of us, you know."

I thanked him, and promised to call him either way by the next day. As I took my leave, I inquired about Mitzi. He assured me that she was well, although not too happy about the prospect of leaving her native country. He promised to have her call me in the evening.

As I left his office, my mind was in total confusion. I would have to give his plan very careful consideration, but this was not the time. I needed to get back to my shop to attend to all the things that had piled up in my absence. I promised myself to give it further thought that evening, in the privacy of my home.

Chapter VI

THE VOLCANO'S EDGE

It was nearly 6 PM when I arrived at my apartment that evening. I had worked at my studio a little later than usual on some sketches I needed the next morning, and had stopped on the way home to pick up some groceries. As I opened the door, I could hear the phone in the living room ringing. I threw my bag of groceries on the couch, and after warning Peggy to stay away from them, I picked up the phone. I immediately recognized Mitzi's voice on the other end. She sounded frantic.

"Alice, is that you? I've been trying to reach you for an hour. Where have you been?"

"Hi, Mitzi! I just got in. What's the matter? You sound very excited."

"I am. I know you just got home last night. Bob told me what happened to you in France. Listen, I need your help, and I need it quickly!"

"Sure, dear. You know I'll do anything. What's wrong?"

"Well, you know that thing Robert was talking to you about today?" She sounded somewhat secretive, but I knew what she was alluding to. "We think it's gone sour. You know, kaput. We just got a phone call from Switzerland. They've arrested several of our people, and I'm afraid they're coming after us next. I'm sure someone will talk. Can you help us?"

"You know I will." The words came out before I had a chance to reflect on what I was saying. "What can I do for you?"

"We need a place to stay overnight. We're afraid they'll arrest us if we remain at home. Do you think you could put us up just for one night? We're planning to leave the country early tomorrow morning."

This sounded serious, but Mitzi had always been a close friend. She had done many favors for me in the past, and I knew I could never turn her down. It didn't take more than a second of reflection to make up my mind. "You know the answer. Come and stay as long as you need to. I've got lots of room since my family left. Only Peggy and I are here now. How soon can you get over here?"

"Oh, Alice! How can I thank you enough? You're such a great friend!" I could hear her telling her husband what my answer had been. "Bob says, 'God bless you!' We'll be right over, we're all packed. See you in a little while. And thank you so much!" She hung up the phone, and I was left standing, phone in hand, wondering about the possible consequences of my decision.

Well, I knew that I didn't have time to stand around thinking. I was hungry, not having eaten a decent meal in days, and the groceries were still waiting to be unpacked. Furthermore, Peggy was wagging her tail, hoping to draw my attention to her empty dish, and I needed to make up the bed in my mother's room for my guests. So I put away the groceries, and began making the necessary preparations. I hadn't moved this fast in years, and felt quite proud of having completed all my tasks before my guests' arrival. I glanced at the old grandfather clock and, to my surprise, noted that it was already 7:30. I hadn't been that swift after all!

"Where can they be?" I asked myself. "They should have been here by now!" I knew that they lived less than a half hour away by car. "Guess they couldn't get a taxi," I reassured myself. But when nobody had arrived by eight o'clock, I began to worry. I put on my coat and walked down the stairs into the cool evening air, hoping to spot a taxi carrying my friends. But there was none, nor would there be one that night. After several more failed attempts to contact them by phone, I decided to retire, for there was little else I could hope to accomplish by staying up. I fervently hoped that nothing had happened to them, but I feared the worst.

It wasn't until I had picked up the newspaper at my studio the next morning that my worst fears were realized. Under the headlines blaring Hitler's latest achievements *in* Poland was a smaller article that immediately caught my eye. Entitled "Jewish Spy Ring Smashed," it told of the arrest of seven Hungarian Jews who had been caught attempting to cross the Hungarian border with bogus Swiss papers. According to the story, the police found documents in their possession that detailed armaments and troop strength of various Hungarian and German forces. After intense questioning, the perpetrators admitted that their mission was to turn these military secrets over to an unnamed embassy official of the French government in Zurich. It seems that the Gestapo had been investigating the spy ring for months, but had avoided making arrests until they uncovered the person who was masterminding the scheme. Finally, they were able to trace the illegal papers' origin back to a Frank Tishman, and his associate, Robert Gilbert, both prominent American businessmen residing in Budapest. Implicated along with the two Americans was Gilbert's Hungarian wife, Mitzi. It was because of their outstanding reputations in the Hungarian community that they were able to conduct their espionage activities without fear of discovery. Fortunately, the intervention of the Gestapo had enabled the authorities to successfully uncover their true identity.

I put down the newspaper to wipe my eyes, which were beginning to well up with tears of anger and frustration. "Those anti-Semitic bastards!" I murmured. "They've arrested those people on trumped-up charges."

It was altogether impossible to conceive that Robert and Mitzi had been actively engaged in espionage without my getting an inkling of it. True, Bob had been friendly, but slightly reserved in our relationship. But Mitzi and I had been close friends for years and had shared many intimate secrets. Surely, she would have given me some hint of her involvement in any nefarious business dealings. Besides, I reasoned, they never would have risked my life by asking me for shelter. The whole idea sounded totally preposterous, a mere excuse for fanning the fires of Hungarian anti-Semitism.

After wiping my eyes, I finished reading the article. In condemning the acts of espionage, it implied that this was hardly an unusual case. Most Hungarian Jews were known to hold antinationalistic sympathies and could never be trusted in times like these. It lauded the Gestapo's handling of the case, and its swift and thorough investigation, noting their vast experience in these matters from having handled the "Jewish problem" in their own country. It went on to speculate on the fate of the accused spies, noting with regret that they probably would have their lives spared since the country was not presently in a state of war. Thus, the most severe sentence that could be imposed on them was "life at hard labor." It was to be hoped that such punishment would deter others from contemplating crimes against the state in the future.

By now I was totally overcome by my feelings, and my hands were shaking. "This was no way to start a day at work!" I reprimanded myself. But how could they get away with such outrageous and unjust treatment of my friend and all those other poor souls? What would become of Mitzi? How could I help her? Could they really send her away to one of those labor camps? I had heard about them, and if what I had heard was true, she might have been better off getting shot by a firing squad.

It was then, and only then, that a horrible thought crossed my mind. I realized that my own name could very easily have appeared alongside the others in that newspaper article! Those poor people were probably just trying to flee the Nazis, like me. They probably weren't spies any more than I was. And Bob and Mitzi were hardly "ringleaders!" Bob was merely guilty of furnishing them with false papers as he had offered to do for me. Thank God I had not accepted his offer! I couldn't help remembering what Bob had said about wanting to get Mitzi to the United States. I remembered Mitzi confiding in me about his nagging her to apply for her American citizenship and how she had stubbornly refused. She could have gotten it so easily, being married to an American. But she loved Hungary, and would never even consider relinquishing her Hungarian birthright. She was so proud of it! I wondered if her feelings had changed following last night's events. She and I were so close, and yet so different in our feelings about America. I knew, without a single doubt, what I would have done had I married an American. But perhaps she saw things from a different perspective, not being of the Jewish faith. Perhaps she felt immune from the growing anti-

Semitism surrounding them. How wrong she had been!

My train of thought was abruptly interrupted by someone knocking on my office door. It was Miss Havas, my capable assistant. As the only full-time sales person, she had been given the responsibility of running the studio in my absence. She was ambitious, and quite obviously enjoyed being the boss, even for short periods. She was there, standing in the doorway, studying me.

"Miss Dunn," she began, "are you all right? I saw you reading the paper. The girls in the shop also saw that article about the spy ring. They were wondering if the Mitzi Gilbert mentioned in the story was the same person for whom we made that silk evening gown last summer. I told them that it couldn't be the same one. I know our Mrs. Gilbert could never have been a Jewess."

I was shocked by her remark. It was a very insensitive question coming from such a close business associate. But I chose to handle her with as much tact and discretion as I could muster, considering my present frame of mind.

"Yes, Miss Havas, that *is* the same Mrs. Gilbert. As you probably know, she was not only a valued customer, but a very good personal friend as well. As you can see, I'm quite upset by her present plight. But you are right, Miss Havas. You have a very keen sense of observation. She's not a Jewess, as you put it." I was beginning to let my emotions get the better of me, as I added, fighting back the tears and the lump in my throat, "And neither is she a spy. She has more patriotic feelings in her than you or I will ever hope to have. Please tell that to the other girls."

Miss Havas gave me a strange look and walked out of my office without another word. I wondered what I had accomplished by my outburst. It certainly wasn't what I had intended. Perhaps, I had just now fallen into the trap they'd set for me. I was positive that Miss Havas, and the rest of the girls on my staff knew my religion. I just never considered it any of their business. But these were strange times, and perhaps I needed to observe greater caution in what I said to them. I hoped I wasn't getting paranoid, but in the last two days, since my return from Paris, I had felt a strange coldness from them, even a reluctance to follow my suggestions and directions. It was something that called for greater observation and thinking on my part.

But for the meantime, I needed to concentrate on the appointments I had scheduled for the morning. As I emerged from my office, I could see Miss Havas already engaged in conversation with my first customer. Mrs. Hetenyi, the wife of the president of the First National Bank of Hungary, was a frequent visitor to my shop. I greeted her cordially, and excused myself for not having welcomed her personally.

"Oh, it's quite all right, Alice," she smiled, as she acknowledged my greeting. "I know how busy you must be these days. My friends were saying that your winter fashions are superior to anything they've seen in all of Budapest. And now, with the publicity your boutique has gotten in the papers, I'm sure that everyone will be flocking to your doorstep. I doubt that you'll have a moment of peace all day. I don't envy you, but then that's what you're in business for, isn't it?"

As it was, she turned out to be quite correct in her assessment. My business was beginning to flourish as never before. It seemed that everyone, even the visitors from abroad, sought me out. Among the list of my more prominent customers was the Archduchess Katherine, a well-known society figure in Budapest. To my delight, she even mentioned my shop when she was interviewed in the society pages of the Budapest press.

But the joy at my ever-increasing professional success was tempered by a total lack of any kind of personal life. I hardly ever went out on weekends anymore, preferring instead to stay at home with Peggy. I shared with her every piece of correspondence with my family.

The excitement of opening the first letter from my mother in the United States was unequaled by any other event in my secluded existence. She had seen my letters to Erno, and was totally destroyed at having left me behind. She wondered what plans I was making to join her. She also related a real horror story of her crossing aboard the *Île*, which included daily "abandon ship" drills as the crew sighted floating mines and U-boats in its path. She mentioned the crowded conditions aboard ship, staterooms that were packed with passengers with scant regard for berth class or capacity. She was made to share her cabin with three other women, each of whom had to take her turn sleeping in an armchair, or on the floor, every fourth night. When they finally arrived in New York harbor, after eighteen days at sea, the thrill of sighting the Statue of Liberty was the highlight of her trip. Yet, her arrival in the States was not entirely without mishap. My brother Erno was not there to welcome her, and in fact, failed to put in an appearance until two days later. Mother was worried out of her mind, but she was not sufficiently fluent in English to obtain help in contacting him. When he finally showed up, he attributed his lateness to the confusion caused by the delayed arrival of her ship. Finally, with a certain lack of enthusiasm, she described New York as a crowded and noisy city. While I was able to sympathize with Mother's negative feelings, I nonetheless wished that I had been there with her to share those experiences. I imagined myself sitting in a taxi with her, gazing at the skyscrapers I had read so much about. It seemed as though I could almost hear the honking horns and the noisy pedestrians on every crowded street corner. I would love it all, every bit of it, I told myself.

But the prospects of personally experiencing the New York scene were becoming more and more remote. Each passing day made me ever more reluctant to try leaving Hungary. Mitzi's experience had robbed me of all my former courage. "Besides," I told myself, "my life here is not all that bad." I still had a successful career, a lovely and peaceful apartment to return to each night, and more than enough money to meet my every need. Why be impatient? I could always find a legal way to get to America after this political mess was over. I would wait it out, and hope for the best.

Thus, when another letter from Argentina arrived at my shop, I was less than thrilled to discover its contents. My brother Laszlo had thoughtfully, and I presumed at great personal expense, decided to send me an Argentine passport. It bore the name, Maria Rafaela Dunn, and contained my picture, which I assumed Laszlo had taken with him. It was even embossed with the country's official seal. In the accompanying letter, Laszlo confided his great concern for my safety, and assured me that his contact at the Argentine embassy in Budapest stood prepared to help me escape. In addition, he related meeting an attractive English girl in Buenos Aires, with whom he had fallen madly in love.

I was quite taken by my brother's generosity and concern for my welfare, yet I knew that his good intentions would go for naught.

Without a dated entry stamp in the passport, it would be invalid. I could envision myself being caught by the Gestapo, which would then be able to use my false Argentine papers to brand me a spy, and send me to a forced labor camp. No, I would have none of that, I decided rather easily. I wrote Laszlo of my reasoning, making sure to include words of gratitude for his kind and thoughtful efforts on my behalf.

Yet another problem arose to complicate my existence. Because of the ever-increasing amount of time I needed to devote to my thriving business, I was less and less able to look into the needs of my family's fifty-year-old custom clothing business, located around the corner from my shop. Now, with Mother gone, it was showing signs of neglect as operating expenses outstripped income. Mother wrote me her decision to liquidate when she heard the news. Naturally, when I was forced to share the news with her employees, many of whom had been with her for years, the announcement was met with a great deal of disappointment and resentment toward me personally. I felt more and more isolated, surrounded by enemies who stood ready to abuse me at the first opportunity. I felt totally helpless; I was dancing on the edge of a volcano, waiting for it to erupt at any moment.

Chapter VII

THE ENCOUNTER

The spring of 1940 was notable for two things: the coming of age of my specialty boutique, and Hitler's rapid-fire conquest of Denmark and Norway in April; the Low Countries (Belgium and the Netherlands) in May; and, finally, France in June. This was culminated by Hitler's triumphant march into Paris on June 14th. All had been accomplished by means of a new military tactic, the *Blitzkrieg*, which combined the use of German air power and armored units. Against such speed and maneuverability, the famed Maginot Line, France's answer to the trench warfare of another era, proved totally impotent.

Mention of that ill-fated relic brought with it memories of my friend, Mlle. Thomas, and I wondered what fate might have befallen her. While I felt great sadness and sympathy for the poor, hapless victims of the Nazi onslaught, its impact on my own life was hardly noticeable. I became so totally involved in running my shop during the day, that I had scant time to think of anything else. I welcomed the success that was bringing the daily crowds of women, some browsing at the fully stocked accessory showcase, others looking through the books of fabric samples, and still more waiting for their turn to view the sketches that I had personally prepared for them. Although I realized that only a small portion of the visitors to my shop would eventually become my customers, I took great pride in having my store selected as the place to rendezvous in downtown Budapest. I frequently chose to mingle among them, greeting those I recognized, and welcoming the strangers, especially the foreign visitors, with whom I conversed in their own language, whenever possible. But the first time I encountered a German customer, accompanied by her uniformed Nazi escort, I became totally paralyzed. Something within me made it impossible to feign cordiality, so I quickly excused myself on some pretext, and promptly summoned Miss Havas to attend to their needs.

But I should not have been surprised at my reaction to the Germans. I had ample reason to hate them. Each night, upon returning to my apartment for dinner, I tuned in to Radio Free Europe to listen to the news. I had recently purchased a short-wave radio that carried these forbidden broadcasts. The Nazi propaganda on the local stations sickened me, and I had yearned for the truth, no matter how bad it got these days. The detailed stories of Nazi terror inflicted on the civilian populations of the conquered countries drew a predictable response. It was altogether natural to have transferred those feelings to all Germans. As the horror stories continued, month after month, I wondered how long it would take for my beloved America to drop its neutral stance and join the Allies' efforts to stop the bloodthirsty aggressors who took increased encouragement from the Allies' attempts at appeasement.

Finally, in the summer of 1941, the all-too-familiar script took on a substantive change. Russia, a military power of a greater magnitude, was experiencing first-hand Hitler's thirst for *Lebensraum*. It was now, quite unexpectedly, on the receiving end of its former ally's military fury. Yet, despite its proximity, the widening conflict scarcely touched us. It was as though we were separated from the destruction around us by a protective wall.

In the meantime, Hungary was fast becoming the center of the black market trade for the European continent. In Budapest, business flourished, as visitors from abroad sought to buy goods with their inflated currencies. Things were going so well for my salon that I was forced to hire another salesperson.

Then, at last, the evening broadcast on December 7, 1941 brought the news I had waited so long to hear. The United States, the victim of a sneak attack by the Japanese on its naval forces in Hawaii, had been brought into the war on the side of the Allies. But my hopes for a quick and favorable resolution to the conflict were soon dimmed. The magical powers I had somehow attributed to my American friends were being sorely tested in the Pacific. It wasn't until almost a year later, in November 1942, that Radio Free Europe broadcast the welcome news that American troops had landed in North Africa. An American general, Dwight Eisenhower, had been assigned to command the troops that would eventually rid the European continent of the Nazi menace.

By the next month, I began to hear reports that the tide was beginning to turn against the Axis powers, with the British Royal Air Force carrying the air war to several German cities. Simultaneously, Hungary ordered its citizens to commence practicing air raid drills. In my case, this meant turning out all lights, and descending to the basement of our apartment house. But the drills were of short duration, and soon Peggy and I found ourselves back in familiar surroundings. I was loathe to participate in these silly and altogether useless maneuvers, but I was quickly told by Mr. Skenyi that those who did not put in an appearance would be considered spies. It was a clear message for me, and I soon learned to put up with these petty interruptions. But what bothered me the most was the cessation of letters from overseas. After the end of 1943 I never heard from any member of my family, although I continued writing to them as before. Even Peggy showed her disappointment as she jumped up on the sofa next to me and waited for me to read the latest family news to her. But all she ever got now was the contents of notices and bills . . . neither of us relished. But the feeling of isolation was mitigated by the upbeat news we heard on our short-wave radio, which we kept hidden in the linen closet. The tide was finally turning against the hated Axis countries on all fronts. Hitler's Sixth Army was devastated at Stalingrad in an amazing turn of events, while Field Marshal Rommel's Afrika Korps was being defeated by the combined forces of General Montgomery and General Eisenhower. At the same time, General MacArthur's ground, sea, and air forces were beginning to take the offensive against the Japanese, although at great loss of American lives. Finally, Sicily was ours and *Il Duce* fell as Italy surrendered on September 8th. It became the first of the

Axis powers to do so. Even the Yugoslav partisans, under Marshal Tito, were successfully liberating their country of Nazi oppression. At Teheran, meanwhile, Roosevelt, Churchill, and Stalin met to plan combined strategy for the end of the war. But, in a less publicized event, the ruthless head of the German Gestapo, Heinrich Himmler, took control of Germany as minister of the interior. He became the architect of the infamous "Final Solution" to the Jewish "problem," a grisly plan that would systematically eradicate an entire people. Simultaneously, Hitler, in a bizarre speech, denounced Hungary, claiming that she had failed to fulfill her obligations toward her Axis partners. That revelation had hardly been a secret here.

As the first day of March arrived, bringing with it the promise of even greater Allied victories, my spirits were buoyed by the realization that I had virtually made it through the war. I began to congratulate myself, perhaps prematurely, for having made all the right decisions. "We may be toasting the New Year with Mother in New York, Peggy," I crowed optimistically.

As I entered the shop that morning, I greeted my staff with unusual enthusiasm.

"You had a phone call from Mrs. Hetenyi this morning, Miss Dunn. She would like you to call her back as soon as possible." Miss Havas' greeting was accompanied by a slip with a phone number on it. When I rang the number, I heard a familiar voice on the other end.

"Hi, Alice. How are you? Thanks for calling back." It was Eva Hetenyi.

After assuring her that I was splendid, I inquired about the reason for her call.

"Oh, I wanted to let you know that I'm sending the daughter of a friend of mine to you. Her name is Magda Fugazy. She's an aspiring young concert pianist who will be making her debut at our upcoming charity affair in Vigado at the end of the month. That's the one being sponsored by the Archduchess Katherine. I'd like to help her find the right gown for her appearance. You know how important image is to one's career. I want to treat her to the outfit, she's such a charming and talented girl. So please, Alice, send me the bill."

"How generous of you, Eva. Of course I'll be delighted to help her. I'll take care of her myself. Please ask her to call for an appointment. Perhaps you could even accompany her. I haven't seen you in ages."

"Ordinarily, I would love to, you know that. But we're leaving for the country in just a few minutes. That's why I called you so early this morning. Carl needs to get away from the bank for a few days. It's been very hectic down there this week, you know."

"No, I didn't," I admitted. "What's been happening?"

"Well," she answered, "that last speech by Hitler, the one in which he accused us of not helping enough in the war effort, has everyone convinced that the Germans are about to put some kind of pressure on us. It seems everyone was frightened into withdrawing all their money on deposit at the bank. It's causing quite a problem for Carl.

"But I know Magda will be in good hands. You always have my complete confidence, you know that. Whatever the two of you decide on will be fine with me. I'll call you when we get back."

We said our goodbyes, and I rang off after thanking her.

By that afternoon I had almost forgotten our conversation when I noticed a young girl, whom I judged to be about sixteen years old, entering the shop. "What an attractive young girl," I mused. Her long hair, which was almost jet black, hung down on either side of her Madonna-like face.

As her shimmering, dark brown eyes caught mine, I wondered how many young men would soon be overpowered by that gaze.

"You must be Alice Dunn," she remarked breathlessly. "I'm so thrilled to find you in. I'm Magda Fugazy. Mrs. Hetenyi called you about me." She rushed towards me, holding out her hand.

"How do you do, Magda?" I responded, a little annoyed. "I'm very pleased to make your acquaintance. But didn't Mrs. Hetenyi tell you to call for an appointment before coming to see me? I've got a store full of customers right now. If you leave your phone number with Miss Havas over there, she'll call you with an appointment after checking my calendar. I'll look forward to seeing you then. In the meantime, goodbye." I shook her hand once more, noticing her long slender fingers. I could see the look of disappointment on her face as she walked away from me and gave her telephone number to my assistant.

She had left the shop by the time I had a chance to speak to

Miss Havas. "She's quite something, isn't she? What a combination of spirit and beauty! Please set up an appointment for her. She's a concert pianist, the daughter of Mrs. Hetenyi's friend. I'll need to take care of her myself."

Miss Havas nodded agreement. I could see a smile on her face as she went into my office to check the calendar on my desk.

A few weeks later, as I was just about to step out for a late lunch, I bumped into Magda as she was entering the studio. I was caught somewhat by surprise as I had failed to check my appointment calendar before leaving. It had been a busy morning, and I was a little later than usual.

"Hello, Miss Dunn," she greeted me with that charming youthful smile. "I guess I'm a little early for my appointment, but I just couldn't wait another moment."

"I know the feeling, Magda," I interrupted, smiling, "I guess I'm a little late myself. Why don't you accompany me to Gerbeaud's for some tea and pastry? I was just on my way there. We could use the opportunity to get to know each other a little better. And perhaps," I added, "we could discuss some ideas for the gown we'll be creating for your debut. I've already made some preliminary sketches, but we can see them when we return."

Magda was absolutely delighted, I could see that. We walked together down the Vaczi-utca toward my favorite pastry shop, chatting along the way.

Gerbeaud's was always crowded. It was the favorite meeting place for many of Budapest's elite. Artists, writers, and business people who lived or worked nearby could be found there on most afternoons. It always intrigued me to guess as many names as I could of the famous customers.

It was no different on this visit. But Magda and I were able to squeeze through the crowds toward a rare empty table I spotted in a far corner. Magda began chatting about her gown as soon as we were seated, but I was already tuned into another conversation that had caught my attention at the table behind me. Pretending to adjust my lipstick, I scanned the faces of the three men through my compact mirror. I was able to recognize two of them as owners of prominent businesses on the Vaczi-utca, the famous shopping street we had just strolled down on the way to Gerbeaud's.

"It won't be long before we get rid of those Jew-owned businesses, now," I heard one of the men remark.

"You're right, Eric. I just heard this morning that two of them have already been taken over by their Aryan staff. You know, the jewelry and the luggage stores across the street from you," the other one answered.

"Really? What happened to the owners?"

"Oh, they arrested them and took them away yesterday."

"Good riddance! I hope they'll all be gone soon!"

I returned my lipstick and compact to my pocketbook. I had heard enough. A sudden nausea was beginning to suppress my desire for food. I wanted to get out of there as quickly as I could.

Magda evidently had not overheard any of the conversation I'd been listening to. She looked totally puzzled as I rose from our table and grabbed her by the arm. I began steering her out of Gerbeaud's as quickly, but unobtrusively as possible.

Once out on the street, I attempted to explain my seemingly odd behavior.

Magda's eyes grew very big as she listened to me. "My mother was just talking about this very thing yesterday. She's quite worried that something bad might happen to us also. But I reassured her that the Archduchess would protect us. She's my official sponsor, you know. And she has a lot of influence in Hungarian politics."

I nodded my head in agreement. But I knew in my heart that the Nazis would hardly permit an Archduchess to get in their way. Their ruthless behavior had been all-too-well documented on that subject.

"Why don't we go back to my office so I can show you the designs I created for your gown?" I offered halfheartedly. "We can have our tea there."

"I'd love that, but are you sure you're feeling well enough? I could come back tomorrow, if you have the time. I'll gladly rearrange my practice for your convenience."

"That's so thoughtful of you, Magda," I said, accepting her offer before she could withdraw it. "I really don't feel very good right now. I'm still very upset. But we'll get together tomorrow. Same time?"

"Great! I'll look forward to it. I'll probably dream about my gown all night. Goodbye till tomorrow then."

We shook hands and parted. I walked the few blocks back to my studio in a daze. I was totally unprepared, therefore, for the next surprise that greeted me as I entered my shop. There, on the wall behind the counter, hung a poster of Adolf Hitler delivering his Nazi salute, arm outstretched. Beneath his picture were the German words: *Ein Volk, Ein Reich, Ein Fuhrer!* (One people, one nation, one leader!) I could feel my throat tighten as a new wave of nausea came over me. Without a word I retreated to my office, sinking into a chair.

Miss Havas, who had observed my entrance into the shop, followed me in. "Miss Dunn, are you all right? You look white as a sheet!" she remarked, with somewhat feigned sympathy.

"Yes, I know, but I'm really not feeling too well right now. Can you tell me who put up that poster out there?"

"One of the girls," she answered, all too quickly it seemed to me. "Two policemen came looking for you while you were gone. They left the poster with orders to mount it. They also left you these," she added, handing me several yellow Stars of David mounted on a cloth background. "You're supposed to wear them on your outer garments, they said."

I took the emblems, dismissing her from my office. So, this was it! The final indignity! I stuffed the pieces of cloth into the pocket of my coat, postponing for the moment the decision about wearing them as instructed. Then, glancing down at my appointment calendar, I dutifully marked down Magda Fugazy's name for the next day, March 19, 1944, at 3 PM. But the young pianist would not get a chance to keep her appointment. The Nazis would come in her place.

Chapter VIII

THE NEW REGIME

The late afternoon sun was casting an orange glow on the display windows. I sat slumped in my office chair, looking at it. The enthusiasm with which I had greeted this infamous day had by now totally left me.

Miss Havas stood looking at me with pity in her eyes. "Would you like to leave early tonight, Miss Dunn? I'll be happy to close up for you," she offered.

It had always been my custom to be the last one to leave. Everyone knew that, especially Miss Havas. Was her offer now a genuine response to my downcast appearance, or was this her way of telling me that she was prepared for the expected takeover of my shop? Doubtless, she was the natural heir, especially since she was conversant in German. But I was getting ahead of myself. There was no takeover just yet, except for what I had overheard at Gerbeaud's.

"No, Miss Havas," I finally responded, "but thank you for the kind offer. I'll do the usual closing up, but you can tell the girls to leave whenever they're finished. You can leave now, too. The store seems empty, and I don't think that we'll get any more customers tonight."

Miss Havas nodded. When she got outside the office I could hear her whispering something to the girls. Then they all broke into laughter. I noticed them waving goodbye to me as they left, one by one.

I was about to leave myself, a few minutes later, when I saw the door to the shop open, and a familiar figure enter. It was the Archduchess Katherine. I had gotten to know her from several previous visits. She was a striking woman with a youthful appearance. Her light brown hair was piled high on her head. She was wearing a long, dark overcoat with the fur collar turned up. I spotted a yellow Star of David on the lapel of her coat.

I was so dumbfounded that I could hardly greet her. But she offered her greeting as though I were an old friend.

"Hello, Miss Dunn. I see you're ready to leave. I promise not to keep you very long. I just happened to be in the neighborhood and wanted to stop by to say hello."

When I finally recovered my composure, I invited her into my office, offering her the chair next to my desk. "It's an honor to have you visit us anytime," I started. "Please tell me what I can do for you today."

"Nothing really, Miss Dunn. But I would like to do something for you. You may have noticed the insignia on my lapel. By tonight, many of our finest citizens will also be wearing it. The Nazis intend it as a symbol of shame, but as for me, I wear it proudly. Not because I'm a Jewess, but because I feel a unanimity with those who are now required to wear it. We're all Hungarian citizens and, as such, we deserve to be treated with respect commensurate to our accomplishments, regardless of our persuasion. I have always been a firm believer in that principle, and I hope you share my belief." She rose from her chair and threw her arms around my shoulders. Then, without waiting for a reply, she walked out of the shop and onto the darkened street.

It took me several minutes after her departure to gather my thoughts. Her whirlwind visit, together with her brave display of personal conviction, had made a lasting impression on me, one I would never forget. Yet, I felt an urgent need to get away. This place, in which I had invested so much of my personal time and effort, and which had been the ultimate source of my self-esteem, no longer held the same attraction for me. I wanted to be within the friendly confines of my apartment, my home, where my only true friend awaited my return. She would apply the required salve for my wounded ego.

I picked up my coat once more. I was about to pin the star on it, intending to follow the Archduchess's example, when something made me change my mind. I would put discretion ahead of bravery for tonight, I thought. So, instead, I pinned the symbol to the lapel of my jacket. Then I put on my coat over it.

As I stepped out onto the sidewalk, locking the door behind me, I noticed two policemen approaching. I froze in my tracks as all kinds of horrible thoughts crossed my mind. But they were interested in one thing only. One of them took a decal out of his pocket and applied it to the front of my display window. As they walked away, one of them muttered something under his breath, while the other one spat at the front door. As I watched them leave with a feeling of relief, I thanked God that they had not looked for the emblem on my coat. Then I took notice of the new decoration on my door. It was a Star of David, as I had expected, with the word "Jew," in Hungarian, printed beneath it.

As I set off to follow my usual path back to my apartment house, I noticed an unusual amount of traffic through the downtown section for that late in the day. Every few minutes, it seemed, truckloads of soldiers and motorcycles with sidecars drove past me. I was walking rather quickly, with my eyes fixed on the sidewalk, so I didn't notice the symbols on the vehicles until I got to the corner. Then, as I was about to cross the street, I looked up in time to see another military vehicle whiz by. Without a doubt I was able to recognize the emblem of the German Army which I had seen in the newspapers many times before. I realized then that something big, something of great import was taking place. I wanted to get home to my radio as quickly as possible.

Suddenly, as I made my way down the next block, I saw a band of hooligans on the opposite side of the street running toward me. I heard the breaking of glass and the shouts of the youths as I watched them rush inside the breached establishment to loot its contents. I could hear their chants of "Jew! Jew!" as they moved on to their next target. I wondered about the fate of my own shop, which now also bore the hated symbol, but I never gave a second thought to going back there. As I continued to walk quickly along the sidewalk, close to the empty stores, I saw two more policemen approaching.

My heart jumped into my throat, but I managed to force a smile as they passed by without giving me a second look. Their attention was obviously focused on the looters, who were now far behind me. I felt great relief at their inattention and wondered if their reaction might have differed had I been wearing the star on my coat.

I was within sight of my house now. I congratulated myself on having successfully negotiated the chaos of the business section behind me. I could now observe a new phenomenon in my neighborhood. Everywhere I looked, I saw banners with swastikas hanging from rooftops and windows. They certainly hadn't been there this morning, I was sure of that. As I arrived breathlessly at the threshold of my house, someone opened the door from the inside. It was Mr. Skenyi.

"Miss Dunn," he began, "I see you're back just in time. A curfew is on for tonight. No one is to leave his apartment, unless we have an air raid drill, of course. Do you understand?"

His tone was that of a superior, giving orders. It was not one I was accustomed to hearing. Then I noticed the swastika armband on his sleeve. So, he was one of them also!

I nodded my head and started to walk up the stairs. As I got to the first landing I heard him shout after me. "Oh, by the way, Miss Dunn. You are not to bring your dog with you to the basement. Kindly leave her in your apartment from now on. Understood? We've had too many complaints about her from the other tenants."

I knew that was a lie, but I wasn't about to argue the point with him, especially not tonight. All I wanted was to get inside my apartment to experience its warmth, its comfort, and, above all, its safety. Peggy was at the door to greet me, as usual. I welcomed her enthusiastic demonstration of love tonight as never before. Then, I heard the phone ring. It was Julia, a friend and confidante, with whom I hadn't spoken for ages.

"Alice, is it you? I've been trying to reach you for hours. Where have you been? Do you know what's happening out there?"

I related to her my experiences of the evening, and Mr. Skenyi's greeting. She didn't seem too surprised.

"Please listen to me, Alice," she pleaded. "You must leave the city with me as soon as possible. We're all in mortal danger now. The Germans have occupied the country. They've just arrested Horthy. Now they're giving the orders, just as in Austria. You remember what happened there, don't you?"

"You know I do, Julia. I had family there. But how can we leave the city in the middle of a curfew? And where would we go?"

"Listen, Alice. I have a plan all worked out. I know a farmer who'll hide us from the Nazis. He's just an hour away, in the country. Please say that you'll come with me."

"Dearest Julia, I'm most grateful for your concern, but I'm not sure I can go. I just can't pack up and leave. Besides, there's Peggy. I won't leave her behind and I don't know if your farmer would take her in. It's too much to ask."

"For heaven's sake, Alice. Be sensible! Who'll take care of your dog if they take you away? Please listen. I'll meet you in the lobby of the Vadaszkurt Hotel at 9 AM tomorrow. The curfew should be off by then. I've arranged for a service truck and driver to transport us. And, please, don't tell anyone about our plan."

My head was spinning. I didn't know what to say. It was a time for quick decisions.

"All right, Julia. I'll try to meet you there. I'll go by taxi."

"Good!" she exclaimed, sounding relieved. "I'll see you tomorrow, then."

I hung up the phone. Uncertainty and fear gripped my brain. I wasn't at all sure if I was doing the right thing. And I didn't know where to begin.

"A cup of tea, that's what I need to clear my brain," I said to myself. I prepared a cup in the kitchen, and, after taking off my coat, I settled down on the couch to think things over. In a flash Peggy was next to me, her head in my lap. Her big, trusting eyes looked up into mine, waiting for a word from me.

"How can I leave you, darling?" I asked her. "Who'll take care of you?" Her answer was a big wet lick of my face.

Right then I determined that I would never leave her behind again. She was my family, all I had right now. She would come with me, no matter what the destination!

Chapter IX

MURDER

The grandfather clock chimed the hour of ten as Peggy and I began our frantic preparations for the next morning's departure into the unknown. Julia's phone call had gotten me quite upset and raised all sorts of questions in my mind. Where were we actually going and what would our destination be like? Where would we hide, and for how long? Who was this farmer at whose mercy we would be forced to place our lives? And how much was it going to cost us? How would I pay him after my cash ran out? And, above all, would he object to Peggy's presence?

I needed to know the answers to all these questions, but right now I also needed to concentrate on my packing. This was not going to be some vacation or business trip to Paris where shops and shopkeepers stood ready to serve my every need. I would have to make careful choices about what to take along.

It wasn't until my suitcase was nearly full that I remembered the pieces of jewelry I had hidden upon my return from Paris. "You should have reminded me, Peggy," I admonished my faithful companion as she lay on my bed, watching my every move. "We could have been in big trouble had I forgotten to pack them." I got up on a kitchen chair and reached into the darkened light fixture. They were still there, thank God, just where I had left them. As I delicately removed each piece from its hiding place, I tried to estimate its worth, in case I needed to sell it. But I soon decided that the sentimental value of each item far exceeded what I could possibly sell it for. There was the diamond necklace, a family heirloom for four generations, originally worn by my great grandmother; and the 18K gold watch that had belonged to my father's mother, but which no longer kept time; the diamond rose with petals that could be used as earrings; and the antique bracelet that had found its way into our family from the wrist of some unknown aristocrat; and, finally, the ruby-diamond-emerald wedding band, my late father's proudest gift to my mother on their twentieth anniversary. Mother was very sentimental about it, but after my father died she had given it to me as a reminder of my parents' love for each other. I gathered them all up now, and brought them into the bedroom to pack away in the side pocket of my suitcase. All of a sudden, a thought struck me. This was going to be a trip like no other I had ever taken. It was quite conceivable that my bag and I could become separated. I would need to find another place to hide the only source of real funds I would have with me. They needed to be in the clothing I'd be wearing on our trip. I decided that my everyday coat, the one I would be wearing tomorrow, would provide the ideal hiding place.

I got a pair of scissors from the drawer and began opening the seams in the lining of my shoulders. After removing the shoulder pads, I stuffed each of my gems, after wrapping it in a handkerchief, into the two empty shoulder recesses. Then, with shaking hands, I restitched the seams, making sure to use the matching color thread. After completing my little chore, I tried on the coat in front of the full-length mirror in the bedroom. The coat looked exactly as it had before. "Nobody will ever suspect," I promised myself.

Just then, the air raid sirens began wailing. I grabbed Peggy off the bed, and was about to descend the stairs to the basement shelter with her, when I remembered Mr. Skenyi's stern directive. Peggy would have to remain in the apartment tonight, I reminded myself. As I reopened the apartment door, I could hear the tenants from the upper floors scurrying down the stairs. Once inside my apartment, I placed Peggy on the sofa, cautioning her to behave while I was downstairs. She looked up at me with the saddest eyes as she whimpered not to be left alone again. Right then, I decided that

Peggy and I would not be separated on this night, perhaps our last evening at home. I turned off the lights, and the two of us sat together in the darkened apartment.

"We're family, Peggy," I whispered in her ear. "We'll always be together, no matter what anyone says. If the bombs happen to fall, at least we won't have to go looking for each other."

Peggy wagged her tail in agreement.

Without lights there was little we could do while we awaited the "all clear" siren. It was still a little too early to retire, so I retrieved the short-wave radio from its hiding place and plugged it into one of the living room receptacles. Then, I settled down once more next to Peggy to listen to the latest developments.

The Germans had indeed sent their troops into Hungary, their erstwhile ally, and had taken full control of the government and armed forces. Admiral Horthy and the Hungarian General Staff had been arrested on charges of treason. The new Hungarian leaders, all Nazi puppets, promised sweeping changes that would make the country a more effective deterrent to the onrushing Red Army. General Zhukov, the Russian commander, had his forces advancing along a five-hundred-mile front to within a hundred miles of the old Czech border on one flank, and within fifty-two miles of Rumania on the other. The rest of the foreign news was equally optimistic. There was even speculation that an invasion of Europe, by Allied forces poised somewhere in Britain, was at hand.

Suddenly, Peggy started barking excitedly. She jumped off the couch and ran over to the apartment door. Now I could hear the cause of her agitation. It was a noise coming from the hallway just outside our door. I quickly unplugged the radio and ran with it to the linen closet, stubbing my toe on the way. I limped back to the living room to find Peggy still on alert at the door. Then I heard a key turning in the lock. "It must be Mr. Skenyi, Peggy. He's the only person with our keys. He's probably checking to see if I'm all right after missing me in the basement. Please calm down and stop your barking."

Peggy calmed herself somewhat, but she seemed unconvinced. She remained at the door, ever on alert.

Suddenly, before I had a chance to open the door from the inside, it was flung open, and someone shone a strong beam of light directly into my eyes. I was completely blinded.

"Alice Dunn," a strange voice addressed me from behind the beam, "you're under arrest. Get your things and come with us now! Quickly!"

The order was clear and direct, but its meaning got jumbled by the time it reached my confused brain. I could hear my heart pounding as the questions leaped uncontrolled from my mouth. "What do you mean? What have I done? What are the charges?" Was it I who was saying those things? It seemed as if another person had taken control of my body and brain.

"Never mind the questions!" The voice was gruff and unfriendly. "Just do as we say and you won't get hurt. Get your things and let's go!"

"But I haven't done anything." My voice continued to argue in spite of myself. I had lost control of it! "I only stayed upstairs to be with Peg..."

I felt something strike my mouth and I could feel instant pain. The force of the blow sent me hurtling against the back of the sofa. Before I realized what had happened, I found myself sitting on the floor, staring at the carpet on which was collecting a pool of dark-colored liquid from my dripping chin.

In a flash I saw Peggy charge the voice behind the flashlight. The light hit the floor with a bang. Her snarls sounded more fierce than any I had ever heard.

"You dirty bitch!" I heard a voice exclaim. "Let go of me!"

A shot rang out. I saw the muzzle flash in the darkened room as the acrid scent of sulphur entered my nostrils. Someone picked up the flashlight and turned on the beam. The small circle of light shone on the floor in front of me, revealing a quivering, whimpering body.

"Oh, God!" I heard my voice exclaim. "What have you done? You've shot Peggy! God damn you!"

Something from within was forcing me to get up and rush to the quivering body. As I stooped over to pick her up in my arms, I felt a sticky substance coating my hands. Her legs were making short, uncontrolled movements in the air as a whimper escaped from her throat. Then all her movements stopped.

Peggy was dead. She had been my companion, my friend, and my protector, all wrapped into one small body. Now, she could be none of them. My mind refused to believe it.

My inner weeping was interrupted by the all clear siren. Suddenly the room lights went on, and I could see three men standing in the open doorway. One of them was Mr. Skenyi. The other two were strangers. The only similarity in their appearance was the swastika armbands they were wearing. The short stranger wore a jacket over his pants. He had a dark mustache, similar to the one I had seen Charlie Chaplin wear in his movies. He was holding a pistol in his right hand. The other stranger was tall, thin, and dark-haired. A long scar extended from the bridge of his nose to the middle of his right cheek. A twisted, ugly smile accented the scar's appearance. He held the flashlight that had blinded me earlier.

The short man spoke first. "You'd better get moving if you don't want the same treatment as your dog. Right now." He was pointing his gun at me now.

"You bastard . . . ." I heard my voice exclaim. "Why did you have to do it? She didn't mean any harm. She was just trying to protect me."

I walked slowly over to the sofa and placed Peggy's motionless body on her cushion, the one she used to lie on when we sat together in the living room. I could clearly see the bleeding bullet hole in the right side of her neck. I bent down to kiss her head, as I had done on so many previous occasions. Then I pulled the eyelids over her eyes, those reproachful eyes that I can still see today.

"Goodbye, my love," I whispered in her ear. "Sleep well. Perhaps we'll meet again . . . in better times."

I picked up my coat from the couch and wiped my hands on my skirt before slipping it on. Then I picked up the suitcase I had packed with such care a few hours ago. I had left it standing beside the couch.

The tall man grabbed the suitcase out of my hand. "You won't be needing that where you're going." He pushed me toward the open door.

I followed Mr. Skenyi out into the hall. He hadn't looked at me once since the lights had gone on. The other two followed close behind. The apartment door slammed shut behind us. I could feel a sob coming, but I stifled my tears so as not to give them the satisfaction of seeing me cry. As we began descending the stairs, I asked myself if I would ever see my beautiful home again. The other person in me, the one who had done all the talking before, said nothing.

Chapter X

FEAR COMES TO STAY

How can one adequately describe the collapse of one's life? It is much more than a feeling of emptiness, although that is certainly one of the more dominant sensations. There exists a kind of puzzlement, a disorientation through which your senses become distorted and out of focus. In time, all of it, the confusion, the denial, the rationalization, gives way to the loss you have felt from the beginning. It is an uncommon emotion because the chaos is behind it, and the unknown is yet to come. And, as the accompanying panic feeds on itself and begins to permeate the spirit, it grows constantly more primal. In the beginning, before there is anything for your eyes to see, before the first German tank rounds the corner, before the first Stuka drones low overhead, before the house-to-house searches begin, before there is looting and arson, that panic is growing constantly. You try to ignore it a little while longer, but it will not go away.

On March 19, 1944, that fear came to me. And it came to stay.

Terrible thoughts began to plague me as I descended the last two flights of stairs in a state of near shock. What had I done to cause this awful nightmare? What accusations would they level against me, and would I have the opportunity to defend myself? What unthinkable punishment awaited me? Was I to become just another of the thousands of victims of the ruthless Nazi purge of which I had so often heard? I shuddered uncontrollably at the thought. No, I would not permit myself to even think of those things! Besides, didn't Mme. Boriska predict that I would be a survivor? Was this, then, the beginning of those horrible experiences she had foreseen? If so, God help me!

Before I had a chance to ponder my uncertain future further, we arrived on the ground floor. Mr. Skenyi, who had led our small group, now beat a hasty retreat into his apartment without a remark or even a glance in my direction. The brief light from his open door enabled me to read my watch in the darkened hallway. It was just after two o'clock. Good timing, I thought to myself. The appropriate hour for predators and victims to be about.

The two gangsters who had followed me down the stairs now grasped my arms from either side and led me unceremoniously toward the entrance door. As it opened, I was propelled forward, stumbling down the front steps. Before I could regain my balance, I had crashed against a dark-colored van parked at the curb, its engine running. One of the men, the one with the scar, grabbed me by the hair and half dragged me to the rear of the vehicle.

"Where are you taking me?" I demanded with a naive defiance. "What are the charges against me? You know I haven't . . ."

I was answered with another swift, hard blow to my face. I could feel the blood spatter down on my coat as the wound reopened. Now, I felt myself being grasped by both of them as I was flung through the open rear door of the van. I scrambled into the dark blackness on my knees, scraping them on the rough metal floor. As I grasped for a handhold inside, my hands felt a bench and I sat down on it. On the opposite wall I could see a tiny barred window through which the early morning chill penetrated. I pulled my coat tightly around me and sensed the rough outline of my new shoulder pads. I reached inside my coat to reassure myself that the stitching was still intact. Then I wiped the blood from my face with my sleeve.

By this time, the van was starting up and I grabbed the bench to keep myself from falling off as we careened through the darkened streets on our malevolent collection route. At the first stop the open door produced an old man clutching an unlit pipe, and two younger men wearing only bathrobes that they held tightly closed as they stumbled into the dark interior. Without a word of complaint, they sat down dejectedly on the opposite bench. One of the younger men wore the same badge of futile defiance as I did. His face was covered with blood from a cut over his right eyebrow. I gingerly fingered the cut on my own face. It had almost stopped bleeding. I could feel the moist edges of the wound and hoped that it wouldn't become infected. Perhaps our destination would have a first aid station.

Now, the van screeched to another stop. Through the open doors I could see the tall apartment houses as they stood silent witness to yet another injustice. This time it was a middle-aged man accompanied by a pair of elderly ladies. The man clutched the remains of two crutches against his chest. They had been broken in half, rendered totally useless. The ladies held each other in their arms, sobbing softly.

There were to be more stops and more victims that morning. Each time, the van slowed and crept up another unlit street claiming more victims, who were devoured through its open jaws. The new day was rapidly approaching, a gray, misty dawn. I was able to see my companions a little more clearly now. We were all alike, all victims of some strange, inhuman justice. Each of us wore the same dazed look. Each smelled of the same fear and confusion. As the interior of the van became more crowded, it was easier to keep from being tossed about. But that was of little solace. No one spoke or complained. Not even the frightened little boy who sat sobbing beneath the tiny window. Perhaps his parents had offered too much resistance. He had entered the van unaccompanied.

One more stop. This one, just before daybreak, made no pretense at stealth. The sound of breaking glass shattered the early morning stillness. I could sense the drama unfolding outside as the youngster across from me stopped his sobbing to peer through the window. His whole body shuddered at the sight he was witnessing. The sound of harsh voices mixed with frantic, high-pitched pleas as an object hit the side of the van. The door was yanked open, and I could hear the grunts and groan of an old man. We all turned to watch a young girl with long blond braids help her aged companion inside. As the occupants of the bench made room for him, he sat down on the edge with a loud groan. The young girl bent over him to straighten his prayer shawl and skull cap. He offered a weak smile in return and, reaching up, gently touched the side of her face where a dark bruise had already formed. As the van, now filled to overflowing, pulled away, with its doors slammed shut, I began to wonder about our destination.

Chapter XI

BAPTISM OF TERROR

We finally stopped at a rabbinical school, the Rabbikepzo-Rokszilard-utca. What irony!

The stone and cement building looked more like a barracks than a school for holy men. Square windows were the primary source of light on all three floors, but on this day they only reflected the gloom, like so many shadowed eyes.

We were led to massive double doors that opened onto a dusty courtyard where vans parked only long enough to disgorge their unfortunates before speeding off, scattering gravel and dreams.

Inside, the building had been stripped of any comforts it might have once had to facilitate the study of the scriptures. Now, it was just a great hall a floor beneath the towering cathedral ceiling.

It was just as well that there were no seats, as they would have made the scuffle for space even more feverish than it was. While more unfortunates were constantly being jammed through the doors with rifle butts, those already inside were desperately clinging to what precious patch of floor they had secured.

The cries of those imploring others to give way mixed with the anguish of the confused. A man waved his hat at a screaming woman only a few bodies away, trying to catch the attention of someone calling his name. Elsewhere, there were simple embraces, with neither finding comfort in the heaving sobs of the suddenly lost. There was barely enough room to breathe and the heat and smell of confusion and fear made the atmosphere increasingly unbearable.

A mother tried hard to calm her two young boys, who were screaming for milk. Their wailing made the people next to them talk more loudly. And the confusion grew. It grew beyond an echo, to something that permeated, that penetrated one's hearing so that only the din itself remained. It was truly chaotic. The noise trapped us all.

Still more vans came, and the doors swinging away from the building let in a little more light and many more yellow Stars of David. One man tried to go back out through the doors, shouting for his wife, but he was met with a boot in the stomach. No one stopped to help him as men wielding clubs chased him back inside the building. Newcomers stared in disbelief. Those who had come earlier hovered nearer to the ragged bundles they had brought, and pulled their children ever closer to them.

In one corner a young girl, in a perfectly pressed linen suit, with hat and gloves, sat on the floor and wept silently. Near her a handful of students sang familiar or religious songs at the tops of their voices, hoping the melodies would mask their fear. The girl did not seem to hear them as she compulsively combed her long, blond hair.

An elderly man sat in another corner, a neatly folded blazer beneath him, half of a loaf of bread in his hand. He stared blankly in front of him and didn't move, except to sink deeper into himself and hunch his shoulders when someone squeezed closer.

In the turmoil I hear a plaintive cry: "Let me out! Let me out!" I craned my neck to look in the vicinity of the doors, but they remained closed. The lost plea had come from elsewhere. It went unheeded.

I looked around. All the faces were strange.

"I don't belong here," I said aloud to no one but myself. But I did belong. I was no longer the celebrated designer of Budapest. I was undistinguishable from the others. My name was the same. My uselessness was the same. It was marked with the Star of David.

No one noticed Alice Dunn. No one even noticed the dried blood on my skirt, Peggy's blood. We were all very much alike, with that one badge as the common characteristic. To our captors, it was all that mattered.

Still more came through those doors. I had previously been able to find privacy in the quiet moments when I needed solace, sometimes even in air raid shelters. But it would not be so here. Bodies pressed against bodies and elbows pressed back. Soon it would be a crush, with no one able to move from his or her shrinking space. I began to perspire heavily and breathe shallowly of the musty air. The windows remained closed. My skirt and sweater began to itch. I could barely move enough to get relief.

Suddenly, desperately, I needed a bathroom. I had never taken care of these needs out of doors, much less in public. The thought was both degrading and disgusting.

I remembered seeing a sign for a restroom. I turned and saw the Hungarian spelling high on the wall about sixty feet away. That was where I had to go. Hours ago, when I had first arrived, the journey would have been much easier. Now there was nowhere to step. Those who had been reclining were now sitting up with their feet tucked in close. Someone else was leaning against their legs, another against their back. I had to step over each, and around those still standing who thought I intended to intrude on their places.

When I finally reached the wall a few feet from the door under the sign, I turned and looked in dismay at a line of people stretching back to where I had come from. As the door they were facing opened, each moved forward in turn, waiting for their chance.

I could ill afford to wait much longer. I shouldered my way toward the door at the front of the line. A soldier stood next to it on the opposite side of the line from me. I squeezed closer to the entrance.

As the door opened, inward, I sensed a sickening stench. It made my stomach turn. But I had no choice. I rushed forward, the man coming out, still zipping his pants, noticed me and grabbed my arm.

"What do you think you are doing?" he shouted in Hungarian. "You were not behind me. Get back in line with the rest of them! You don't belong here!"

I tried to wrench free, but his hold was firm.

"Officer!" he shouted.

The soldier had already noticed the struggle. He pushed his

way through the line toward me. Putting his hand around my throat
he backed me up against the wall. People nearby shrank back. Some
of them looked away.

Not much older than I, the soldier slowly looked me up and
down. His eyes lingered on me for a moment. Then he turned his
gaze on my coat. Snatching it away from me, he turned sideways to
watch me out of the corner of his eye.

"That is only an old wrap to sit on," I said. "What could you
want with it?"

"Silence!" he ordered, as he turned toward me, watching me
intently.

Holding the coat with his left hand, he slowly explored the
hemline with his thumb and forefinger. Then, he squeezed the
sleeves inch by inch, and did the same to the collar. He examined
the inside lining and for an instant seemed defeated. Then, as he
glanced at me for a clue, his hands fell on the shoulder pads. In a
flash he was smiling.

He struggled briefly before the seams parted. He fished out the
jewelry from one shoulder pad and then turned his attention to the
other.

When he was finished, he examined each piece carefully. I
stood there waiting, a hollow feeling in the pit of my stomach. My
arms and legs felt numb. The soldier slipped several jewels into his
pocket and rolled some of the smaller ones into his fist.

"Ignorant Jew," he hissed through his rotting teeth. "You
thought you could outsmart us."

He used his fists like clubs, beating down on me as though he
were swinging an ax. The cut on my forehead reopened with the first
blow, but the sight of my blood seemed only to spur him on.

I tried to flee, but he blocked my attempt to lunge past him.
Propping me up against the wall, he continued to pound my face and
shoulders. Finally, I fell sideways onto the threshold of the
bathroom. As I curled up to protect my ribs he viciously kicked me
in the back.

"There," he said, kicking me once more, "you have earned
your turn at the toilet. Go ahead, use it!"

He stepped over me, resuming his place against the wall near
the door. He didn't look at me again. I saw him finger his pockets,

where the remnants of my past were located, before I closed the door behind me.

When I emerged, I tried to move as far away as I could from the toilet until the pain in my back and the throbbing in my head made me dizzy. I leaned against the wall near a corner and felt someone give way a little as I sank to the floor.

I woke up with a humming in my ears. It was cold. Through the upper windows I could see pink clouds. I must have slept, but the pain and numbness in my body were still there.

I became aware that the man next to me was pulling at the sleeve of my sweater and his lips were moving. I must have given him a quizzical look because he leaned closer.

"Can you hear me?" he asked. His words barely penetrated the hum. "Whistles have blown and they are preparing to make an announcement. You must listen closely."

Slowly, painfully, I pushed myself upright. Most of the people were still slumped on the floor, jammed together. We were all alike. There were no longer any distinguishable features, no outstanding manners of dress or jewelry, no distinctive hairstyles. We were a gray mass.

It was all for the better, but I did not know it yet.

The soldiers had cleared a space on the floor by the entrance, and it was now occupied by a half-dozen officers. One stepped forward and produced a piece of paper from his jacket pocket.

All fell silent as he announced in perfect Hungarian, that each of us was guilty of plotting to overthrow the government of Hungary. We were all to be sentenced to death.

This is what the man next to me relayed as the room once again erupted in a crying and wailing that competed with the buzzing in my ears.

"We will not be tried?" I asked him, my voice sounding tinny. "Just like that, the death sentence?"

"We are mostly Jews," he said. "Not all, but that does not matter."

The soldiers saluted each other and left the building. The verdict was final. There would be no appeal, no need for justice nor justification. Only a need to solve the "Jewish problem" in Budapest, just as was already being done throughout Europe.

A woman sitting on the other side of me cradled her baby.

"Where is your daddy?" she asked aloud. I noticed that my hearing in my left ear was better than my right. "Where is your daddy?"

The woman turned to me.

"My husband and I were separated when they brought us in here," she said. "I don't know where he is. I know he is in here, somewhere. I have to find him." She began to sob.

"How long have you been here?"

"They brought us in last night. They came to our house in the middle of the night and took us away. We barely had time to dress." The woman was wearing a simple dress, the baby was wrapped in a blanket.

"He will find you," I said, consoling her.

She looked at me, and then down at her child. The baby was sleeping. Suddenly she thrust the bundle at me.

"Please hold my baby for me," she said, scrambling to her feet. "I must find my husband." And she disappeared into the mass of humanity.

At first I held the baby at arm's length. I looked at the sleeping child's face, a face that did not know the horror around it. Did not know of the frightening choice its mother had made. Did not know yet that the hands holding it were unfamiliar to the task.

I slowly brought the child onto my lap, trying not to wake it. I hoped the woman would return soon. I knew that shortly they would have to begin emptying out the hall. They would have to take those of us already here to another prison elsewhere—to some other terror.

And I thought about the horrible stories I had heard about the Nazi experiments on mother and child. They would never believe the child was not mine.

I did not hear the baby crying at first but I felt its trembling. Little hands pawed at my breasts. It was hungry, and still didn't know that I was not its mother.

I stroked the baby's temple. Sadness overcame the awkwardness of the moment, sadness from a feeling that a battle was inexorably lost before the chance to fight had ever presented itself.

I had only been with the child for thirty or forty minutes when, suddenly, a pair of hands reached for it. I drew back. When I looked up, I saw the baby's mother.

"Thank God I found you," she cried. As she picked up the child, it immediately stopped crying. "Thank you so much for caring for him. I don't know how to thank you."

I knuckled tears from my face.

"I am glad you came back. Did you find your husband?"

"Yes. He is standing in line for the restroom. It is the only one in the building. He will be back soon. He is close to the front now.

I smiled at the mother and her child.

Before the husband found us, the doors to the hall were flung open. About a dozen soldiers poured in, and I could see more outside. People started pushing toward the doors amid the ever-present shouts of *"Schneller! Schneller!"* It had grown uncomfortably warm inside, and people had been shedding their coats. Now there was a scramble to retrieve their few pitiful belongings. We were farthest from the doors, so we went out last. There was sufficient time for the husband to return. He could only offer his wife a gesture of helplessness. I suspected she had seen that gesture before.

The soldiers seemed in a hurry. The nearer we got to the door the more restive they became. People were being hurled through the opening, and those who lost their footing were prodded to their feet by kicking boots. The young couple and their child disappeared as I ducked through the door and into the courtyard.

"Where are we going?" I asked a man near me, as I stepped up to the waiting van, squinting in the afternoon sun.

"We are going to Csepel Island to work," he said.

"How do you know?"

"The driver used to be a neighbor of mine."

Csepel is a small island in the Danube, south of the center of Budapest. Its use was primarily industrial. It had been chosen as our next stop because the only way off the island was by a bridge leading to Pest, and it could be easily guarded.

The warehouse where we would be incarcerated was surrounded by a high fence, permitting us to remain outside the cramped building, if we so chose. That is where many of us waited, in preference to the steaming vans, while the Hungarian guards practiced their German efficiency in getting our new prison prepared.

By the time our van was finally emptied, the sun was going down. But the day still seemed unseasonably warm. Chimneys from the many factories surrounding the warehouse loomed over us like sentries. I found an empty spot against the wall of the warehouse and slumped down. For me, another day had come and gone.

It was morning and I felt cold. I had never gotten my coat back. I awoke to a man shaking my shoulder. I did not know why he woke me; there seemed to be nothing going on. Nothing but the interminable waiting.

But I could tell he was trying to say something to me.

"Pardon me, but I cannot hear you."

"They are calling names for people to come inside," he said, almost shouting.

I listened, straining to hear. Every so often another name would be called over the loudspeaker. I wondered what they were up to.

As I sat up the man who had awakened me moved away. He found a shadow, closer to the door, and sat down.

I wondered about the names until they called mine.

It was the first time I had heard my name called in three days. Wonder turned to apprehension. There was every reason to believe that the summons had a sinister intent. What would they want a Jew for anyway?

"Alice Dunn. Alice Dunn. Report to the police table at once."

My heart skipped a beat. I couldn't move.

Later the loudspeaker blared again. I heard the noise, but could not distinguish the words. The same man who had awakened me earlier, returned. He looked even more disheveled than before. His dirty coveralls made him look like a factory worker. Now, his shirt was grimy as well, and a streak of dirt crossed his forehead between his shabby dark eyebrows and his unkempt black hair.

"They are calling for translators," he said. "Do you speak German?"

"Yes," I said, when I comprehended his words. "But I don't think I want to go in there. I don't trust them."

The man didn't offer any advice and I was thankful for that. But as I had a moment to think I had time to notice that the day would again turn into a cold night. Perhaps it would be warmer inside the building. Maybe it wasn't a trick after all.

I stumbled through the heavy wooden door nearest to me. I was met by the foul smell of desperation. To my left, in another enormous room devoid of anything but a dusty floor, I saw several soldiers gathered around a table. A bedraggled woman in a torn dress was holding up a document, straining to read it. A Hungarian officer stood nearby.

Slowly, I made my way over to the table and stood in front of it. One of the soldiers, decorations gleaming on his chest, turned to look at me. He spoke, but I couldn't hear him.

"I have been beaten, as you can see, and am not hearing well," I said, leaning toward him. As I did so, he backed away slightly. "I was told you need translators."

He snatched the document from the other woman and handed it to me. Then he pointed to some pencils and blank paper.

"Write down what is said in the orders," he ordered.

There was plenty of light to work with but I still had to squint to read the German words on the paper. Everything was blurry. I had suffered from astigmatism since my childhood, though it had never been this bad.

I blinked several times to get the type into focus. The printing was poor, the paper yellowed, and the type a washed-out gray. When I did discern the words, a literal translation was almost impossible. But there was no mistaking the intent.

Beginning the next day, all those who had been found guilty of treason would be transported to Poland for extermination.

I wrote out the translation and handed it to the officer. He tossed me a moldy piece of bread.

It was the first food I had seen since this nightmare had begun. I thought about the supper I had forgone that last night at home. I knew that most of the people watching me also had not eaten in more than two days. There were so many of them. I slipped the bread into the pocket of my skirt.

The trains began moving the next day, but it wasn't until another day passed that I was wrenched from sleep and sent staggering toward the waiting railroad cars. Those of us left behind during the first loading had watched in horror as more and more people were crammed into each freight car. They had tried to get us all on one train of twelve cars, but there were just too many people. By dawn the next day, when the soldiers came for me and the other leftovers. More had been added overnight, so there really was no wasted space.

As usual, the soldiers limited their vocabulary to "*Schneller!*" punctuated by boot kicks, rifle butts, and clubs. We scrambled onto the freight cars and, when we thought that capacity had been reached, more were herded in.

When they finally did slide the door shut, the pink clouds of morning had disappeared, leaving only the pressing bodies and the encompassing fear.

I stayed close to the door. The cool iron felt less suffocating than the press of strange, warm flesh. We all had to stand for there was not enough room on the floor to sit. I had to struggle to cross my arms in front of me.

Somewhere in the car another felt as I did. A man's voice began screaming, "Out! Out! I must get out!" I could hear him pounding on the side of the car and then scratching at it with his fingernails. Eventually, the man's voice grew weaker and his pounding and scraping slowed. Eventually he became exhausted.

People clung to each other. I had no one to hold on to and never felt more alone than on that train. Even with the mass of humanity pressed against me I was completely alone.

I wondered if it was a dream, and at once another thought came to me. I remembered Silbiger Boriska's prophecy that I would be among screaming, struggling people behind bars. I didn't even know if that recollection was a dream. Reality seemed illusive.

Had we been able to see outside, we would have known that the morning sun was in the face of the engineer as we climbed the Carpathian Mountains toward Poland. The only sense I had of time was that the morning we had boarded was long ago. Every so often, a sliver of light would sneak in through the loosening seams of the car, but we could not tell whether it was sunlight or a searchlight beam.

Consciousness came and went as well, and as irregularly. A sudden jolt of the train would shake me back to awareness; then the rhythmic chugging of the engine and click-clack of the wheels would cause me to doze off. That, and the creeping exhaustion. A few slumped halfway to the floor before being propped on the shoulders of others who no longer cared. Others just stayed wedged in a corner or between two or three more faceless strangers.

The last time I wondered about time was when the train finally picked up speed and continued at an even pace for a while. But, like my silent comrades, the thought didn't linger. No thoughts did.

Perhaps that is the best way: Never aware, never conscious, never unconscious. Not thinking. The past was gone, and the future had nothing to offer. To think meant to connect the rumors we had heard with what was happening. That was not something anyone wanted to do.

Without light and without focus, everything was in slow motion, nothing was defined. I tried straining my eyes to see the rest of the people in the freight car. All I could make out were silhouettes reaching, crawling, squirming. Arms and legs were twisted, interlaced like tentacles. It was a swarm, a cobweb, without order.

I must have gotten used to sleeping standing up because it came as a surprise that I woke up lying down. I couldn't see the woman who had been standing next to me; an unfamiliar shape had taken her place. For a moment, I wondered if I was alive or dead.

The one certainty was that I was too exhausted to move. I felt heavy, weighed down, too drained to get off this lumpy place of rest.

Someone nearby stirred, touching me. Suddenly a hand gripped my shoulder, shaking me violently. I saw a tall, stocky figure. He moved his face close to mine and I could see his eyes widen. He had the fearful eyes of someone who had seen his nightmare come true. He screamed.

"Get up! You've squashed her to death. You have killed my Susan. Look what you have done. You've taken the air from her."

The man's horror had come before that of most of the rest of us. He shook me fiercely, almost lifting me off the floor. I felt like a puppet in his hands. All of us were weak. He had found strength.

I reached out to balance myself and touched the lifeless mass under me. It was a feeling I had never known before. I was bewildered and afraid. Despair followed.

The body was cold, like marble. And the accusation was clear and formidable. Had I collapsed on top of the woman, somehow bringing this on? It was easy to believe.

His rage turned to lament, from anger to tears. His heart broke in front of me and I understood his pain. I respected that pain and was silent.

He held his head in one hand while the other reached out to caress his wife. His body shuddered as his shoulders heaved with every labored breath.

I barely made it to my knees, remaining close enough to touch the woman's shoulder. With the slightest sound, I recited the *Kaddish*, the ancient prayer for dead souls. The solemn words of communion with God brought me a glimmer of solace.

It was the first time I had ever recited the prayer.

I had been dry-eyed at the passing of my father. Now, abruptly, I felt tears on my face. I had fought those tears since 1939, and had suppressed them when Peggy was killed. Now as they gushed forth, I welcomed them.

I wept for myself, for that wretched woman, for all the souls on that train and all the other trains. I cried for the child I had held in my arms—how long ago had it been? That child would never smell a flower or chase a ball. Beauty would never be a part of its young life. It was destined to be a lost child.

I tried to shut my eyes and ears to my wretched surroundings. And, quietly, I said goodbye again. This time, to everything. I bid adieu to memories and dreams, and cast my fate to the unknown.

And the fear disappeared.

Gradually, the familiar rattle of the train slowed and stopped. Even the widowed man had stopped sobbing, leaving the quiet of the freight car intact.

Noises approached from outside. Something was about to happen.

Chapter XII

PURGATORY IN POLAND

LOCKS CLICKED OPEN AND DOORS CRASHED BACK—
"Schneller! Schneller!"—stumbling out, blinking, blinded by the
powerful klieg lights . . . "Where's the step down?" . . . falling,
feeling and tasting the mud . . . "Where are we!? . . ." "I can't see,
I can't see! . . . "Come, you must get up or . . ." "I can't walk, help
me . . ." "Please don't take him away. You mustn't take him! . . .
"No, no, give me back my baby! . . ."

An endless line of men disappear into the darkness. Women
this way, prodded by boots and rifle butts. One falls from a blow to
the temple . . . others drag her along, but she cannot escape the
kicking boots. Doors close on a truckload of children, and the vehicle
pulls away into the night.

A strange, acrid, sulphurous smell coming from the chimneys
. . .

Hard, faceless Germans . . . robots . . . shiny buttons . . .
uniforms . . . polished boots and rifles . . . whistles . . . *"Schneller!"*

Filthy Jews . . . mud-stained . . . bleeding . . . tattered clothes
. . . crawling . . . a little farther . . . a little farther . . . another
muddy field.

Away from the lights, the sky was fading to gray. Morning was
coming slowly. A handful of German officers stood between us and

a boxlike barracks. One of the soldiers stepped forward.

"*Achtung! Schweinhunde.* On your feet," he shouted, his voice harsh. "Take off your clothes and shoes and line up. Now! *Schneller!*"

As we struggled to stand, we glanced around. The only true reactions were disbelief or horror. But the order was obeyed. What had become rags were slowly peeled away, clothes that had been slept in, soiled, torn. Some held the garments against their bodies, trying to cover their nakedness. Many wept in the face of the overpowering shame. Cries came from those whose rags were ripped away by passing guards.

Some were able to slip quietly into shock, their eyes glazed and staring absently. Others kept their eyes downcast, avoiding the sneering guards. For many, the dawn was coming too quickly.

The soldiers stood like a tribunal, singling out those who were injured. They were taken out of line and led away. We did not know where. Only those of us who could stand were permitted to stay.

I followed all orders completely and quickly. But to do so I had to ignore those penetrating eyes. I disregarded them, refused to think of them as human eyes. I stopped thinking about them entirely as I shed my blood-stained skirt and sweater, undergarments and shoes. I held my head high and stared straight ahead. After a while I didn't feel the chilly breeze.

No one's head turned. The tears of those next to me were felt rather than seen.

There were hundreds of us waiting to be counted. Hundreds of haggard bodies. Women of all ages, their bodies and their spirits stripped to reveal their secrets. More German soldiers came to replace their comrades, and inventory was taken again and again and again.

Still we stood, motionless. The sun rose and fell and another inventory was taken, another few naked, hobbling, broken women were singled out and led away.

Again at dusk and again at full night. Again when the most weary sank to the ground to find sleep in the damp mud and sparse grass. To fall was to be taken away. The rest of us were counted once more.

Again before dawn and again as the new day glimmered.

Throughout the next day. Whistles, more Germans, another inventory.

The lines continued to grow smaller. Only those who could endure would see tomorrow—even though tomorrow would be no different.

In the middle of the third day, the final test came. There was work to be done and the laborers were waiting, naked. It was time to make use of them: Those who passed the test and survived the scrutiny of the camp doctor. His name was Josef Mengele.

It was Mengele who decided who was capable of working and who would help him in his experiments. He was a curious man who did not waste anesthetics on his test animals. He was most curious about the physical and psychological aspects of pain. His tools, his test animals, were the inmates of the camp. He was curious to see how they would react to electric shock.

He was also curious about the effects of brain, liver, and heart surgery on unborn children.

Mengele filled pages and pages with notes, and thousands of hearts with fear and hatred.

His eligibility test was simple: Mengele walked slowly down the line of women, studying each. As his inspection began, we were all commanded to raise the left arm. If Mengele saw bones protruding he lifted his finger. The next victim had been selected.

Few went quietly; they had heard of Mengele. And of Ilse Koch, whose experiments began with Mengele's leftovers.

For Mengele this inspection was a solemn ceremony. His Nazi uniform was impeccably tailored and he moved slowly down each line, gently tapping his riding crop against his leg. His face was expressionless. It was as though he was looking over a meaningless toy.

He turned onto our row.

I felt my heart begin to beat faster. My mouth became dry, while my right palm turned clammy.

I sensed, rather than saw, him coming. He moved very slowly. He was very deliberate in his decisions. A girl screamed and was dragged away. I glanced over. Mengele's expression did not change.

I felt my body grow damp as beads of perspiration formed and then dripped down my face, chest, and legs. My heart was already pounding, and Mengele still had two more decisions to make before he got to me. Would he lift his finger here? Would he ever get here at all? For a moment I wanted it over with. In another I wanted more time.

I told myself that when he reached me he would pass, barely noticing me at all. I told myself to stop trembling. I told myself it was a nightmare and I would wake up soon. I wanted very much to wake up.

Then Mengele was in front of me and I knew I was really awake. I tried to look past him, look through him, look around him, as he looked through me, over me. I shivered in spite of the fact that I felt warm. He looked at me slowly, as though he was musing over a new shirt. I felt my legs weaken and wobble. If I fell it would all be over. I tried hard to pretend he wasn't even there, that I had nothing to worry about. But still I trembled and fought to keep from collapsing.

I prayed silently.

He moved on.

Sunrise and sunset were the only way to keep track of the days as we stood. The German inventories slipped into a routine of dawn and dusk. In between they waited for more to collapse. Many did. Mengele got them too.

The rest of us stood until even the sunrises became sunsets and dusk became no different from dawn. It was another day, sometimes rain, sometimes the bright sun parching our skin.

But always standing. Sitting or squatting on the barren ground was forbidden. Our bodies relieved themselves where we stood and still we were not allowed to move.

Those of us who passed Mengele's test were fed on the third day following the dawn *Appel*, the German word for head count. I remembered the voices when we arrived echoing, "Eat! Eat!" I forced myself to swallow the brown slush. It was served up in rusty cans and usually contained small bits of turnip. It also included pieces of stone, wood shavings, and even nails.

There was little encouragement in either the food or the passing of Mengele's test. Yet, it raised the question that maybe death was not imminent. At least, I thought, today was secure.

As long as we could stand.

"We must hold each other," came a voice next to me. It was a young woman, her long, black hair flowing down over her breasts.

Almost subconsciously we drifted closer together until we were side by side. Then we linked arms. The strength of one became the strength of several and the weakness of one was reinforced.

The woman on the other side of me, on my right, fainted. The rest of us kept her standing. The guards did not notice.

They noticed two who fell in front of us and swept them away.

We quietly shifted our weight, first to this foot, then to that, keeping each other awake. I felt my head bobbing, my neck bending more and more forward. I drifted in and out of consciousness. I saw a multitude of twinkling lights. What is happening to me? Am I in heaven? Or are these the shimmering lanterns on the many bridges over the Danube? Then, all of a sudden, I played hide-and-seek, running between the century-old baroque buildings, stumbling on cobblestones, trying to escape from some unknown pursuer. Those next to me gently tugged at my arm to keep me alert. All of us were weary and we took turns bearing the weight. There were no words; it was just done.

We held on for several days. I had lost count of them. Then, the soldiers marched us toward the barracks. It was empty. The ones before us didn't need the room. Ashes don't take up much space.

The camp was divided into about thirty sections, each designated by a letter of the alphabet. Ours was *Lager* C. It was windowless, damp, dismal. The bunks were three feet high, with mattresses filled with straw and smelling of urine. The mattresses were about the size of a double bed. There were thirty racks of bunks, fifteen on each side of the barracks.

They were to accommodate more than six hundred prisoners.

It was up to us to select our bunkmates and to keep the barracks clean. Both tasks were important. The forced intimacy made us want to be clean, at least made us want those around us to be as clean as possible. The overseers— "*Aufseherinnen*" —some of whom carried whips, wanted the barracks to be kept clean. Each day someone new was appointed to clean the barracks. Each day there was an inspection. Just about every day there were consequences.

German efficiency began displaying itself less than two weeks after we arrived. We had to be cleansed, naturally, because we were a threat to our Nazi captors.

We were marched into an enormous brick building, one of many we could see throughout the camp. It looked like a factory without windows. This one stood at the end of our section. Four chimneys poked through the roof. They belched the heavy smoke that spread soot over the *Lager*.

The efficiency came in the speed with which they were able to perform our delousing. Through the entrance, guarded by a pair of soldiers, we moved into a corridor smelling of disinfectant. Then, we were herded through a great, open hall and into another room full of cubicles. We went in two at a time, one person for each of the spigots on the wall.

But only one of the spigots worked at any one time. One released steaming, scalding water. The other only hissed, waiting its turn. We knew its function. We stood in the cubicle, each week, and waited. This time, each of us was bathed.

I didn't realize that while I waited my turn, staring at the ceiling rather than at the spigots, the remains of my fingernails were piercing the skin of my palms.

A whistle, sharp yet soothing, commanded us out of the cubicles. On to the next hall. Still dripping, naked, we were met by more soldiers and a mountain of old clothes.

The guards took a sporting pleasure in throwing us the rags we would wear until the next delousing. For me, this first time, it was a man's flannel shirt, several sizes too big. Lucky for me. The woman in front of me had gotten only a pajama top. It barely reached her waist. My shirt was scratchy from all the fumigation, but it reached all the way to my knees.

I welcomed the castaway clothing, even though it was a far cry from what I had known. In time, we would all come to trade clothing when it was useful. That first time, though, was a selfish time.

So it was with the shoes, even more so. Shoes meant life. If you couldn't walk, you couldn't work. And walking on stones and broken roots all day meant scratches and infection. No one could afford that.

On the day after our first delousing, we were all given new life. A truck backed up after the morning inventory and the tailgate opened. A pair of soldiers dumped what looked like a thousand pairs of shoes out onto the ground.

There were tennis shoes, riding boots, hiking boots, galoshes, even evening slippers with rhinestone buckles. Shoes of every kind.

We couldn't count on getting a second pair, especially after the *Aufseherinnen* told us this would be the last visit by the shoe truck. So, when the guards released us from formation, there was nothing else on anyone's mind. Finding the right shoe, and finding its mate, was all that mattered.

Only food would have attracted such a frenzy. I tried to get through the crowd several times only to be pushed back.

One woman came away with a pair of silk opera pumps. They were hardly a thing to wear in the mud. The soles, though, were firm.

Two others argued over the same pair of shoes. One had the left shoe and the other had its mate. I didn't wait for the outcome as I finally found an opening and began my own search.

I ignored a pair of giant boots, perhaps size twenty, despite the black patent leather and gold trim.

Most of the women had made their choices by the time I began foraging in earnest. I had to settle for some wooden clogs, the kind worn in the Netherlands. They were too big and they were clumsy, but time was running out. And I had them in my possession. Learning to wear them without socks, and learning to answer the *"Schneller!"* promptly would have to come later. Learning to cope with the blisters would come much sooner. To help I collected some grass and leaves made sticky by the soot from the chimneys and stuffed them inside the clogs as padding. I made them wearable and in a few days I was able to walk normally.

There was a positive aspect to those awkward shoes. At night, when we slept, shoes were often stolen. Mine, I knew, were safe.

We were able to mark the weeks by the delousing schedule. At least, we could have. There really was no measure of time in the camps—only in hindsight. Only at the end of the day did you know that you had lived one more. To count days or weeks would mean having something to look forward to. We had nothing.

That is the way the Nazis wanted us to feel. They continued to take efficient steps to reinforce that feeling. They began again the day after we got our shoes.

An enormous *Aufseherin*, tapping a coiled whip against her thigh, marched us toward the building they used for delousing. Each of us knew that a week had not passed. We entered single file through a dark passageway and into the auditorium.

Tables were scattered throughout the room, with a single chair next to each. Some instruments were under a cloth on each table. We were directed to the tables and shoved into chairs. A uniformed woman waited at each table.

When I sat down, a swift, cold razor glided over my scalp. For a moment I feared that blade would travel toward my throat. But that was not the point of this exercise. The blade scraped my scalp again and again and again. The cold sweat dried on me, giving me a chill.

There was another chill to come. A pair of hands wrenched me out of my seat and I looked down to the floor. I saw my hair on the ground. In a panic I reached for my head. It was incredibly, horrifyingly smooth. It wasn't meant to be that way.

I was supposed to feel the curls my mother had once adorned with delightful colored ribbons.

I was supposed to feel the softness, the shining, the flowing.

I was supposed to feel my pride, my vanity, my womanhood.

After everything that had happened to us, our hair was all we had left. The last vestige of our dignity, our femininity, our innocence.

Mine was there on the floor.

I looked around. Several other women were standing, bald, touching their heads. Guards were leading them away. Many were crying.

I began to laugh, louder and louder. I couldn't stop. A guard slapped me and the sobbing took over, shaking me. I felt hollow and empty inside. The Nazis were efficient, indeed. I wondered what they could possibly do next. I only had to wait a few days.

My answer came on a bright morning with just a hint of spring in the air. This time the tables were set up in the courtyard where they counted us each morning. By the time inventory ended, the sun was already high.There were actually two long tables and several chairs at each. The tables were narrow and a uniformed woman sat on the other side of the table across from each of the chairs. At the order of *Nächste* (next), another prisoner was taken to a chair. I watched in horror as each member of my barracks was tattooed. Some cried out, some tried to resist. None escaped.

When my turn came I sat slowly in the chair. I saw only a uniformed arm grab my left hand and hold it firmly. With her other hand she held the needle, the same one she had used on her other customers. I looked straight ahead. I could neither watch nor look away. The blue ink penetrated my arm through the needle, down through several layers of skin. I thought of cattle being branded.

I bit my lip to keep from screaming. The operation was over almost before it started. But the tattoo would remain for a lifetime. Mine was on my forearm; others were branded under their shoulder. The craftsmanship was precise and lasting. That, above all, we knew.

I kept staring at my forearm while the others were being dealt with. Eva, who had helped me in those first few days, had gone after me. Now she scratched and rubbed at the mark on her shoulder that her hair, those long black tresses she had wept over, would have covered.

Our identities—my identity, Eva's identity—were gone. I was now No. A 135,000. I said it aloud. And I wondered what difference it would make in a mass grave. To the Nazis I was just a number. The one they had given me, so they could keep the books straight. This one's gone, this one's not.

Each of these steps that the Nazis took brought more people to the bottom of their psychological reservoir. Many more dried up each time. Many gave up, became lifeless, emotionless, faceless. All feelings were gone.

In a way I became one of them. But the mark on my forearm wouldn't let me. I searched for a positive possibility, a positive reason, for having the mark. Then it came to me. If they wanted to keep track of us, they meant to let us live.

I wondered again what else the Nazis had in store for us and began to prepare for it in my small way.

I became two people. One struggled for water, for the daily slush. Struggled to keep the clogs on and to keep them safe under my head at night while I slept.

The other gave the orders and kept the sanity. I blocked out the atrocities, the fear, the helplessness. I balanced reason against hope with the will to survive in between.

We shared the last bit of strength we possessed. I shared mine with Eva and those others who were close to me. And they shared what little they had left.

We had been lucky. I had the good fortune to find three women with whom I could feel comfortable in the closeness that we were forced to suffer through. In the bunk at night, we calmed each other's fears and relieved the humiliations each of us felt.

We had met and held each other up in the line those first few days, and we were still holding each other up. We had chosen each other because, for one thing, we had the right odor. Or, at least we were acceptable to one another. Under some circumstances, and in the most intimate ones, that consideration is very potent.

The four of us shared somewhat similar backgrounds, tastes, and aspirations. We took turns sharing our confinement and its horrors.

One, Agnes, was a former actress. Eva was a practical nurse. The third, from the outskirts of Budapest, had her own clothing business before the Nazis arrived. Anne always trembled. She would never be able to thread a needle again. Fear was closest to her.

We four stayed together day and night. We were all we had.

We were together when the Nazis brought the children.

Instead of another head count, one morning, the guards walked us in columns to the entrance of *Lager* C. A huge circular court bordered by an iron gate stood in front of us. A fence separated us from that courtyard. We kept away from that fence. It was electrified.

Enlisted men in uniform paced randomly between our fence and the gate. Now and then one would glance at the gate, then continue pacing. Someone was coming. Perhaps overdue.

We were formed into a semicircle facing the fence. Before long the soldiers also fell into formation near the gate. It swung open, and about thirty young girls filed into the yard and stood in a row to face our pitiful gathering.

The girls were dressed in spotless blue and white uniforms with little straw hats and ribbons on their heads. Many of them had stray curls peeking from under the hats. None looked the least bit unkempt. Patent leather shoes and gleaming white stockings completed their identical outfits.

They quickly assembled into two rows at the direction of the only adult to arrive with them. On a subtle command they produced violins from under their arms. They proceeded to play the *Blue Danube Waltz* by Johann Strauss.

We watched them play, each note mocking us, each note bringing back some private memory of when we had been human beings. Each stroke of the bow was a reminder that we were the tarnished ones, the filthy ones, the nonpersons. Each bar of the melody served as a reminder that this was our last glimpse of a more genteel world. A world that no longer existed, at least for us.

Some inmates covered their eyes, others cried aloud. Many were simply numb. A few more had sunk to a new low.

The rendition was flawless, but it sounded more like a march than a waltz. That night the four of us were sleepless.

I never did fall asleep. Each time I closed my eyes, I saw the children moving their bows across the violins. I wondered how I must have looked to them. I could feel the filth on my body. I sat up on the bunk.

"What are you doing?" Eva asked.

"Could you watch, please, to see if anyone comes. I have to go outside and wash. I don't want to feel like an animal anymore."

Eva nodded and I slid off the bunk. Seeing those girls had made cleanliness suddenly more important than safety.

I was lucky. That night a damp snow had fallen. Even on the coldest days the snow fell wet, softened by the smoke that belched constantly from the chimneys. And this time of year—what I guessed was late April—it didn't last long on the ground.

So I shed my meager clothing and took what I could. There was no moon, so I had a better chance of going undetected.

Naked in the night I picked up two handfuls of the wet snow, scraping it off the ground. I scrubbed my feet, my legs, my hips, until the snow was gone. I grabbed for more, rubbing it fiercely against each arm with the other. A couple more steps for more snow and I scrubbed my chest and neck. I couldn't find enough snow, so I just rubbed my wet, cold hands against my body. The night got colder, even for the short time I was outside. For a few precious moments, though, I was away from the barracks, away from the press of people who, like me, had not bathed for some time. And would not for some time to come. Perhaps never again.

When I was finished I took a last handful of snow and let it melt on my tongue.

For awhile after that I just stood outside, breathing in the cool air. There weren't many opportunities to be alone with your thoughts. It had seemed like months since we had come here and yet it had only been a few weeks.

And the snow was beautiful, the air crisp, the night dark.

And I was alone. There was solitude, or the illusion of it. No guards, no *Aufseherinnen*, no other prisoners. Just myself and the beautiful dark night. The camp was silent, almost peaceful . . . almost.

I left my clogs off and made my way back to the barracks. Creeping along carefully, I found my bunk. My bedmates were glad to see me, but not happy to feel my cold, wet body in the bunk. I didn't care. For a moment I was clean, and I drifted off peacefully to sleep.

There was still more to learn about captivity and being a prisoner. The next lesson came the following morning.

Our line-up and the delousing were routine. But this time, after leaving the showers, we did not return to the barracks. Instead, we were herded into the hospital.

We went into the *Rewier* (barracks) in one long line. Waiting for us was a former Hungarian internist (we knew she was Hungarian because she told us what town she had practiced in) and two uniformed women. The internist had a single hypodermic syringe, a single needle, and several vials of an unknown serum.

Each of us was vaccinated.

Some of us found out what had happened sooner than the others. The internist, when pressed, had said something vague about terminating the menses for reasons of cleanliness and sanitation.

What the Nazis were really looking for was a way to make sure that, even on the off chance any of us escaped, there would be no future generations of Jews. They were experimenting with sterilization drugs. They had found one that worked.

All of us came to know it, a fail-safe component in the final solution.

Medical science was able to help some of those who made their escape. Some of the damage was successfully reversed. We were not cognizant of that at the time.

Nor did we fully comprehend the appearance of the infectious swelling caused by the use of a single needle on six hundred souls. Those who did suffer from these lesions, some of them the size of grapefruits, were tested and retested. Samples were taken and studies made. They were not taken away, these victims, as had happened to others with minor injuries. They were left to suffer and be tested further.

Most of them wouldn't have cared had they been taken away. We were thinking more about that little bit of possible future that had been erased. That little, tiny "if" that had been there and was now gone forever.

Vanity had already been taken. Now womanhood was gone as well.

I was spared the infection and thus the testing and sampling. I hardly noticed. I was thinking about the children I would never have.

Evidently the Nazis, Mengele, and Ilse Koch, had used up their creativity and we were left alone. I don't know how long it had been summer before I noticed. It really didn't matter. What mattered was inventory in the morning, the slush, our once daily trip to the outhouse, roll call in the evening, and sleep. When it could be found.

Our greatest challenge, other than thinking of a reason to stay alive, was keeping clean—or some semblance of it.

Privacy certainly wasn't a consideration: there wasn't any, not even in the outhouse. Larger than the other barracks buildings, it was simply a huge room with boxlike seats with holes in them. Presumably, there were also holes in the floor underneath. The smell made that uncertain.

The guards watched everyone. There was nowhere to go without the ever-present uniforms.

And the Nazis didn't waste paper on us.

Along the way I learned that my right index finger would work as a toothbrush. I learned you had to be quick to get to the water spigot before the dawn *Appel*. And you had to be strong to keep your place when the others arrived. I learned how just a few moments alone could seem like a lifetime, and how a few months of sleeping in a double bed with six other people seemed like an eternity.

I learned, finally, where we were. I overheard it. The Polish spelling was Oswiecim. It is a little commune west of Krakow. It is better known, and I will remember it, as Auschwitz.

I also learned that there are a few things that cannot be taken away, blotted out, or smeared with brutality.

It was on a morning that started out in the deep darkness of hopelessness and only brightened reluctantly. I was there, shivering. The days had been growing shorter, but *Appel* was the same every day. Or so we guessed. We had little way of knowing.

The night left grudgingly as the dawn arrived, only because of its persistence. The horizon grew purple and the clouds magenta. Somewhere, the darkness gave way to the sun and the clouds were shaded in orange, fuschia, and light blue.

The counting went on without me as I watched. The splendor reminded me of long ago, of seeing El Greco's *Toledo*. The looming, threatening, menacing majesty of the sky.

It was something the Nazis missed. Something they could not control or conceal. Something for us that we could internalize and retain.

Chapter XIII

AUFSEHERIN MARGIT

A flicker of light, a glimmer of hope, a thread of a chance. Even all three together can't stand up to the degradation, the disappointment, the despair. Those things add up faster and weigh heavier. Before long even that trickle of a chance of survival becomes lost beneath the shards of a shattered spirit. And the Nazis continue to grind away at what's left.

The burden can breed many things. In me it brought defiance.

The bright mornings had become fewer and shorter. El Greco was a fleeting memory. The Nazis were winning and I knew it.

I could see it happening. There were fewer trainloads of people, the chimneys were belching more smoke than ever. The rest of the camp seemed to be less crowded. Work transports carrying loads of prisoners departed from the other side of the compound, far enough away so that the engines were barely audible.

They were taking the able-bodied to other camps. We were again left behind. If we were not to work, then what? The answer was undeniable and unthinkable.

It was difficult enough to sleep without these thoughts, without the recognition that time was now once again precious. What had gone by was not countable. What might be ahead seemed infinitely more dear.

I had seen the fate the Nazis held for me in the half-light of the last dawn. A great pile of refuse had been left on the other side of the fence from *Lager* C. I had slipped out prior to *Appel* and had seen the mound, at least twice as high as I stood.

As I got closer I could hear the hum of the electricity in the wire. I warned myself not to get too close. Yet, I was curious and wanted to see.

As I approached I could see the mound better. It looked alive! Parts of it were moving! Perhaps it was a mountain of leaves and branches swaying in the wind. I would have liked to believe that.

The approaching sun was behind me, leaving the mountain in gray light. I got closer. Something pulled at my stomach and fanned the back of my neck.

The mound was made of people. They were the sick, the nearly dead who had been pulled from the line-up and the barracks and were bound for the ovens. I heard a moan. I saw a hand coming out of the pile, trying to make a fist.

I ran back to the barracks, but had to go out again for roll call. The mound was still there. Sometime during the day, after we had all seen the mound, it disappeared. More smoke belched from the chimneys.

I still saw the chimneys as I tried to close my eyes against the day and sleep. This is what the Nazis have planned for us. The others might be going to work. We are not.

The night was still. It seemed there were far fewer restless souls in the barracks that night. Where the bunks had once squeaked with sleepless nightmares, now there was silence.

I thought again of the smokestacks and the destiny the Nazis had chosen for us. I chose my own. Suddenly, inexplicably, I found a way to extricate myself from the plans of the Nazis and create my personal destiny. To exercise my last individual choice. To grasp my last morsel of dignity.

For a moment, as I slipped quietly out of bed and out of the barracks, I remembered the other decisions I had made in my young life. The path that had taken me to a career, to independence, to a free and creative existence. They were not as important as this.

I walked slowly to the wire. Long ago its buzz had ceased to be part of our consciousness, as had the clattering of the trucks on their way to the crematorium. It was just there, carrying high electrical voltage and a tool the Nazis didn't realize we could use to determine our own destiny.

As I came closer I took solace in the silence of the darkness.

For a moment, standing there an arm's length away from the fence, I may have had second thoughts. But I do not remember them. Once again I thought only that the *Reich* would be denied its decision. Slowly, I reached out, took a half-step forward, and grabbed the wire.

In that moment, I realized the silence was unusual. There was no electricity in the wire! The Nazis had denied me this escape. I sank to my knees and covered my head in my hands.

"Please, God," I cried, "I want to die. Please let me die!" I grabbed the wire again, this time with both hands. Again, there was nothing. I toppled onto the ground on my side, facing the wire.

I had little chance to mourn when a raucous, searing voice pierced my thoughts.

"What are you doing here? How dare you leave the barracks?"

I looked in the direction of the voice and could barely see a huge silhouette. It didn't matter. I could feel. And in a moment the whip came hard against my back.

I tried to scramble to my feet as the lash came again, snapping a welt on my collarbone. I kicked off my clogs and reached for them as I saw the huge arm swinging again. The short piece of leather on the end of the riding crop snapped across the back of my neck.

The whip was faster than my protecting arms. And it always found a new target. The fury of the beating and the speed of the whip grew.

This huge body had me backed against the fence and was nimbly following and foiling my attempts to get around. I got too close and the riding crop slapped against my forehead, snapping my head back and opening a cut that quickly sent blood streaming into my eyes. I feinted one way, then dodged around as the whip slit my earlobe. I opened my mouth to scream, but choked back my cry when the whip bit my bare ankle. I discovered how stern the punishment was for failing to die.

This night prowler wasted few strokes on the shabby garment that came to my knees. My head, hands, and bare legs suffered the most. The barracks seemed far away. The beating followed every step. I didn't notice the stony ground under my feet. I could see only the doorway to the barracks and what I hoped was safety.

I finally had my hand on the knob, but I wasn't quick enough. My other arm was suddenly held very tightly.

The whip was resting against my neck, my shoulders hunched. For a moment there was nothing to hear except my heavy breathing. Then the voice came again, this time in a whisper.

"We will finish this in the morning at line-up," it said, and I was flung against the door. I turned to look and, in the light of the lantern by the door, I recognized Margit. She smiled, then walked off, tapping the whip against her immense thigh.

Though we did not see Margit often, she was not unknown to us. She was, after all, the superintendent of all *Lager* C. She left the lesser *Aufseherinnen* to handle the daily chores. It was Margit's duty to oversee all the operations of this section. It was up to Margit to determine punishment and fate, even the punishment and fate of those who were punished enough.

It was Margit who escorted the Nazi officers on their rare appearances at *Lager* C. Had she not been born of Jewish Hungarian-Czech parents, which was all we knew about her, she might well have been embraced and accepted by the Germans. Instead, she was simply in charge of carrying out their bidding. She had a reputation of doing so with a macabre flair.

The trust the Nazis had placed in Margit was well founded. This was a special Judas they had found, who seemed to enjoy the work delegated to her. Though she rarely engaged in the dirty work necessary to keep inmates cowed, she relished in its execution and could often be seen in her office window, watching.

She ordered punishment for everything. Too long in washing meant a beating. An inspection of the barracks by Margit, though infrequent, was a dire time for whomever had been designated to clean that day. Margit always found something she did not approve . . .

Most often, some minor transgression resulted in the deprivation of the slush. Or the denial of washing privileges.

And, always, Margit could be seen at her window, surveying her fiefdom.

We knew also that she had been shipped to Auschwitz in the early days of the war, as the Nazis had overrun the Eastern European countries. She had been ambitious then and had found work in the newly organized camp. She was strong, and strong workers were needed to handle the defiant prisoners. Margit had cooperated ruthlessly with the Nazis. She must have; she was still alive. Margit lived apart from us and ate the same food as the Nazis. The daily administration of *Lager* C was her responsibility.

At five feet eleven Margit's only resemblance to a woman was her name. She was fleshy, like an overripe fruit. Her body and enormous breasts were jammed into a tight, ill-fitting uniform that strained at the buttons. The cinched belt made her immense hips seem to protrude even more.

She carried her head high, seemingly more from a stiff neck than from dignity. She had a dark, oily complexion with traces of old blemishes. The skin on her nose was taut, yet puffy, and the corner of her small mouth turned down in a pinched expression. She had a small chin which would one day be bracketed by heavy jowls. That chin stuck out when Margit was provoked, which happened often.

Her eyes had two prominent expressions: blank and angry. But, sometimes, those wild, penetrating brown eyes would dart from one place to another and take on a haunted look—the look of an animal that is running out of territory.

Still she swaggered. She had an overbearing confidence and her huge body exuded the force of a well-fed animal. There was no trace of femininity in her curves, no softness. The motion of her huge body was strangely fluid, like that of a prowling predator.

In our own darker moments, we whispered that even Margit was a prisoner and that her fate was sealed as well. The Nazis would want no witnesses, no traces of their atrocities. For Margit to sell her soul might mean a few years of survival, but the chance that this woman had taken, without remorse, had her looking ever more over her shoulder.

Most of the time she paid no attention to the ghosts and tapped the whip against her leg. She polished her boots daily, or had someone do it for her.

And there was the hat, perched atop a round head of unruly, curly black hair. Though it was a military beret many sizes too small, it was a man's cap and therefore accentuated her authority.

I wondered less about her past and her fate put together as I did about her hands. She always wore gloves and was the only one of the *Aufseherinnen* who did. Perhaps there were ugly scars on those huge hands, perhaps the ravages of a childhood disease, or a defect. It was said she wore them because she enjoyed persuading victims to cooperate in the bathhouse.

Though we did not fail to obey the other *Aufseherinnen* in *Lager* C, it was Margit who commanded the most fearful respect. When it was announced that Margit would personally oversee the *Appel*, each of us made an extra effort to be still, even though it was often hours before Margit would arrive. Then, she would stroll up and down each line, stopping to stare at each inmate. She wouldn't move on until the prisoner trembled.

The commands she shouted at the select prisoners working in her office and at the other *Aufseherinnen* could often be heard in the barracks. Her voice had grown hoarse and had ultimately remained that way.

Now, I was expecting to hear that voice. And though the others didn't know how much, their help in getting me to *Appel* was important. They saw the scars, some still bleeding, and raised quizzical eyebrows. I told them only that I had fallen.

I remembered the whispered promise. The finish would be this morning.

Margit appeared at her office door. She was holding something up to the light, examining it carefully. There were two more uniformed women behind her on the platform, and they were all laughing. Though the early morning had been clear, the sun had climbed high behind some clouds. We still waited for Margit.

She glanced at the line-up then went back through the open office door. We heard Margit shout angrily. She emerged again holding a sheet of paper. She examined it quickly, then handed it back through the door to an unseen aide.

Margit stood on the platform, staring in our direction, and finally took two steps down and strolled to where we were assembled. She stopped next to another *Aufseherin* who had snapped to attention at her approach. For a moment she was silent. Then she spoke, clearly and firmly but without emotion.

"Which one of you is Alice Dunn? Step out."

I heard, but followed the unwritten rule in camp: Never, ever, reveal yourself. Do not volunteer. Do not be visible. Remain in the shadows. Remain colorless. Remain anonymous. Too many had been noticed and never seen again.

She spoke again, once more without emotion.

"Alice Dunn, step forward now." I had seen her eyes searching. They had come to rest on me.

I slowly came forward despite the whispers of my three friends. Whispers or gasps, I didn't know which. Along the way, squeezing between the other rows, I prepared myself to become an example. I finally reached Margit, stood in front of her, and returned her stare.

"So, it is you," she growled. "What a pleasant surprise. Be in my office after line-up."

She had spoken for only me to hear. And then she had looked at the other *Aufseherin,* nodded toward the assembly, and walked away.

As I made my way back to my place, I saw the glances—and frightened looks—of the other prisoners. They did not know what had happened the night before, nor what Margit had said. Even I had no idea what Margit had in store for me. All I knew was that we lived vulnerable lives and that even an attempt to take one's own life was punishable.

When I got to Margit's building I was met at the top of the steps by another *Aufseherin* who we rarely saw. She escorted me down a hallway to the middle of the building and knocked on a door. Before there was an answer, the woman pushed open the door and stepped back.

The room was small, holding only an iron stove, a desk covered with papers and a couple of straight-backed chairs. A wood fire was smoldering now in the stove—it had probably come in handy during the early morning chill. I could still smell the scent of the pine logs. It was a clean, earthy smell and it kept the repulsive odor from the chimneys at bay.

On the desk, situated on the window side of the room, with a clear view of the assembly field and our barracks, was a clutter of papers, two military caps, a large jug, dirty drinking glasses, beer cans, and three loaves of bread. Behind the desk was Margit, whip in hand, tapping it on her desk.

She stared at me with a mix of disdain, arrogance, and a faint glimmer of curiosity. I detected a twitch of a smile. Evidently, I had masked the disgust I was feeling.

The smile turned quickly into a sneer. "Finally, I discovered you, Alice Dunn. From now on, you'll be working for me, exclusively."

I didn't know what to make of her remark, but I tried very hard to remain calm in spite of the turmoil taking place inside of me. Margit noticed the confusion and fear showing on my face. She extracted her fleshy body from her chair and waddled over to the door.

"Mitzi! Come in here! There is someone in my office to see you."

The door was flung open and I observed a female figure enter the room. She was dressed in the same ragged prison garb as I, and her bald head revealed the stubby remains of her bright blond hair. At first, I didn't recognize her. But as she walked toward me, her face breaking out in the familiar, beautiful smile I knew so well, my heart began to pound. Anyone else in her place would have appeared hideous, but to me, at that moment, she was the most fantastically beautiful sight I had seen in many days. Could it really be her, or was I dreaming?

"Alice! It really is you! Oh God, I thought I would never see you again."

She threw her arms around me, kissing me on both cheeks over and over again. It was only then that my frozen brain began to make sense of what was transpiring.

"Mitzi! Mitzi Gilbert! What are you doing here? My God, you're alive!"

I could feel a rush of emotion well up inside of me as we embraced and clung to each other. Tears of joy, evidence of feelings that had been foreign to me for the past several years, cascaded down my cheeks and onto our clothes.

In the background I head Margit's footsteps as she returned to her seat behind her desk. But this was our moment, Mitzi's and mine, and I was not about to let anyone spoil it for us. Not even

Margit! I wanted to savor it, to take full measure from it, to hold on to it. It was the first positive emotion I had felt since Peggy. "Let me take another look at you, Mitzi," I said, wiping the tears with my sleeve. "You know, you really haven't changed at all. But tell me, what are you doing here? How long have you been here? What happened to Carl?"

"It's a long story, Alice. One I'd rather not think back on." She took a step backward, looking at me with a wry expression on her face. "If only I'd listened to you and Carl, this would never have happened. How could I have been so naive, so stupid!"

"We've all made mistakes, Mitzi. And now we are paying the price! But you haven't answered my questions. How did you know I was here? And what is your connection to the *Aufseherin*?" I stole a look at Margit who was watching us intently from behind her desk, a dour expression on her face. I tried not to notice her stare.

"You remember the trial, don't you? It was in all the Budapest papers. Well, Carl and I, along with the seven others, were shipped here the very next day. I haven't seen or heard from Carl since. I can only hope that he's still . . ."

The remainder of her account was lost in sobs. But she brightened almost immediately as I took her hands in mine, squeezing them sympathetically.

She continued speaking in a low whisper. "The *Aufseherin* was very kind to offer me the opportunity to work for her when she learned of my background." She smiled shyly in Margit's direction. "Then the other day I noticed you in the line-up. At first, I couldn't believe my eyes. I thought I was fantasizing. But when I observed your gait, your mannerisms, I knew it really was you. I intended to greet you at the first opportunity, but then I couldn't find you. I thought I lost you . . . that something had happened to you. It wasn't until this morning, in the warehouse, while we were sorting clothes, that the *Aufseherin* mentioned something about a Hungarian inmate who had tried to kill herself . . . well, you know what I mean. When she pointed you out in the line-up, I told her who you were. I mean your profession, and all. She recognized you instantly from the pictures she had seen of you in the Hungarian press. She wanted . . ."

Margit interrupted. "Yes, it's true." There was a certain

childlike pride in her voice. "I recognized you from your pictures, even though your appearance has changed somewhat." There was a touch of sarcasm in her voice now. "But that's enough explaining, Mitzi. Go back to your work. I'll finish with your friend here myself. We must not let these personal matters interfere with our jobs." She dismissed Mitzi with a wave of her hand, and Margit and I were alone once more. She stood up behind her desk, looking at me with a strange expression. "I am well acquainted with your reputation in women's fashions. And Mitzi, as a former client of yours, has corroborated what I have read in the papers." She paused for a moment, studying my face. "I want you to make those lovely clothes for me now. I need to feel—well, you know—like a woman again. I could never afford them before. But now that you have come to me, well, I could hardly pass up the opportunity."

This turn of events was too unexpected. I had anticipated more punishment from her, as she had promised. And now, this monster, this horrible excuse for a female, was asking me, Alice Dunn, the designer from Budapest, to outfit her with my creations. It was all a cruel joke. What could she have heard to change her mind so completely? What could Mitzi have told her about me? But I didn't have time to ponder the answers as Margit walked toward the door, motioning me to follow.

"We'll get started immediately, unless you have some reservations about working for me, of course. I can always find other things for you to do." A sly smile crossed her face as she looked to me for a reaction.

"No, I assure you, I'm delighted with the prospect of designing your outfits. I'm sure you'll be happy with them. It's something I have done all my adult life, as you can imagine. I was only concerned about where we'll obtain the tools, the materials. I can't imagine that this place will have . . ."

She nodded impatiently at my doubts. "You'll have to do with whatever we can find. Your friend, Mitzi, told me how good you were with your hands and your creative mind. Now we'll find out if she told the truth. Won't we? But enough talking. Come with me to the warehouse. We'll look over its contents to see if there's anything we can use. I'm most eager to get started with our little project."

There were several warehouses at Auschwitz. Many of them

held the spoils of the most recent conquests of the Third Reich. They held the property of those who had arrived here—what property they might have brought with them. Some of the warehouses held old clothing, furs, shoes. Others housed the jewelry, gold teeth, religious items. All of it was supposedly destined for Germany. What we didn't know was how quickly Germany—at least, the Nazi empire—was shrinking.

It was in one of these warehouses that I discovered the extent of what Margit wanted. She wanted everything.

"What do you want to choose for me?" she said. "What do you think would suit me best?" We had come and I had been given a free hand, but I needed a few more hands.

Margit was virtually wading through a mound of old blankets in the musty warehouse. "Do you see this," she said, her voice bubbling. "It reminds me of one of the skirts I saw you pictured with. Let's pull this one out."

Margit gave a heave, putting all her weight into the effort to free one great maroon blanket. As it came free, pieces above it on the mountain of fabric began to tumble down. In one long moment, Margit was suddenly up to her waist in Persian lamb coats, fur pieces, a long, fluffy fur boa of silver fox over her shoulder. Blankets of camel's hair and mohair with beautiful Stuart tartan patterns were near her feet.

There were yards of knitted cloth. I caught sight of a skillfully knitted lap cover, discovered a worn mink coat with a knife in the pocket, a hand-woven afghan from the softest wool I had ever felt, long woolen scarves big enough to cover one's body, a huge paisley piano cover with long fringes. It was similar to the one we owned in Buda. I didn't want to think about it. Buda was on one side of the Danube, where our summer home nestled in the hills.

"I want this," Margit commanded. "And this. Perhaps this?"

She wanted it all. She wanted glamorous dresses. She wanted, above all, to be a woman.

There was another, hidden side to this dreaded *Aufseherin* —vanity! Here was a woman whose long-time dream was to be and look fashionable. She wanted the things she had longingly remembered from years ago, from pictures and from her imagination. And she had never been very patient.

"I will need help," I said boldly, as Margit concentrated on touching every garment her searching eyes noticed.

"Fine," she said. "Who?"

I told her about my three bunkmates.

"Yes. I have seen the four of you together. You will all work for me. And you shall not disappoint me."

The child had returned from the sea of cloth and gone back to being an *Aufseherin.*

"No, we will not disappoint you," I agreed.

"That will be your responsibility," she said. The implication was clear.

The three of us were no longer required to attend dawn *Appel*—that was our reward for working for Margit. By the time the others were counted, we were already at work at our bunk on another of Margit's fantasies.

Of course, the others shunned us. There were no words, no threats, no acts of violence. We were simply outcasts, barely noticed, never approached.

It bothered me that they saw us in such a different light. We were so misunderstood by them. It shouldn't have been held against us that we were forced to satisfy Margit's fashion fantasies instead of cleaning the latrine, or the barracks, or working in the warehouse. Work is work. It is expected of you. One is in no position to decline.

Would it have been more honorable to refuse Margit's orders? Would it be more honorable than accepting this fate? I felt the other prisoners looked upon us as collaborators. We were simply forced to work, like everyone else.

There did come a time when we were briefly accepted back into the ranks of our fellow prisoners. While searching for some food in the garbage, I found a pair of tweezers. That night, and every night for the next several days, I was the toast of the barracks. We were, after all, women, and tweezers were for women's eyebrows. Before long, each of them had approached me about the tweezers. I didn't let them hold the tweezers, but I did help them indulge this small bit of vanity we had rediscovered in ourselves, one we thought had been long gone.

Even with the four of us working, it took two weeks for Margit's first outfit to be completed. The tools we used were as primitive as our living conditions. The shears were blunt kitchen knives; narrow twine substituted for thread; hairpins became needles. It took ingenuity to turn out the dresses, shawls, and coats that Margit wanted.

We were each given an extra piece of bread for our work.

"I guess," Margit said pointedly, "this must be the first really hard-earned bread of your entire lives." Her inference was eminently clear to us, but we let it pass without comment. We were too smart to chance throwing away our newly found good luck.

There was one necessary tool we could not find, nor could we find a substitute for it: a mirror. We really didn't want one. Margit did, especially when I presented her with the first of the outfits, more of a frock than a dress and only glamorous in her imagination. But for the moment it satisfied her.

What had been a blanket, in a deep blue color, had become a gown. For accessories we used a sequined, shirtwaist jacket, trimmed it down, and made a sash and belt.

For her "fitting," Margit undressed shamelessly in her office in front of us, uncovering her grotesque body. I could not bring myself to touch her, so I passed her the garments gingerly.

Grabbing them, she held them proudly against her pasty body. Finally, she put them on.

She paraded around the office preening like a peacock, constantly looking at me for approval. I smiled and nodded, making little sounds of admiration. She postured as though envisioning herself in a restaurant or playing a game of charades. Only Margit knew for sure, and she was miles away. It was all I could do to keep from laughing.

It was like that every time I brought her another outfit, and it lasted for almost two months, until the leaves on the trees outside the camp changed color.

As we worked for Margit, a greater bond developed among the four of us. It grew out of the shabby working conditions and the rejection by our fellow inmates. We had a camaraderie that had been unimaginable before. We stopped short of sharing hopes and dreams. There were none, and we were not about to fool ourselves. One incident I recall vividly vas my birthday. Though I didn't know what month we were in, I felt it couldn't be too far away. With the days growing cooler, winter was definitely on the way.

I didn't remember having mentioned my birthday, but I must have at one time or another, and someone must have remembered. I hadn't paid that much attention to it since we began working for Margit.

But on one of the days when a delivery was imminent, I woke before dawn. We had all grown more tired and undernourished since we had been there and this was one of those mornings when I wasn't ready to face the day.

Stirring slowly, I tried to move as little as possible, so as not to disturb my friends. They were tired too.

When I opened my eyes, I saw four carefully laid out pieces of bread and tiny twigs spelling out "Happy Birthday." They had even used some of our twine to keep letters together to form the words.

My crying awakened them, but it didn't matter.

I was the only one who made deliveries to Margit's office. I didn't think that was fair because that meant I got to take advantage of Margit's stove. We were well into autumn now and the barracks were getting colder.

One late afternoon, as a light snow was falling, Margit appeared unexpectedly at the barracks. She was suddenly in the doorway, causing more than a minor stir. The four of us were sitting on our bunk near the door and Margit signaled for me to come out.

I walked to the door cautiously. She pulled me into the courtyard and, although she had slammed the door behind us, she still whispered mysteriously.

"You must leave the barracks before dawn. Sneak off quietly and go to the end of the road near the loading area by the gate."

I gave her a quizzical look and, as I opened my mouth to speak, she held up a protesting hand.

"Orders to empty out the camp, one way or another, arrived here yesterday. Accordingly, a transport of workers is being formed which will leave here tomorrow morning. See that you, Alice, and only you, are at the selection area at daybreak. I will be there with the other *Aufseherinnen*. And make sure that you are near the front of the line. If there are too many, the ones at the rear will get eliminated." She moved closer now so that her face was just inches from mine. In a barely discernible whisper she added, "And remember, do not tell anyone of our conversation!" After another furtive glance around the yard, she turned on her heels, leaving me standing there alone.

I was dumfounded. I made my way back to the barracks in a turmoil. She had all but admitted to me that the inmates who remained would be exterminated. At least, that is how I interpreted her remarks. Where did that leave my coworkers, my friends? Why had she selected only me to be on that transport? Was this another one of her sick games? Was it a one-way ticket to the gas chambers, the long overdue punishment for my attempted suicide? And why the secrecy? I needed to find logical answers, yet there were none. The most distressing feature was her caution about keeping our conversation from my friends. She knew precisely how close we had all become. But she was a macabre monster, a sadist who delighted in hurting others. I, myself, had been witness to that!

I arrived at the barracks in total confusion. The girls were gathered at the door, waiting to greet me. Somehow, they had observed my meeting with Margit.

"What did she have to say, Alice? What did she want from you now?" they all chimed in together, curiosity showing on their faces.

It was not within me to deny them. So, I quietly gathered them in a vacant corner of our barracks and told them the news. There was utter silence when I had finished. I hoped for a discussion so that our combined thinking might help to shed light on this life and death puzzle. We had successfully used this technique to solve much more elementary problems in the past. I declined to influence them in either direction, as I was myself unsure of the transport's true destination. And, after all, I could hardly assume responsibility for their very lives. But, as the sky outside darkened, we were no more certain of which path to follow than we had been at the beginning. Yet, we realized that we needed to adopt a plan of some kind before daybreak. Finally, it remained for me to propose a strategy. Each of us would independently decide for herself what she would do the next morning. Those who wanted to leave would do so. The remainder would stay quietly in their bed so as not to arouse the suspicion of the other inmates. It was something all could agree with.

As we realized our "team" was about to be dissolved, we cried and hugged each other. We reminisced about out daily hardships and the slim rewards we had experienced together. Ours had been a most extraordinary relationship, forged under the most adverse circumstances imaginable. We had survived as individuals because we had been able to draw from our combined strength when necessary. It had been an unforgettable experience.

None of us got much sleep that night as we agonized over our fate. And, as the black sky began to fade into a purple morning, we realized that the time for decision had arrived. Mine, I must admit, was not based on any strong conviction, but rather intuition. It was all I had to rely on. Yet, according to Boriska's prophecy, which had remained ingrained in my mind, it would be sufficient.

As I stole quietly out of the barracks moments later, I found myself alone. Strangely, I felt an inner determination, a conviction that I was doing the right thing. In the semidarkness I could see silhouettes moving rapidly out of the other barracks. I mingled with them as they moved toward the line that was already forming in the assembly area ahead. I was relieved to see many others dashing into place behind me. I would not find myself at the rear, I was sure of that.

It was not long before we found ourselves being herded into the waiting freight cars, similar to those on which I had arrived last spring. Where would they take us? It was the same question that had plagued my mind at Csepel Island. I knew that I would have to wait for an answer. In the meantime I could only hope and pray.

As I turned to glance back at the barracks and assembly area in the faint light of daybreak, I thought I detected the back of a familiar hulking figure entering through a lit office door. I wondered if her face bore a sneer or smile.

Chapter XIV

THE FACTORY AT TCHOPAU

Another train. Was it to be the last one? Would I find the chimneys at the end of these tracks? Each of the last few trains had brought me closer to destruction. In another life, trains had brought joy and excitement. The rides had always been accompanied by a sense of anticipation of the pleasures to be experienced upon arrival. Now there was only doubt, dread, and fear. And it was showing on all the faces around me. None of us in that crowded boxcar seemed convinced that we were being freed from the terrors of Auschwitz without becoming subjected to an even more terrifying ending.

My eyes began the search for a familiar face. Perhaps Mitzi, or even one of the others from my barracks, had also boarded this train. No. It was not to be. I was alone among strangers once more. The vision of my friends' faces was only in my mind. They would remain in my memory forever.

I huddled within myself to keep out the cold. Suddenly, it occurred to me that no one had been counted. We had not been given work clothes. We had not been deloused prior to leaving. We had not been given the scarves that most others had received when they were leaving Auschwitz.

There was no indication we were bound for work.

I felt better for my friends.

We could feel the train climbing, straining through the passes and leaning against the turns. Outside, rocky heights looked out on green valleys. We were in the Erzgebirge, the Iron Mountains, the natural border between Germany and Czechoslovakia. But we were as unsure of our location and destination, crammed in those closed boxcars, as the people of the little villages, tucked away in the majestic giant spruce and pine trees, were of the dismal cargo the train carried.

I wondered aloud to an emaciated woman nearby. "Where do you think we are going?"

She looked somewhere across the car, her eyes not focusing on any of the fleeting shadows. "I don't suppose we'll know until they let us off," she said.

"We probably won't even know then," I replied, surprising myself. "We are in the mountains and it will probably be dark again when we stop. How will we determine our location from our surroundings of mountains and trees?"

She made no sense. I thought the woman insensitive and a fool. Yet she was likely more right than I was? But, ever since Margit's warning to leave, I had been torn by distrust. In spite of that, I had decided to follow her advice. One aspect had already come true: we had left Auschwitz. But so far that solved little. We were still in the merciless hands of our captors. Our bodies belonged to them.

And which of us could work? Dr. Mengele certainly would not have given us a passing grade at this juncture. I wanted to tell the woman that our destination would probably be no better than our previous location, that the Nazis were undoubtedly just shifting the burden of the ovens, redistributing the ashes.

I listened to my own thoughts and wondered why I was now failing an endurance test that had seemingly started ages ago in my Budapest apartment. When my mind and body still worked in concert, when I met challenges with a different attitude, optimistically.

In most cases it is common for the handmaiden of the unknown to be fearful. Yet, this was different. I didn't know where we were going, but it had to be better. At the very least, it could be no worse. So, for a while, the unknown brought hope.

Two days ago, prior to Margit's advice, leaving Auschwitz

would have been a wild, unlikely dream. Riding a train to somewhere, anywhere, would have meant a rekindling of a spirit too long dormant. I repressed all negative feelings and let hope return. I found it not uncomfortable but awkward in its newness. Yet, the possibility of being human again, of becoming functional, of being capable of loving and accepting love, of finding old friends alive, was still remote. Letting the possibility creep briefly into my mind was unfamiliar. I tried it a few times, and I decided that I would worry about where the train was going when it came to a stop.

I finally noticed the cold, and the scratchiness of the dry, fumigated flannel shirt I had gotten at the last delousing. My knees and legs were stiff and I pushed hard to raise myself into a standing position. When I was erect, the whistle on the locomotive suddenly shrieked and the brakes screamed against the wheels, jolting the cars. I was pitched sideways toward the front of the car and fell in a heap by the door. A moment later the train ground to a stop and the door slid open.

Outside I could discern only darkness. No klieg lights like those that had greeted us at the end of our last journey. The stars seemingly hung from the branches of the huge spruce, birch, and pine trees. There was snow on the ground, highlighting a shadowy track that separated the trees on each side. As I debarked, the ground seemed damp and cool, like the air, and I breathed deeply. For a moment I allowed my mind to escape to a better time, a better world.

We were soon to learn that we had arrived in the southern part of Germany, in Saxony, where the Auto Union Werke had produced automobiles, sewing machines, and agricultural machinery during peacetime. Now it housed an aviation parts factory that, despite the ravages of war, was still operating at full speed.

Only a handful of guards, most of them barely teenagers, and the rest grandfathers, were there to meet us. They shouted their commands like all the others had, but there was less conviction in their voices. Perhaps they were weary. Perhaps they just didn't feel threatened by us anymore.

We were lined up in columns five across. As we marched down the stony road through the forest, the night seemed to brighten. At first, the distant lights simply filtered through the trees, indefinable.

Then came faint beams and, finally, individual globes of brightness could be discerned.

We emerged from the forest into the shadow of a gleaming "palace." It was a huge building, seemingly carved out of the rocks.

There were no chimneys.

There was a sign, at first hard to read, but as we got closer we could make it out easily. Our hearts skipped a beat. It read Auto Union Werke Tchopau. To us, it read survival.

In eastern central Germany there were three major industrial centers: Leipzig, Dresden, and Chemnitz. We were closest to Chemnitz, protected by the trees and the Erzgebirge. Allied bombardiers knew the areas well, and knew where the factory was located. But how they knew was a mystery, and it was not something we counted on. Yet, they had never chosen to bomb a forced labor factory.

By some miracle we had been sent to a factory that worked day and night. The Auto Werke was a steel and glass structure five stories high, glittering in the moonlight in contrast to the forest darkness. A circular courtyard occupied the area leading to the entrance. A wide, pebbled lane brought us to the courtyard where we were assembled, counted, and counted again. The head count alone was a reassuring sign.

While we waited, we could hear men's voices coming from the other end of the courtyard, submerged in the darkness of the rocks and the trees. One of the voices started to sing, and immediately others joined in. They sang as they worked to widen the road leading to the back entrance of the building.

To the casual listener, or the Nazi, it seemed they were singing to themselves. Even to me the song began more as a low hum than as a recognizable melody. Then the melody became clear. It was *Frère Jacques*. But the lyrics were different. The words were invented. It didn't matter that nothing rhymed.

"You're our brothers. You're our sisters.

Have no fear, have no fear.

Nothing here will hurt you, if you follow orders

We'll soon be free. We'll all be free!"

I was overcome by the sentiment of the lyrics. They meant more to me at that moment than all of the beautiful arias I had ever heard. Tears came to my eyes as I remembered the last time I had heard that tune. It was on my way to Mme. Boriska's. I recalled my feeling of eager excitement and anticipation. But, curiously, the others in my group showed no signs of being equally affected. Their faces only showed the doubt and fear of facing the unknown. Perhaps they couldn't understand the very original French lyrics, I reasoned. So I moved quietly among them, translating the French into Hungarian. Soon there were smiles all around, more smiles than I had witnessed in my last seven months at Auschwitz.

The singing faded and reality returned. Orders were read and quarters assigned. It was near dawn when we were directed to enter the building.

We were to sleep on the fifth floor, just above our fourth-floor working area. Some had to be helped up the stairs. Though the sleeping quarters were not ready—the room was bare—no one needed help falling asleep. We slept where we dropped.

It was barely past daybreak when the whistles blew. Against one wall of the room, the guards had set up a slush line. Bread and slush was disbursed for the morning meal. It was not something we were used to. When the last person dipped into the pot, the whistles sounded again. Time, it seemed, for another head count. This one would be downstairs, in a room near the main assembly line.

The head count took place as expected. This time, though, there was more to it; a more elaborate roll call, yet less efficient than you would expect from the Nazis.

I watched as the uniformed guards selected some prisoners individually. I was surprised, even startled, because it seemed that the prisoners were being questioned. I should have known better than to assign some meaning to this exercise. It was a very brief interlude, exposing for the present, my naiveté.

As each prisoner approached the long table on one side of the room, he was instructed to step on the scale. Then, after a few questions, a guard made a notation on a form. Coveralls, a shirt, and canvas shoes were handed out, and the prisoner was shown to his work station.

I took this to mean that they were assigning jobs based on a prisoner's qualifications. In a way, I was right.

My turn finally came; I stepped on the scale. It stopped at the equivalent of seventy-five pounds. I stared at the figure for a long moment. The guard broke my reverie.

"What is your background?"

For a gullible instant I envisioned a clerical job.

"I have an extensive education through *Gymnasium* (high school) and owned my own dress shop in Budapest."

"That's enough!" he interrupted, and made a notation on his ledger. "Next."

My education had impressed him. I was escorted to my work station and informed that I would operate five machines simultaneously. When we were all in place, we were given a brief demonstration of what we would be doing. Then we were assigned our quotas for the day and left to our work. The machinery began humming.

The primary function of this part of the factory was to make holes in metal aviation wheels, test them with a rod which had to fit precisely, and approve them for use. Failing to deliver the amount expected, we were told, would be punishable as sabotage. Ruining a piece counted as the same.

The workday lasted from dawn until well after dark. The only breaks we got were during the frequent air raids. At first, the Germans sent us out of the factory while they occupied the bunkers. It wasn't long, though, before they locked us in. After all, they reasoned, if the factory was destroyed, they would have no need for us.

The rest of the time the machines ran in a continuous horizontal motion. They had a hypnotic effect on me. Often I would close my eyes tightly for a split second in order to focus more clearly.

"Do you get dizzy from the machines?" I asked Ruth, a worker who operated a single machine next to my set.

"Yes. It is almost a Godsend when we have to leave."

"I feel the same way," I said. "But I get lightheaded at work. It could be the hunger. When I am running back and forth between the machines, the whole building seems to sway. You are fortunate to have just one machine."

Ruth smiled at me sympathetically. She could not volunteer to take over one of my machines.

Though the air raids and the bombs never hit our factory, they came close enough to shake the earth with an unholy trembling. We could see beautiful trees burning like torches. At night, the sky over Chemnitz glowed an eerie orange. In the daylight, we could only see smoke.

One night was especially frightening. I had taken a moment to use the one bathroom on our floor, steadying myself against the heaving building. There was an open window near the hallway with icicles hanging from the top sill. I broke one off and sucked on the cold treat, which reminded me of the lollipops of my youth. As I turned to go back to my place at the machines, the first of the bombs fell on Chemnitz, shattering my reverie and knocking the icicle out of my hands. When I looked back to the window, there were no more icicles to be had.

We were all hurried outside to the growing glow over Chemnitz. White snow covered the ground and capped the rocks around the factory like toupees. We scrambled into the rock formations, looking for what shelter we could find.

The constant rumble of the bombs shook the ground and, as terrible as it was, the devastation evoked a certain curiosity in me. We hunched behind the rocks the size of buses peeking out to look toward Chemnitz.

I was peering out from behind my shelter when I saw a shadow steal through the night. I watched it come closer, finally slipping behind another rock nearby.

It was a man, one of the other prisoners, I presumed. But, somehow, he seemed different from us. Over his clothes he wore a cloak, its hood pulled up over his head. He made a most unusual appearance. I could barely see his face in the darkness. He addressed me in French.

"*Mademoiselle*, do not be afraid. I am a friend. My name is Fleury . . . André Fleury. Is it true that you understand French?"

"Yes, I do. But how did you know? Who are you?" I answered somewhat suspiciously, afraid that it might be a Nazi trick.

"I am a prisoner here also. One of the others in your group pointed you out to me. She heard you translate our song . . . our greeting to you when you arrived last week."

"Then you were one of those singing. I can't tell you how

much your greeting meant to me . . . to all of us . . . It was the most beautiful song I have ever heard. But what . . ."

He interrupted. "Listen carefully. I do not have time to explain everything. The *Boche*, they are losing the war badly now. We will all soon be liberated. Be patient. You will soon be free. Don't try anything foolish. And listen to our songs. They will tell you what to do. Tell the others also. And remember, take heart and don't give up!"

In a flash he was gone. The shadows swallowed him up. They were his camouflage. There seemed to have been an air of competence, of *savoir-faire* about him. It was reassuring.

Yet, I was unsure. I sat there behind the boulder as the air raid subsided, wondering at what I had just witnessed. Who was this man? Could he be trusted, or was he part of some bizarre Nazi plot? I was still trying to solve this puzzle when Hilda and some of the others from our group approached.

"Alice, who was that strange man you were talking to? What did he want?" They all wanted to know.

I looked at them, not knowing what to tell them. But they had the same right to know as I. After all, he had only selected me to talk to because of my knowledge of French. So I told them about Fleury and the good news he had brought with him.

"Do you really believe that man, Alice? Don't you think the Nazis could be using him to trick us, to send us to the ovens?" It was Hilda speaking now, echoing the same fears I had felt just a few moments ago.

But some of the others took a different view. They wanted to believe in Fleury and the good news. It was Gina who spoke with the greatest conviction.

"I too am afraid, just like Hilda and some of you. But I'm also saddened by the way we seem to have lost faith in everything around us. Will we ever again believe that there are decent human beings left in this world? Because, if not, there is little sense in going on living. Yes, I believe in this man and his message, and in the others in his company."

"Perhaps you are right, Gina," I concurred.

My mind still was not made up when we went to bed that night. But, at least I was prepared to accept the "good" he represented—albeit, with caution! As Gina had so aptly put it, if we were not prepared to believe in something, life would have little meaning for us. And I wanted very much to live!

Restlessness kept me from falling asleep. Hilda, who was closest to me, as usual, crossed herself and finished her nightly prayers, then turned to me and whispered, "Alice, you know memories haunt me night after night more than ever before. Now that hope seems to be more than a glimmer, I ask God fervently to stand by me no matter what happens."

She was quiet for a while. The others must have been overcome by fatigue and fallen into a dead sleep.

Then, as if driven by an inner urge, she murmured under her breath, "The nuns were hiding me for several days before the Hungarian Secret Police found me behind the organ in our little church. I turned gray overnight as a result of a week-long interrogation at gunpoint. I held out strong but shaken, without disclosing any financial or personal information about the president of my company, which was one of the biggest in Europe. I can still feel the vehemence of their blows to my head.

"Although I am a Catholic, the ultimate punishment was to be shipped out to a concentration camp. It was Auschwitz. They spared me the bullet."

Chapter XV

THE OUIJA BOARD'S MESSAGE

Something was wrong. It wasn't the lights, which cast their usual glare onto the machines. Nor was it the hypnotic motion of the equipment. It was something else. Something infinitely more ominous.

I was trying to load one of the machines and couldn't do it. I was unable to fit the rod into the slot. I couldn't locate the slot with the end of the rod. It was far easier than threading a needle, something I had done countless times, yet suddenly I couldn't do it.

Blinking, trying to focus my eyes, I became dizzy. The rod clanged to the floor. As I reached out to steady myself, the machine caught my hands.

Everything stopped. All the machines came to a halt; the clanking, chattering equipment fell silent. In place of the factory noises, came the screech of sirens and the chiming of warning bells. Eight guards, all of them crippled in some way, closed in on me. They were shouting orders at me and at each other. The deafening alarms added to the chaos of the scene.

One of the guards reached over and released a safety device. My hands were freed, but blood was gushing from both, covering the machinery. I remember screaming and counting my fingers over and over again. Each time there were ten.

I cried for help, but if anybody heard, none came forward, not even Ruth or Hilda. Not even the Germans, most missing an arm or a hand but still able to carry a rifle, came near.

They could shout, though. And they did. *"Schweinhunde! Sie Sabotiert! Bring Sie zum Oberschahrführer!"* Pigs! Saboteurs! Bring them to the commander!

Their conclusion was sabotage. Why else would the machines have stopped? It was simplistic reasoning.

Four of the guards, two for each arm, came forward. They practically carried me from the room. Still, the other prisoners stood motionless. I could not blame them. We were far down the hall when the alarms stopped and the clanging of the machines could be heard again.

The commandant's office was spacious and overheated. Windows opening onto the courtyard offered a bare view of the snow-covered ground. A bookcase adorned one wall. A massive desk beneath a huge portrait of Hitler contained scratch pads, pencils, a cigarette lighter, and an overflowing ashtray.

The heat and pine wood smell competed with the cheap patchouli scent worn by the commandant. He was in his mid-forties, a haggard-looking man, yet his uniform was immaculate. The buttons gleamed and the ribbons on his chest flashed brightly. He sat behind his desk stiffly, yellowed fingers constantly bringing a burning cigarette to his small, pursed lips.

He was another example of the rubble of the Third Reich. Those who were still able to fight, did. The rest, like the commandant and the guards, had been reduced to watching over half-dead enemies of the German empire.

I offered no sympathy, then or now.

The commandant's thinning brown hair was combed carefully over a bald spot on top of his oval head. He had enormous ears, a Hitler moustache, and a beak of a nose, which made him look like some kind of predator. One brown eye glared at me, looking me over carefully. The other was covered by a black eye patch.

"We know how to deal with your kind," he said without emotion.

The commandant seemed about as interested in me as he would be in sharpening a pencil. He lighted a fresh cigarette from the butt of the last. Blowing out a plume of smoke, he waved off the guards.

"Your act of sabotage was reported to me," he said as the door closed on us. "You caused an interruption in production and damage to the equipment. You are an enemy of the *Reich*."

He scratched his forehead above the eye patch as though it irritated him.

"Who else is connected with this plot?"

Now my sabotage was a conspiracy. Maybe he would lock up the entire factory.

But he had done something I had never heard a German officer do with a prisoner. He asked a question. Usually only commands were shouted at us. I took the chance to answer. He was impatient and probably would only hear what he wanted, but I would have no other opportunity to explain. I took a deep breath to calm my pounding heart.

"Sir," I said, feeling lightheaded again, "you can check my record. My work has always been what was expected of me, even though I was responsible for operating five machines. Never did I plan any act of sabotage. Since childhood I have suffered from an astigmatism in one eye. I have always worn corrective lenses. In the two weeks we have been here, my eyesight has gotten progressively worse. I didn't dare report it for reasons that you can imagine. My accident resulted from getting dizzy because of my eyes. That is all there is to it."

Out of the corner of my eye I could see a wall clock. The pendulum kept swinging, counting the long seconds. The heat became suffocating. I was glad we were alone, and the commandant didn't need to put on a show.

The commandant sighed, grabbed his note pad, and jotted down some instructions. He called the guard, who burst through the door and went directly to the desk. The commandant, lighting another cigarette, handed the guard the notes and turned his attention to some imaginary problem on his desk, effectively dismissing me.

The guard led me back to our sleeping quarters.

"I will be back for you in the morning," he said.

As I bound my hands with cloth I tore from the hem of my

shirt, I pondered what fate might be in store for me. Everything pointed to another train, probably back to Auschwitz. My hands were useless and my eyes were bad. What use could the *Reich* find for me here? There was none.

The other prisoners left me to my thoughts. The night passed slowly as I tossed on the flimsy mattress they had given each of us. As the shock wore off, my hands began to throb. No position was comfortable on the makeshift bed, not comfortable for my hands and not comfortable for my heart. I was awake when the sky began to lighten.

Before the others even stirred, the one-armed, limping guard who had brought me from the commandant's office came for me. We left the factory, taking a wide, stony road through the woods. In ten minutes we reached the depot of Tchopau. The train was waiting.

But it was a passenger train! The people boarding were commuters, working people, somber businessmen and weary laborers. Some carried attaché cases, others led children. The mothers were adorned in their Bavarian costumes, many of them seemingly headed for a festival.

And there was the *Hitler Jugend* (Hitler Youth), never a welcome sight before. They carried tents, backpacks, helmets, and walking sticks. Surely they were not going to Poland?

The station men announced the train's destination as Chemnitz, one of the large industrial cities in eastern Germany.

An old-fashioned steam locomotive belched great clouds of steam into the cold morning air. It was pulling about a dozen cars. I was weak, but I climbed the four steps leading to the entrance of the last car in front of the caboose and pushed through the heavy door.

Those passengers who noticed gave us quizzical looks. I doubted they had ever seen a crippled guard carrying a rifle and leading a prisoner whose faded gray woolen coveralls were adorned with a white phosphorescent stripe on the back.

The rear seat in our car was unoccupied and the guard motioned me to it. At least I had a kerchief to cover up my fuzzy head.

The train chugged away as the passengers leaned out the open windows, letting the cool air in. My coveralls protected me little against the cold, but I hardly noticed as the lurching train knocked me back against my seat.

When the windows came down, the baskets of food came out. As the scene unfolded, I could not remember the last time I had seen so much food. Women pulled homemade bread, fruit, and sausages from their baskets. Pastries were everywhere. Sauerkraut in covered dishes sent its pungent fragrance into the air. All of the aromas wafted toward the rear of the car.

I was practically overcome. I watched a man, one seat up and across the aisle, smacking his lips, gobbling a huge knockwurst. A mother shared a drumstick with a young boy. Two women in front of me shared a loaf of bread. I imagined it must have still been warm. Up the aisle, a man turned, facing across the car. He had an open beer bottle in one hand from which he took great swigs in between tearing voraciously into a slab of ribs.

Everyone seemed to be chewing. Wet lips smacked, fingers were licked, sleeves passed across mouths. I closed my eyes. All I could see were giant lips devouring bread, sausage, fruit. When I opened my eyes again, the train was slowing. The whistle sounded. "Chemnitz!"

The guard gestured me to follow him. He was confident I would not try to escape. We left the train, moved through the station, and emerged onto a cobblestone street. Two blocks away, he turned right onto a quiet avenue bordered by stately chestnut trees. There were sidewalks on either side of the street, and two-story buildings embellished with white stucco stood away from the sidewalks. Each building seemed to have the same balcony, Italian columns, and iron lanterns.

Wherever the bombing of Chemnitz had taken place, it was not here. This avenue had been spared. It was peaceful and tranquil. The pavement seemed to have been scrubbed. Even the gutters were cleaner than I was. And I felt it.

Less than a block up the avenue, we came to a smaller house. The guard opened the gate and we turned up a walkway lined with clipped hedges. Behind one of the hedges was a well-kept garden. It was a straight walkway leading us to a single door decorated with a polished brass knob. We entered without knocking.

The room looked like a doctor's waiting area. Diplomas from

three different institutions highlighted one wall. Two of them bore silver medallions, the other gold. There was no one else in the room.

One overstuffed armchair and a large couch offered respite. I chose the armchair. It felt like a cocoon as I sank into it and I remembered a chair from another life.

An elderly gentleman—he had to be past seventy—came out of a room down the hall and approached us. I assumed him to be the doctor. I tried to get out of the chair and couldn't. He smiled warmly and walked over to where I was sitting.

"Good morning," he said in German. "I have been expecting you."

His voice was kind. He looked at the guard as he helped me up. "You can come with us if you must."

The doctor didn't wait for an answer. He simply turned and walked back the way he had come. The guard followed and I was last.

I still didn't know if my eyes were to be examined or if my fingers were to be mended. I got the answer when I followed the doctor and the guard into a room off the hallway. The equipment in the room served an ophthalmologist.

The guard stood by the door while the doctor gave my eyes a thorough examination. He seemed indifferent to the procedure. There was nowhere for me to escape.

The doctor was careful. When he was finished, he smiled and stood up. He reached out and took my hands in his. I flinched from the pain.

"What is this?" he said, speaking for the first time since we left the anteroom. "We will attend to this in a moment. First things first. I will explain what is wrong with those eyes."

He led me gently to another chair and motioned me to sit down. He slid his stool near.

"My dear child," he said in a rich baritone, "you have a very bad case of astigmatism. You also have an infection. I know this is of great concern to you. Don't worry, you will be able to work. I will give you medication and some glasses that will get you through."

"Thank you, doctor," was all I could manage.

"Now, let me see those hands."

He used the same amount of skill in checking my fingers as he had used in examining my eyes. Each of my fingers on both hands had deep, oozing gashes just below the knuckles. He carefully stitched the deeper wounds and bandaged all of them. He gave me more of the ointment he had used on them to take with me.

Then he gave me glasses, and eye drops, and stood up. Before I could follow the guard out into the hallway, the doctor put his arm around my shoulder.

"Everything will be all right," he whispered. "Just believe that with all your heart."

I looked into the eyes of a compassionate old man, a concerned man, from a forgotten, better world. I smiled a thank you and left.

We had to wait awhile at the station for another commuter train to take us back and, by the time we arrived at the factory, the workers were finished and back in our quarters. They were astonished to see me, glasses on my nose and bandages on my hands. The fact that I was back at all seemed to astonish them.

Hilda and Ruth rushed to greet me. We embraced, and once one of my battered hands got between us. I winced.

"How did it go?"

"It's wonderful to see you, a miracle."

"We didn't think you were coming back!"

I didn't answer or reply as the rest of the prisoners gathered around. They had never seen anyone come back, either.

The welcome ceremony ended when the bread was being distributed. It was the first time I had eaten since before the accident. By the next day, my recuperation period was over. At least for the time being I was given only one machine to operate.

The air raids continued. Hilda, Ruth, and I took to huddling under a staircase leading up to the fifth floor. Often, we waited there for long periods as persistent Allied attacks kept the all-clear from sounding.

To pass the time, we played a little game in which one of us posed certain situations, while the other two speculated on what their actions would be under the given circumstances. The situations presented were usually positive ones, like being liberated, or having the guards disappear, or the war coming to an end. It was a way to keep our spirits high and to prevent us from giving up hope of survival.

On one of those late winter nights, when the snow fell less heavily and melted more quickly, we sat there in the stairwell, trying to cheer ourselves in the usual manner during another lengthy air raid. But, on this night, the doubts and fears about our eventual survival predominated. What if the war ended too late to do us any good? We fully realized that our daily diet of "slush" accompanied by a lone piece of bread could not sustain us indefinitely. Our growing hunger pangs and the deterioration in our appearance and outlook bore this out. The basic question of survival came up in our discussion time and time again. We needed a new game, one that would provide us with the real answer to our predicament. And I had just the right game to propose to them.

"Tomorrow night, when the guards abandon us during the air raid, I want you both to help me gather some materials for a new game. I'm going to construct a Ouija board that will provide us with answers. I'll teach you how to play. It's quite easy. Really! I learned when I was only ten."

"Are you serious, Alice?" Hilda wanted to know. "A Ouija board? How is a board going to predict our fate? I don't believe in the supernatural! Do you?"

"Why not try it? It could be fun!" Ruth interrupted with eagerness in her voice. "I don't believe in those things either. But what can we lose? It might be better than that stupid game we've been playing every night. I'm growing tired of it!" She turned toward me. "What materials will you need, Alice, to build that board of yours? We'll help you find them."

"Good! Is it agreed, then?" They both nodded affirmatively. "We'll have to search around the rubbish piles on the first floor. I'll need a good-sized flat piece of metal. At least a foot and a half square. We'll also need a small block of wood. You decide between yourselves which item you'll be responsible for. I'll look for a rock with a sharp point outside the building. But, remember to keep this a secret. And don't get caught by one of the guards! We'll meet here two nights from now to play. Good luck!"

The appointed night arrived quickly. We eagerly awaited the usual air raid sirens around 6 PM, but there were none.

"Isn't it ironic?" I muttered to myself impatiently, as I lay on my bed. "Just when you want those planes, they don't come!"

It was getting late, I judged about 11 o'clock, and I was just falling asleep, when the sirens startled me awake. I could hear the guards scattering, their footsteps disappearing down the stairs. I reached under my mattress for the hidden rock. It had been selected with great care, and I hoped the other two had done equally well.

We met in the familiar stairwell with great enthusiasm. Even Hilda's face seemed flushed with excitement. It took less than half an hour to etch several "yes" and "no" words in various locations on the metal board.

"Let me show you how this is going to work," I began. "When it's your turn to go, you must ask a silent question of the board, one that can be answered with either a 'yes' or 'no'. Then you must place your right hand on the wooden block in the center of the board. With your eyes closed, relax the muscles in your hand and let it move the block across the board in any direction it seems to want to go. When it stops moving, open your eyes and see where it's landed. That will be your answer. If it hasn't landed on anything, try again. Just remember to relax your arm and hand muscles, and keep concentrating on your question. Hilda, why don't you go first?"

Hilda seemed reluctant to be the first player, but she quickly got into the spirit of the game. We watched breathlessly as her hand began to twitch and the wood block moved ever so slowly across the metal plane. Suddenly it stopped its movement, coming to rest on the "no" in the upper right hand corner of the board. She gasped as her eyes opened and a pained expression crossed her face.

"What was your question, Hilda?" Ruth wanted to know. "What did you ask the Ouija board?"

"Don't answer, Hilda!" I blurted out the caution before Hilda had a chance to answer. "You mustn't tell anyone what your question was, or the power of the board is lost forever. But you may go again, if you want to. You can ask as many questions during your turn as you desire."

Hilda was looking positively ill now. It was apparent by her appearance that the answer she had gotten did not promise good things for her. "I don't feel too well right now. Besides, it's getting quite late. Maybe I'll just go back to my bed. If the bombs fall it won't matter much anyway. Please excuse me." She got up and walked up the stairs. We could hear her footsteps on the floor above us.

"Well, I'm sorry about Hilda. But perhaps the board will be kinder to you, Ruth. Why don't you go next?"

Nodding her head, Ruth moved closer to the board. Her question must have been a complicated one because it took nearly a minute before she closed her eyes and grasped hold of the wooden block. I watched as her hand moved slowly but steadily across the board, finally stopping directly on top of another "no". When she opened her eyes, a look of disappointment crossed her face.

"This is a stupid game!" she shouted, as she flung the wooden block down the stairs in apparent anger and disappointment. "Where did you learn this game, anyway, Alice? I don't believe in it! I should never have played! You can have it to yourself, now. I'm leaving also."

I retrieved the piece of wood as soon as she had disappeared, and began to concentrate on my question.

"Will the Nazis kill me?"

It was a simple question, yet a basic one. Would the Ouija board supply the answer? I had to find out.

I closed my eyes and felt a strange numbness in my hand and lower arm as I grasped the block, placing it on the board. I closed my eyes and began concentrating on my question. I could feel my hand moving slowly across the board. Then suddenly it stopped. I opened my eyes. The block was resting squarely on a "no" in the lower left corner.

"A good start," I muttered to myself. "Worth another try!"

This time I decided to ask, "Will I be rescued?"

The answer was "no" also.

I was disappointed, but not enough to keep me from trying again.

"Will I escape?"

Another "no" answer would surely seal my fate, but I felt compelled to try.

When I opened my eyes, I was truly surprised. The board had given a "yes" answer for the first time tonight!

I had become so engrossed in the game that I had failed to hear the all-clear siren. Now it was too late! Two of the guards were standing over me; the looks in their eyes foretold trouble.

"You are coming with us!" The angry shout in German was all too clear to me. It came from the guard who had only one arm. His pistol was out of his holster, resting in his hand. He was pointing it at me.

Chapter XVI

THE DEPARTURE

The two guards escorted me to the office of the head *Aufseherin*. They were acting as though they had just captured a master spy red-handed. Their evidence, the homemade Ouija board, was being carried by the second guard, a short fellow well into his fifties, with graying hair and a distinct limp.

"We caught this Jew trying to send signals to the enemy on this," he announced proudly, handing the "evidence" to the *Aufseherin*. She was a short, heavyset woman, with sagging jowls and squinty eyes beneath bushy eyebrows.

"What signals were you sending?" she shouted at me, trying to sound forceful despite her high, girlish voice. "You might as well tell us now, before we turn you over to the Gestapo. They won't be nearly as nice to you. You know what I mean, don't you?"

"You don't understand," I tried to explain, making a desperate effort to hold back a snicker. The situation was becoming more and more ludicrous by the minute. "I'm not a spy. And this is just a Ouija board I was using to amuse myself. It doesn't send signals, or anything like that. It's just a . . ."

"Enough of your lies! We know very well what you are. We've been watching you very closely ever since your little 'accident' in the factory. You may be able to fool some of the others here with your stories, but you can't fool me!" She looked me up and down, her eyes blazing with anger. "The only reason we're not going to turn you over to the Gestapo is that you'll be leaving with the others in a couple of days anyway. You'll get your just punishment there! In the meantime, you'll be confined to solitary, where you won't be able to do any more damage. Guards, take her away!"

We knew that the *Aufseherin*'s threats were lies. Nobody believed her. We knew she did not follow orders when she locked us in the factory during air raids. And she was known among the prisoners to be a brute, whose sadistic satisfaction was to scare the life out of us.

For the next two days, my home was a tiny concrete block cell in the basement, barely five feet high. It had a metal door and a tiny barred window just below the ceiling on one wall. I was grateful for the window, because it enabled me to keep track of the passage of time. There was hardly any room for movement, just barely enough space to sit and cry.

When my two days were up, I was led back to our barracks on the fifth floor, where I found my friends gathered at my bed, awaiting my arrival.

"Alice, what happened to you? We woke up to find you gone. What did they do to you? And why?"

I started to relate the whole story to them but in the middle of it I began to sob uncontrollably, unable to continue. I felt an aching in the pit of my stomach, and every part of me trembled. But my friends were most understanding. They promptly produced several pieces of bread they had saved for me, and, while the bread had become somewhat stale, I devoured it quickly, with words of gratitude. I had only been given "mush" and water in solitary, and, at that moment, the stale bread tasted like the finest French pasty from Gerbeaud's.

The following morning, the work whistles awakened us as usual, and I was just beginning to think that the *Aufseherin*'s threats had been just a scare tactic, when at midday, without warning, guards with unfamiliar faces appeared from nowhere. They began herding us into the courtyard to be counted, after which we were issued new clothing. I was given a pair of tight canvas shoes with knotted shoe laces, baggy blue slacks, and a striped green shirt with long sleeves. I also got a man's double-breasted overcoat, which was several sizes too large, and had many buttons missing. But it was warm and comfortable, and I was happy to have it. Then, we were ordered to discard our old outfits and don our new ones. This brought no protests from us, as we had been forced to wear our former clothes night and day since our arrival sometime in the distant past, and they had become stained and malodorous.

But what caused me the greatest concern was that there was no delousing, a procedure we had become accustomed to on prior occasions. It made me feel very uneasy about our future, especially in light of what the *Aufseherin* had told me.

Now we were lined up once more in formation to be counted. I made sure that my friends were nearby. I wanted to be together with them on our forthcoming trip. There would be some comfort in that.

As we stood there, awaiting further orders, the wind whipped up a late spring snow flurry around us. I shivered and wrapped my new coat tightly around me, grateful for the warmth it offered. I noted with sympathy that none of my friends had been as lucky as I in obtaining a warm outer garment. I intended to share my luck with them once we got on the train.

The soldiers around us seemed equally uncomfortable in the cold as the dusk of another day settled in. They began to stir impatiently, shuffling their feet to keep them from freezing. They were a great deal younger than our former guards, who were now nowhere to be seen. None of the replacements had any sign of facial hair and their appearance gave no indication of prior combat experience. They were mere teenagers, possibly members of the infamous and fanatic *Hitler Jugend*, I imagined. They carried their weapons with the fierce pride of veterans. One of the guards paraded in front of our formation, a huge German shepherd dog on a leash following behind him. As he passed directly in front of me I looked at the dog's alert, shiny eyes, and instinctively reached out my hand to pet him. The animal, to my surprise, licked my fingers in a gesture of friendship. I was quite touched by this, but I found myself hardly prepared for his master's reaction. The blond, blue-eyed boy in uniform, who couldn't have been over fifteen or sixteen years old, yanked at the dog's leash and grabbed it by its collar. Then he viciously applied the butt of his weapon against the poor animal's skull. The dog yelped in fright as blood began to ooze from the side of its head. As it trailed its master with its tail between its legs, I was overcome with pity. I had been the cause of its punishment through a totally innocent and impulsive act. This poor animal, I realized, was no less a prisoner of Nazi brutality than myself. I vowed never to act so impulsively again.

It took several more hours of standing in the cold before they began loading us into the waiting freight cars. I was just about to board, when I heard men's voices singing in the distance. At first it was difficult to hear the lyrics, but as I concentrated on the familiar tune, I was able to make out the French lyrics.

"*Frère Jacques, Frère Jacques . . .*"

There could be no doubt. It was Fleury and his men, the ones who had greeted us with their song upon our arrival. I wanted to hear the next verse, so I moved to the side of the boxcar opening, permitting those behind me in line, to board.

"Heed our warning! Heed our warning!

"Escape or die! Escape or die!

"At Annaberg we'll greet you. At Annaberg we'll greet you.

"Three kilometers east. Three kilometers east."

The message was clear to me, but it had come too late. Escape was not possible, now, not with all the guards surrounding us. Even given the fact that they were probably inexperienced at using their weapons, we stood an excellent chance of being killed. I had looked into the youthful eyes of that guard, the one with the dog. They had been filled with hate and loathing for me. No, there would be no escape!

And now, having lost my turn in line, I was about to be separated from my friends as well. The boxcar's doors were slammed shut in my face and I was being pushed toward one of the other cars. There would be no way for me to let the others know what I had heard. I was not going to be able to see them until our arrival. By then, it might be too late.

Chapter XVII

THE TRAIN TO A *VERNICHTUNGS LAGER* (EXTERMINATION CAMP)

The door of the freight car clanged shut behind me. I could hear it being bolted in place. I had been forced to board the last car of the train. I was alone once more among strangers, with no one to share my thoughts and feelings. What was it that Boriska had prophesied? "Crowds of strangers with a common bond." I looked around me at the remains of what had at one time been humanity, but what was now nothing but animals packed together like the cattle that had previously occupied our car. The smell from their residue mixed foully with the stench from our own bodies. I was glad that I had been one of the last to board, as I was able to benefit from the cold, fresh air that penetrated the seams of the sliding door. I noticed, without surprise, that on this trip both men and women had been loaded in the same car. But there was little difference between us now. Finally, Hitler had reduced us to the level of domesticated animals to match his perception of us. As I stood there, glancing at the expressions of pain, misery, and suffering, I wondered whether it would finally now come to an end. "Escape or die!" Weren't those the lyrics I had just heard?

The train began to move with a sudden jolt, throwing us against each other. There was much screaming, pushing, and kicking.

Those who had been too weak to stand now provided the others with a soft landing place. I couldn't afford to fall, I told myself. I had to stay upright despite my exhaustion . . . my hunger. We hadn't been fed or given water during our long wait to board, and all of us were feeling the effect. I began talking to myself, repeating the same words over and over, "Don't give up! Hold on! Don't let yourself fall!"

Still, I lost consciousness. Had it been for just a moment or several minutes? I couldn't tell. I jerked my head upright, chin high. I breathed in the cold air deeply. I blinked my eyes. I ordered myself to stay awake. But, soon, the metronome-like clickety-clack of the wheels caused my head to dip forward again.

Suddenly, a deafening explosion shook the train, jolting into consciousness all but the dead on board. The train braked to a stop, wheels squealing. Then came another explosion, followed by another, and yet another. There was sheer terror in the car. People were screaming, praying, and crying. They were pushing each other to get away, but there was no place to go, no escape. The fires from the bombardment were all around us. I could see a reflection of the flames on the opposite wall. I watched and waited for the end, mesmerized, unable to utter a sound. My heart was pounding in my chest. I could hear it clearly.

The explosions stopped as suddenly as they had started. The only sound to be heard now was the crackling of the flames. The smell from the fires entered the car, but it was a pleasant odor of wood burning. It was altogether different from the acrid odor that emanated from the smokestacks at Auschwitz.

There was a sudden lurch as the train started up again. Before I knew what had happened, I found myself lying on my back, on top of someone. I could see the crowns of the burning trees alongside the tracks through the small opening way up high as we passed by ever so slowly. Opening! My heart skipped a beat as my brain began to realize what my eyes had discovered. I pushed myself up to my feet to get another look from an upright position. As I did so, my hand came into contact with something cold and clammy. It was the face of a corpse I had been lying on. I shuddered uncontrollably. But the interest in what I had just seen took my mind off the corpse. It was a small opening up high on the wall against which I was leaning. It must have served as a vent or an opening for throwing hay or feed to the animals that had been transported in our car. And it had been left open and unnoticed by the young guards.

An opening! An exit! A way to escape! My throat became dry and my whole body quivered. I wanted to cry out, but I didn't dare. I didn't know what reaction I could expect from the others in my car if they saw me trying to escape. There was no way to predict it. But I would soon find out. I had to try! It was my only chance, perhaps the last one.

Slowly, surreptitiously, I inched my way in the direction of the opening. That in itself, was no easy task. There was so little room to move, so many bodies in my path. Hands clutched at me, elbows jabbed, and grunts, groans, and insults were flung my way. But I didn't care. I was possessed by a single purpose, a single goal: To escape! I had to get to that opening and I would not be stopped.

Finally I arrived at the spot directly beneath the little window. I could see the stars through it now. They looked so free, so beautiful! I wanted to see all of them, every star in the sky. And the moon as well!

But I soon discovered a few problems I had not anticipated. I realized them as soon as I looked up at the window from directly below it. It seemed so much higher now. Also, it really was quite small. How would I get up to it? And once there, would I be able to fit my body through it? Certainly not if I was wearing my bulky overcoat.

My hands searched desperately along the wall of the car for something I could use to climb up on. Suddenly the train lurched to another stop. I felt my body toppling forward as though someone had pushed me from behind. Instinctively I clutched at the wall to keep me from falling again. I felt my left hand close on something round and cold. A ring . . . a large metal ring. Probably a tether ring for the animals. My mind began to churn out ideas as I pulled myself upright. If I could get high enough off the ground to put my foot through that ring I could push myself upwards toward the opening. But what would I use to stand on? And what would serve as a handhold? Think! Find the answers!

I took off my coat and folded it neatly again and again to make as high a platform to stand on as possible. Then, with my left foot on the coat, I placed my right foot into the tether ring. I could feel the adrenalin coursing through my veins as I pushed down on my right foot and straightened my knee. I stood there, up off the ground, clutching at the wall for a finger hold, when suddenly the train lurched forward again. I was thrown off my perch on top of someone below me. It was a man, a fairly young man in his thirties, I judged. He was furious, shouting and cursing at me in Hungarian.

"You fool! What are you trying to do? Do you want to kill me before the Germans get their chance? Get off, damn you!"

I could understand his reaction, but I was not going to be discouraged from trying again. Not by one man, not even by a thousand! This was my chance to escape. It was now or never! I knew it . . . I felt it!

The train was moving quite slowly by now. I could hear the engine at the front of the train chugging away, motor straining. It was struggling to get its load up a hill, I assumed. I started the climbing process once again, noting beforehand that I could get a finger hold by sliding my fingertips through the partly deteriorated wooden sections. But as I struggled to lift my body close enough to the window sill to grab hold of it, I realized that I was a foot or so short of my mark. I was just about to let go and jump down again when I felt two strong arms pushing me upwards from below. I pulled my upper body up to the window and extended my arms outside the car. The cool air rushed at my face, drying the perspiration on my brow. It was a great feeling! Before pushing my head and shoulders out the opening, I looked down sideways into the car to discover the identity of my benefactor. I was surprised to see that it was the same man on whom I had fallen, the one who had cursed at me. He was waving his hand, asking me to hurry up. "God bless you!" I muttered breathlessly, hoping he would hear.

But I was still a long way from freedom. It was fairly easy to squeeze my head and shoulders through the opening, but try as I could, my hips could barely fit through. I pulled and pulled with my arms, scraping my hips and making a bloody mess of my trousers, but nothing helped. Yet I remained determined. Either my hips or the window frame would have to give! I had come too far to just give up, barely taking notice of the sharp pain in my pelvis. I had to make my escape! The stars and the moon beckoned me. "Please, God!

Help me!" I whispered.

Just then the train reached the top of the hill and started down the other side. I could hear each car being jolted by the one behind it as it followed the engine over the hill. Bang! With an enormous bump we went over also, knocking into the car ahead of us. The impact was strong enough to pull the decayed window sill away from the wall. My blood froze as I tumbled down, clutching part of the wood.

I was filled with horror. "What could I do now?"

As I slowly caught my bearings and started to formulate the next strategy, an instantaneous impulse made me raise my head. And there—up the wall—was a large gap left behind by the wooden section which had broken off.

I hastily straightened up and rolled up my coat again, as I noticed my benefactor behind me, reaching out to help. Once again, I clambered up to the opening. I had a precarious hold now, hanging out of the gap by my knees. But I was through it, almost all of me. My hands searched desperately for something to grab hold of. They found the metal ladder that was attached to every boxcar to enable workers to get to the window or roof from the outside. I grasped it firmly with both hands and pulled my legs through the huge gap, feeling for the rungs with my feet. For a moment I clung there, thanking God!

The train was beginning to speed up now. I quickly climbed down the ladder, but when I got to the bottom rung I froze in place. I knew that I would have to jump off, but the fear of falling to the ground from the moving train seemed almost insurmountable. "Jump, you fool!" I commanded my body. Obediently, my arms pushed off.

I landed heavily on the frozen ground and rolled sideways down the embankment. For an instant I lay there on my back, unable to breathe. But after a minute or so, when I was able to resume breathing normally, I realized that I had not hurt myself seriously. I turned on my side and, with my head propped up by my elbow, I watched the light from the last car fade in the distance down the tracks. I didn't want to move. I waited for the sounds of wheels grinding to a halt, for the shouting voices of guards, for the shot from a rifle.

But there was none. "Could it be?" I asked myself. "Am I really free? Had my miraculous escape really been successful?" The answers were not immediately forthcoming, but I didn't care. For the next several minutes, I just lay back, admiring the sky full of stars. They were twinkling, as if welcoming me to their world . . . and freedom. I felt Boriska's presence.

Chapter XVIII

A WALK IN THE WOODS

Freedom. What a remarkable word! Yet, such an obscure concept. Which of us, who has not been deprived of his freedom at some time in his life, can understand its meaning . . . can fully appreciate it? It is not a right, or even a privilege, as some would have us believe. Is it then a condition of one's life? No, it is life itself! It is as basic as the ability to see the stars in the open sky above one's head . . . to feel the breeze brush against one's face . . . to smell the clean, unsoiled air . . . to listen to the songs of birds in their nests. That is what freedom meant to me that fateful day.

God, in His great wisdom, had seen fit to deprive me of my freedom. Now He had returned it. I was ever so grateful! I thanked Him over and over again. And I made Him a promise as I lay next to that railroad trestle, looking up at the evening sky. I promised Him that I would never again take my freedom for granted . . . that I would cherish it forever.

But freedom is a very fragile thing. It comes and leaves without warning. It was now my responsibility to assure that it remained for me.

My first free act was to test my extremities to make sure that they were still intact and working properly. I would need to rely heavily on them from now on. Although reluctant and fearful at first, I began to stretch, testing each part in turn. I kicked my legs first, one at a time. Then came my arms. I waved them as though they were wings. All responded perfectly. Slowly I pushed myself up to my feet. The legs of my pants felt sticky. Blood was oozing from gashes around my knees where they had come in contact with some sharp rocks during my fall from the train. The material next to my hips was also soaked with blood. But otherwise, everything checked out fine. There was no reason not to go on.

Suddenly I felt lightheaded and dizzy. My body was shaking uncontrollably. I collapsed back on the ground as the whole world began to spin crazily around me. The lack of food and the physical exertion of my escape were taking their toll. I stretched out on my back, waiting for the symptoms to pass. After a few minutes, I tried again. Slowly, and still trembling, I pushed myself up to my feet. I focused my eyes on the tracks. They were maintaining their position in space once again. Satisfied, I tried taking a few wobbly steps. Although the feeling of malaise had not totally left me, I realized that I could not afford to remain in plain sight of the tracks. I needed to hide in the woods from possible search parties, or the guards on the next train that would pass by. I had to find a safe place to stay the night. Then, in the morning, I would plan my next move.

Accordingly, I limped off into the tree line, stopping just long enough to pick a few wild berries off a bush in my path. I was both hungry and exhausted from my ordeal, but I also had a feeling of exhilaration. The pine needles underfoot cushioned my every step. I imagined that they would make an ideal mattress. After several minutes of walking, I turned around to see whether my tracks were still visible. They weren't. I had been swallowed up by the forest. It was time to make my bed. With a huge oak tree forming a shelter over my head, I lay down on the pine needles. My blanket was a pile of leaves that covered me from head to foot. It was a primitive bed indeed. Yet, it was far more comfortable than any of the beds I had slept in during my captivity. I quickly fell into a deep and restful sleep for the first time in many months.

I awoke with a start. From behind the beams of sunlight streaming through the branches, I could see two large, yellowish eyes staring down at me. But I wasn't afraid. Their appearance was more soothing than threatening, and they blinked every time I blinked. Then a wet, cold nose muzzled my face. It was a young deer, poking at me, trying to determine what sort of creature I was. I had never been so close to a wild animal before. As I lay there, motionless, trying not to frighten it away, I felt a real kinship with this gentle being. Both of us, I told myself, wanted nothing but mere survival in a hostile world. We meant no harm, represented no threat, to anyone. We wanted only to be left alone.

Abruptly, as though it remembered another appointment, the deer turned away and went off into the deeper woods. My eyes filled with tears as I bid my innocent messenger farewell.

I felt secure in my little hideaway in the forest, yet I knew I had to move on. I needed to find food and water, and a more permanent shelter. The only place I could think of, that would be friendly to me, was that town the Frenchmen had mentioned in their farewell song. How did it go again? "At Anaberg we'll greet you, three kilometers to the east." Yes, that was it! I had to find Anaberg. But in order to do so, I would have to head back toward Tchopau . . . undetected. It was a simple matter of following the railroad tracks back in the direction from which I had come, the South. But I would have to walk in the woods to escape detection.

The idea was a good one, but somehow it went awry. I became so fascinated with the birds that serenaded me with their sweet songs, and the little brook I discovered that offered me a drink of cold water, that I was unaware of the direction my path was leading me. To my consternation, I found myself back at my starting point near the oak tree several hours later, judging by the position of the sun. I had walked in a complete circle without noticing it!

Now I was overcome with panic. I had wasted precious time and energy, and I had little left of either. But I had no choice but to start out once more. This time, however, I kept close watch on the railroad tracks, keeping them in constant view as I blazed my own path through the woods.

But it was getting late now, and the sun was beginning to set behind the tree line across the tracks from me. Soon, I would find myself alone in the darkened forest again. It was an idea I didn't relish. A second night in the open, without food and water, would be no picnic. How long could I expect to last under those conditions? Had I found my freedom in vain?

Suddenly, without warning, I heard the sound of engines coming from the woods to my left. I froze in place, dropping down to my knees. I could now discern two headlights coming from my left and slightly ahead of me. I crept forward very, very slowly until I could see a dirt road ahead of me, crossing the railroad tracks to my right. I flattened myself on the ground beneath a bush and waited breathlessly. It was a motor convoy of the German *Reich*. The lead vehicle was a motorcycle. It was flying a banner with a red cross from its antenna. The trucks that followed also had red crosses painted on their canopies, which flapped loosely in the breeze. Each vehicle was filled with wounded soldiers, some lying on stretchers, others sitting on the benches.

Many were swathed in bandages. A few still wore their helmets. They had not made it for the thousand years Hitler had promised.

After the last truck had passed me by, I waited, fearful that some straggler might discover me. But, after a few minutes I became brave and walked up the side of the road toward the track, prepared to jump back into the woods at a moment's notice. Up ahead, at the crossing, I could see a road sign. It was pointing in the direction from which the convoy had come. But I was unable to make out the letters until I was almost on top of it.

"Anaberg—8 KM."

I felt the blood rushing to my head as my heart began to pound. Was it possible? I read the sign again to make sure. I had found it . . . almost! My plan had really worked! Would I find the friendly faces there that I was looking for? My hopes and spirits were rising once again.

The answer waited for me, just eight kilometers away.

Chapter XIX

AN UNEXPECTED ENCOUNTER

The time for decision making had arrived. Was I going to spend another night hidden in the woods before heading towards Anaberg? Or, should I use the cover of the approaching darkness to make my way toward town now? There were cogent arguments on both sides of the question. But the excitement and anticipation of some real food and a warm bed became the overriding considerations. Although I realized that I was by now totally exhausted, I hoped that I had sufficient strength left to negotiate the final eight kilometers.

While waiting in the woods for the darkness of night to arrive, I took the opportunity to gather some more wild berries. But they were beginning to hurt my stomach and I had to stop eating them. "Don't worry," I reassured myself. "In less than two hours you'll be eating some real food."

As the darkness of night cast its shadows over the landscape, it was time to start on what I hoped would be the final leg of my lonely journey. I walked rapidly but cautiously among the poplars to my right, intentionally avoiding the canter of the road, which stood illuminated in the moon's bright glow. I remained on the alert for headlights or other signs of someone approaching from either direction. But the only signs of life that night were the cricket-sounding insects who serenaded me on my way into town.

After what seemed an eternity, the road dipped downhill and to the right. I could see signs of civilization now, as lights twinkled in the distance. I slowed my pace to use greater caution and thought I heard the sound of water rushing over rocks. I followed my ears to the bank of a small brook. Up ahead, I could make out a footbridge crossing over it. The path from the footbridge led directly to a small outdoor structure that had been built in the middle of a clearing. It was a gazebo, and I could hear voices coming from inside. I needed to get closer to overhear what was being said and in what language. But I could not let myself be discovered. If they were Germans, even just civilians, they would most certainly take me into custody, putting a quick end to my newly found freedom. My shaved head and ill-fitting clothes were clues to my identity that no one could overlook. I had to exercise extreme caution!

Slowly, without making a sound, I crawled on all fours next to the stream until I was directly opposite the gazebo. I could make out the glow of cigarettes and the muffled voices of the men sitting inside. But their words were drowned out by the sound of rushing water. I could not possibly discern what language they were speaking. "If only the brook would stop its babbling!" I whispered to no one in particular. Suddenly, the occupants of the gazebo stood up and walked outside. I could see them looking around the clearing, as if searching for something. The tall figure of a man began walking toward the bridge. I felt my throat go dry, and my heart began to pound inside my chest. I flattened myself as close to the ground as I could get, hoping to avoid detection. But it was useless. His eyes had found me. He was looking straight at me! I closed my eyes hoping that by doing so he would be unable to see me as well.

"*Avancé!*" His deep voice floated across the bridge.

The words were in French, but I did not trust them. It could easily be a Nazi hoax. They had discovered my escape and were trying to trap me! I did not answer.

"*Avancé!*" he repeated in a slightly louder tone. "Please stand and approach. I will not harm you. I promise!"

It was no use. I could not run away. If I did, he might shoot me. He would most certainly catch me, in any event. In my exhausted condition, I would not even think of running away. Besides, they outnumbered me. I got up reluctantly and walked slowly across the bridge towards the tall silhouette. The closer I got, the more familiar he looked.

"*Mademoiselle*, it is I, André Fleury. Don't you remember me?"

It was a familiar voice. I recalled having heard it in the courtyard of the factory at Tchopau. It was coming together now. My dream, my hopes were about to be realized. Could it be? It was time to speak out and make sure.

"Are you the man," I asked in French, "who once talked to me at the Auto Union Werke in Tchopau during the air raid? And you offered me your help?"

"*Oui! Oui! Mademoiselle*. I am that very man. And this is Louis Mattare, a friend. When the Nazis fled, they left us behind. We knew you and your compatriots had been taken away in the trains. We have been combing the area around here ever since, hoping some of you might have escaped. Are there any others with you?"

"No, *monsieur!* I'm afraid I'm the only one. I was separated from the others on the train. I could not relay your warning in time."

Fleury turned toward his friend. "You see, Louis. It is as I told you. Our song has not been in vain. At least <u>someone</u> has been saved from the savages."

"*Mademoiselle*, we stand at your service!" He bowed low in my direction, a friendly smile creasing his gaunt but classic Gallic features.

Was I delirious? Was this just another one of my dreams? After all the horrors of Auschwitz and the months in captivity, I could hardly let myself believe this was actually happening to me. There was only one way to find out. The words emerged hesitantly, but hopefully, from between my lips.

"I do not know who you really are, or why you want to help me. But if you could provide some food and water, and a safe place to rest, I would be eternally grateful. I haven't had anything to eat for several days and I'm almost . . ."

Before I could finish my little speech, I felt myself sink to the ground as the darkness closed in around me.

Chapter XX

AMONG FRIENDS

André Fleury had been a voice first, deep and resonant though restrained and virtually a whisper. It had been a voice offering help and hope.

I had rejected both because the voice had come from a stranger, inspiring caution instead of confidence, wariness instead of comfort. I hadn't been able to imagine a man who would risk his own life to help others in such a perilous situation. I had been more sure that I couldn't trust him than I had been willing to try.

I had decided that this shadowy figure, whose face had been hidden behind the hood of his cloak, had been too much of a threat. Never had I been so happy to be wrong.

Now I had seen the long, clean, refined hands and the straightforward, cool blue eyes. Eyes that had looked into the world around and seen pain, enough pain so that he rarely smiled. Perhaps, he had forgotten how.

Now I had seen what the light had done to his once-young face. A face now scarred by a world gone mad, yet still willing to embrace a return to sanity. A face willing to seek out some reflection of what had been and, in it, hold a hopeful reality.

Now I had seen his flair for leadership. Even on the bridge, it was evident that he was in charge and his men wanted it that way. I would see more of that in the time I spent with Fleury and his band.

I would also see a little more of Fleury and discover what a good listener he was, attentive to every detail and always polite.

I would learn no more than what I could see.

I would come to trust this man and feel protected in his care. I would trust him with the first few steps I took toward freedom. And he would come to guide those steps carefully.

When I woke up, he was trying to discover if I could take any steps at all. I was lying on a cot, blankets tucked under my chin. Fleury was squatting next to the cot, his slender fingers on my wrist which peeked out from under the covers.

Fleury's eyes were half-closed as he counted. Apparently satisfied, he gently released my wrist. That is when he noticed that my eyes were open.

"You collapsed when we found you. We brought you here to our little hideaway. We are going to take care of you," he said.

It would have been a time for him to smile. He did not. His face was only weary.

I looked around slowly. We were in the basement of a partially bombed-out building. There was still some rubble near the stairway that I guessed gave access to the world above.

In one corner a prisoner, or former prisoner, sat with his back to me. He was wearing earphones and listening, hunched over slightly, to the short-wave radio he had revealed behind the open doors of a small closet.

In another corner stood a stack of confiscated German goods, including maps, canned goods, blankets, and clothing. On the wall opposite my cot were an enormous iron stove, sink, and counter for preparing meals. The men must have slept on the floor, because there were no bunks other than the one they had found for me.

It turned out to be the perfect hideout. The ingenious French had given it all the comforts of home and hidden it beneath what turned out to be a mountain of cracked brick. They had disguised the entrance, only went out at night, and had deftly constructed a chimney of sorts that made the smoke from their fire appear to come up at several different places in the rubble above, as though the building, if inspected closely, were still smoldering.

As they noticed I was awake, the men gathered around my

bed, each of them smiling. Each introduced himself in turn, then went back to what chores they had left. Some of them pitched in to complete the one hot meal they had daily, others looked over some of the maps. The radio man, who had left a compatriot at the earphones for a moment, returned to his machine.

A young man named Gaston gave me a flannel shirt. Another, Gilbert, handed me a box of Dutch cocoa. One of the men turned back the blanket at the foot of the bed and pulled some thick woolen socks over my feet. Louis Mattare brought another blanket.

Fleury had stepped away when the others gathered. He returned with some hot tea from the kettle they had on the stove. Fleury helped me sit up and Mattare pulled the blanket around my back to keep me warm.

The tea burned my mouth at first, but it was delicious. I took a long gulp and instantly felt stronger and refreshed.

Propped up on my elbow in the bed, I looked around some more. Some of the men cast casual glances my way and smiled. I smiled in return.

Fleury took the empty cup and walked the few steps to the stove, poured more, and came back. Along the way, he scooped up a low footstool and placed it next to the cot. Instead of sitting down, he put the cup on the stool gently. Then he joined the men perusing the maps at the center of the room.

I flopped back in the bed and remembered the one I had left behind in Budapest. I imagined the blankets I had were the goose-feather comforters of my past, the thin feather pillow the deepest down. It was not the same, but it was a far cry from straw and the smell of urine.

I assumed Fleury to be the leader. I wanted to talk to him and nearly beckoned him over. But, I decided to wait. I had no idea what I would ask him or what I would tell him. It would be better to discuss the future when he wasn't so busy. And when I wasn't so confused. I contented myself with watching them work.

One of the men chopped onions, while another sliced large chunks of bread into individual portions. The onions went into a soup Mattare was tending on top of the stove. I watched as he frequently pulled the large ladle out of the pot for a quick taste.

Several bottles of beer stood on the counter away from the

onions. A couple of crates held up that end of the cooking table. Occasionally, one of the men would help himself to a bottle, lean over to a concrete sill where a window used to be, prop the bottle cap on the edge of the sill, and hammer down on the bottle with his free hand. The cap would pop off, sometimes silently, sometimes with a grunt. No one seemed to notice.

Next to the man chopping the onions was a young fellow who had introduced himself as Jean. He was making a white bean salad and was putting on the finishing touches with what looked like garlic. I couldn't imagine that with all the garlic he was using he could come up with something edible. But he did.

Mattare called supper and Fleury and the others carefully folded the maps and cleared the table. Mattare brought me a large tin of soup and a hunk of brown bread. Then he rejoined the others and the bread was blessed before being passed around.

It was the best bread and soup I had ever tasted.

I decided to wait until the meal was finished and then talk with Fleury. The tea and the soup had given me some strength and it felt like the right time.

One by one, they rose from the table, thanking Mattare for the meal. Most of them patted their bellies, some in jest, some with true warmth. Mattare offered each a second helping and each declined. Jean came over to me and offered more soup and bread.

"It was delicious," I said. "But I can eat no more, thank you."

He nodded and took away my soup tin.

Before I had a chance to beckon Fleury, he had washed his soup bowl in the two buckets they all used and came to my bed. This time he took my teacup in his hands and sat down.

"Are you certain you would not like some more soup?" he asked.

"Thank you, no. My stomach is full. I'm very grateful."

"It is our pleasure, believe me."

I thought he was getting up to go.

"Mr. Fleury," I said, "I suppose I should have a word with you."

"If you wish," he said, folding his hands in his lap.

"Don't you want to know my name, where I came from, where I'm going"

His eyes, at other times distant, were fixed squarely on mine.

"What you want to tell me, if anything, is entirely up to you," he said. "You need tell me only what you want me to know."

He rolled down the sleeves of his woolen shirt and buttoned them. Then he took out a cigarette, lighted it, and inhaled deeply. As he blew out a plume of smoke, he offered me one. I waved it away and smiled.

"No, thank you. I appreciate your discretion. I'd like you to know."

"Very well," he said, and I thought he tried to smile.

"My name is Alice Dunn. I was born in Budapest, Hungary and I would like to tell you a little bit about the city. Fast-paced, she competed with many of the capitals of Europe in elegance, vigor and culture.

"In spite of becoming one of the Axis countries, she was still overrun by the Nazis. I was living there when they imprisoned me for being a Jew. I was sent first to Auschwitz and then to Tchopau, where we met. I must apologize for treating you the way I did there . . ."

He shook his head and held up a hand.

"I would have reacted the same way," he said.

"Thank you. To continue, my family lives in America. I want to join them. You have already helped me a great deal and I am forever grateful. Please know that. If I can help you in any way please tell me."

"Of course," he said. "I am sure there are some things you want to know about us. Let me start by telling you that our purpose here is to help you get back your strength and to keep you out of danger. The war is not yet over. When it is," he nodded to the radioman, "we will know it."

"I look forward to that day, as I know you do," I said.

"Indeed."

Suddenly a question crossed my mind. "Where are we?"

He never hesitated. "We are in Tchopau. Not far from the factory, really. Does that surprise you?"

"In a way it does," I said, trying to mask my fear. "In another I suppose it does not. Does the war seem to be near an end?"

"Perhaps it is a matter of days, perhaps weeks. We are not

sure. The Russians are very close to us in the east. The Americans are coming from the west. We would rather not meet with the Red Army. But it must be safe before we move."

I shuddered at the thought of being left to the Russians.

"Don't worry," he said, seeming to read my mind. "We will not leave you behind. You are with us now."

"How long have you been prisoners?"

"Almost six years now," he said, and his eyes drifted back. "We were taken, all of us, in the Somme in the fall of thirty-nine."

"Six years," I echoed. "Six years? Mr. Fleury, what is the date today?"

"Today is April 16th, 1945."

"April 16th," I whispered, "1945."

"We are hoping that the second half of April is calm and dry," he said. "Enough talk now. We will talk more in the morning, if you wish."

I smiled at him as he reached over and pulled the blankets up around my neck, smoothing them beside me. As he rose from the stool, I closed my eyes on my first comfortable day in the last thirteen months.

In the five days I spent at their hideout, I learned much from these Frenchmen. They had hurried to build their hideout in the last few days before the German guards fled, when they were permitted away from the factory for short periods of time in small groups as discipline wavered. Fleury had found the hideout and had organized its redecorating.

There were still some elements of the German army in the area and I, most of all, was not safe. Still, they hid me, and little by little my strength began to come back.

There were three dozen of them, though never were all of them in the hideout at one time. A dozen were always outside, scouting the area and watching for a sign that would set us free. Had the Russians gotten too close, we would have had to risk a move. As it was, we were able to choose our own time. Or, more precisely, Fleury was able to calculate the lowest acceptable risk.

While we waited, the nightmares came. Lager C came back to me at night while the others slept. The chimneys and the gas chambers took over my sleep. As comfortable as the French tried to make me, they could not keep the demons at bay.

On the fifth morning I awoke with a start. Someone's hand was on my shoulder. It was Fleury. He must have seen the fear in me, for he continued to hold my shoulder firmly, yet with quiet confidence.

"Are you all right?" he asked, his voice soft. "You had a nightmare."

"Yes. I am all right. Thank you."

It was warm in the hideout that morning, and as I sat up in bed, I rolled up the sleeves of the oversized flannel shirt I had on. I had watched as they burned everything. I picked up the beret they had given me—it had fallen off on the floor during the night—and pulled it onto my head.

Louis Mattare brought me a cup of tea and withdrew as Fleury settled himself on the footstool.

"*Mademoiselle*," he said, "we made an important decision last night. We want you to think about it and be reassured that it is in your best interests."

Fleury's blue eyes looked tired, as if he had not slept. He must have seen the fear in mine.

"Don't be alarmed. We are not abandoning you. But it would be unwise for you to stay here. The Germans might still make some spot checks. Our radio information tells us they are still in the area. Please be reassured that what I am about to suggest will be safer for you than you are now."

I did not know what to say. I smiled weakly and nodded.

"Louis," Fleury called, "come over here and let us discuss our plans together."

Mattare had been busy with three other men at the map table, but he came over to join Fleury and me. As he walked over, he motioned to another man to join us.

"This is Phillipe Gerard, a good friend of ours," Mattare told me. Gerard nodded to me and I managed a weak smile.

"I hope you will like us both; we are to be your personal guardians," Mattare said. "We are going to care for you personally and watch over you until it is time for us to depart."

"Thank you, I said. "That is not such bad news after all. But I sense there is more."

Fleury held my gaze.

"We have found another hiding place for you," he said. "We have been scouting for the last five days, since you joined us. We have finally found a secure place. It is in the woods, not far from here. You will be protected and hidden completely. On that. you have my word. Do not be afraid. We will not let anything happen to you."

"My God," I thought to myself. "He tells me not to be afraid. How can I not be afraid? How can I protect myself? How can they protect me? What if the Germans find me?" All these things I asked myself. To Fleury I said nothing, not at the moment. It would have shown distrust. Yet, even though I trusted him, I was disturbed by his seemingly irrevocable decision.

"Whatever your decision, it is acceptable to me," I said, probably unconvincingly.

"It will be okay," Gerard said, a bubbly smile on his little-boy face. "We will look after you."

"Thank you," I said, and I lay back on the bed. The three of them left me to my thoughts and I fell back asleep.

When they woke me for the evening meal, Gerard brought me the soup and bread.

"Are you taking me away soon?" I asked.

He could see the fear in my face. His voice was somber.

"Fleury said it should be tonight," he replied quietly. "After dinner."

I nodded and he moved away.

They gave me a chance to clean up. Fleury and Gerard hung blankets in the corner opposite the entrance, nearest the radio closet. All the while that I washed and put on a new, enormous flannel shirt, I was tormented by thoughts that I would be left alone in the woods.

I really couldn't blame them. If they didn't want the burden of a weak prisoner, that was their business. They had already done more for me than most would have. They probably just didn't have the heart to tell me that they weren't going to come back for me, wherever it was they were going. I had been conditioned to be skeptical of anything resembling good fortune.

Coveralls, blankets, and pillows were tied together with a length of rope. Each of the men came by to bid me *au revoir*, and before we climbed the steps to the outside world. Fleury led the way with Mattare and Gerard behind me.

When we got upstairs to the remains of the building, I could see we were on the outskirts of town. Gerard moved some bricks and a canvas tarpaulin and uncovered a wheelbarrow full of bags of bread, cheese, apples, milk, and honey. Mattare also had a half-dozen canteens strapped to his body.

We kept the last light of the sun on our right as we followed a winding road into the forest. The road turned into a trail, overgrown with grass, and plunged into the densest part of the woods.

Several times Fleury, walking ahead, motioned us to stop. Each time Gerard and Mattare pulled me off the path and into the trees. When Fleury whistled we resumed our trek.

Finally, in the foreboding darkness of a moonless night, we reached our destination. Fleury was standing next to a huge tree trunk. Barely visible above it was a treehouse. I could see boards nailed to the tree leading up to the small opening in the side. This was to be my new home. It was made of timber and protected by a slanted roof. It was only about four feet square; I could stand up in this little hut, but could not walk around. Most of the time I just sat with my legs dangling out the opening.

A layer of hay and the blankets served as my bed. Though the roof was solid, the hay was damp. There was no light and Fleury had left no candles. In fact, he had warned me against using any type of fire, as if I had any matches. Caution was instinctive for him.

I slept as long and as often as I could, always tucking myself on the far side of the treehouse, away from the opening.

For the first couple of days I used the unsteady ladder to bring down soiled leaves and return with fresh ones. After a while, I ceased making the trip, more afraid of not being able to climb back up than I was fearful of falling. My solitude was broken only by the occasional sound of a bird calling its mate. Otherwise, only the whistle of the wind in the cracks of my home broke the silence of the forest. I drifted off. Memories surged forward in this hushed silence. Mirages, long-forgotten episodes, faces, all that once was dear to me, surrounded me.

I will always remember Budapest the way it used to be on early spring mornings, when the mist from the Danube held the sun at bay, the fog shadowing the bridges, and the Royal Palace looming up from the haze like a darkened lamp against the sky. The castle, once the home of the Hapsburgs, was mysterious and imposing. It rose over every point of the city, as a bittersweet reminder of the once-proud empire. It was this palace, its bronze cupolas tarnished by centuries of patina, that remained in my memory forever.

I was fortunate to have been born and to have lived in that romantic city. I was blissful that I had been afforded an education steeped in tradition. My parents had been careful to make sure that its culture was part of my heritage. They gave me everything, but they could not prepare me for disaster.

The crashing of a dried-up stump brought me back to reality. I was frightened to death. The shattering noise echoed through the forest. I didn't move.

I was told not to reveal myself unless I heard someone whistling the French national anthem. Each evening, either Mattare or Gerard would whistle the *Marseillaise* quietly, wait until I lowered a basket on a rope, and then fill it with fond and canteens.

Often, they also dropped in little notes.

"Hope it won't be much longer.

Also, "Don't give up, brave *Mademoiselle*."

And once, "Chin up!"

"Are you all right up there?" Louis once called, more loudly than I thought prudent. "Just be patient. It won't be long now."

"Patient," I thought to myself. "How could I be anything else? I can't move and I'm far above the ground."

So I was patient. I waited, counting eight sunrises.

On the ninth morning I woke to hear a sharp whistle. It was not the *Marseillaise*, nor was it near dark. I froze in fear, huddling in the corner of my refuge.

"*Mademoiselle*," Mattare called, "we have come to take you away. It is time to go."

My legs would no longer support me, so I crawled to the opening and looked down. A dozen Frenchmen were there, smiling, holding a blanket.

"The *Boche* fled town last night," Mattare said. "Isn't it fantastic? Our plans are made. As soon as we pack up, we leave."

I didn't know how to respond, except to smile. They had not

left me behind.

"Will you be traveling with us, *Mademoiselle*?" This time it was Gerard.

"It would be a pleasure," I smiled. "But I don't think I can get down."

"Ah," Mattare replied. "Fleury thought that might be a problem. That is why we have your blanket waiting. Come, my friends, move over here under the treehouse."

The men holding the blanket followed Mattare's directions, and, when they were ready, they stretched the blanket out between them. It was directly beneath the opening to the treehouse.

Mattare looked up at me. "Try to land in sitting position," was all he said.

I did as I was told, without discussion, but not without trepidation. Still, there was no damage. Mattare bent to help me out of the blanket and I threw my arms around his neck, less to help him than to thank him for the news. He carried me all the way back to the hideout.

By the time we got there, Fleury and the men had everything ready. What they were taking was packed and prepared, makeshift knapsacks waiting to be hoisted onto backs. What was not making the trip was burning in their hideout. Smoke belched from the stairway.

"The Americans are in Weimar, in Jena," Fleury told me. "We are going that way, if you would like to come along for the ride. We may need an interpreter when we get there. None of us speaks English."

"It would be my pleasure to help you, Mr. Fleury," I said. "And it certainly appears that it will be a happy trip."

It was the first time I had seen all the men together and all of them so happy. Throughout the trip, they would laugh, sing, whistle, and clap each other on the back. Even on the one day that it rained, they were as giddy as little children with new puppies. It was understandable. They had waited six long years for this moment.

Though the mood was light, it wasn't careless. Fleury dispatched two men to go in front of us, two to follow. The others took turns pushing my carriage—the wheelbarrow they had used when they escorted me to the treehouse. I would have liked to walk with them, and each day I did for a time, but my legs and feet had cramped up from disuse in the treehouse.

There had never been a question of my walking. It seemed they were prepared even for this. Mattare had asked no questions. He simply put blankets and pillows in the bottom of the wheelbarrow, and, when it was time to depart, gently sat me on top. He was the first to push me, stopping only after another insisted.

It was not long before I discovered that Fleury had planned everything, from the route to where we would camp each night, and how much food we needed. Even rest stops were scheduled. Our march was steady and without complaint.

Each man was responsible for his own food and shelter, though we all ate together. Mattare and Gerard took turns putting up a tent for me. One raised the tent, the other carried it. Only Mattare, though, prepared my food.

"Someday he may know something about good food," Mattare said of Gerard. "But I am finished trying to teach him."

Gerard gave a mock pout and joined the others.

It was also established that Mattare would be the one sleeping closest to me. I assumed that he made that rule. I know for a fact that it was not violated. Even when he was not pushing my wheelbarrow, Mattare was rarely out of whispering distance. At night I could hear him snoring. He made me feel like a pampered little sister.

Our convoy was more of a parade for three days. Then it turned into a party.

We rounded a bend and came out of the trees to find our two scouts, Henri and Jean, waiting for us. In the distance, down a road through a barren field, was a moving van—a troop carrier of sorts. We were in Weimar, in eastern Germany, near Jena, the capital of the region and headquarters of the Allied Occupation in the region.

But we were not in Jena, yet. We were barely in sight of the truck. As we got closer, though, the bright noonday sun illuminated a hand-scrawled message on the side of the vehicle.

In giant red letters it said: "No Man's Land. U.S. Army."

You might say the truck was blocking our way. To me, it was showing us the path.

"Mr. Fleury," I said, "the truck says we have reached no

man's land, occupied by the Americans."

I finally saw him smile.

"Please announce this to our friends," he said, with another dignified bow and a sweep of his hand. The men stood still for a moment.

"My dear friends," I said, "we have reached our destination. The truck in front of us belongs to the American army."

There was nothing more to say and no way to be heard. The three dozen men who had taken me in and gently brought me back to health suddenly became little boys, howling and jumping about as though their feet were on fire. Each, in turn, hugged the other and each came to embrace me. I welcomed them and stood with them to salute our freedom.

Miraculously, there was a toast to be made. A magnum of champagne materialized and each had a cup.

"To us," Fleury said solemnly, "and to our regained freedom."

I watched them all dance and realized again how much they had done for me. They had shared their bread, some of their dreams, and had taken a tremendous risk to find me and care for me. As I had become their sister, they had become my brothers. I didn't know what home I would have, or make, in the future, but I knew I would be among friends until that particular path became clear.

With the red poppies and dandelions along the roadside as my witnesses, I pushed my way into the midst of my celebrating brothers and banged a broken branch I had used as a cane against the wheelbarrow.

"*Attention!*" I cried, "*S'il vous plait*. Please listen to me."

They calmed for a moment, gathering around me quietly.

"It is hard for me to find the words," I said, looking at each of their smiles. "I have something to say to all of you and don't know what it is. I just know how it feels. You have all become brothers to me. You have stood by me and helped me back to life. You have protected me when I needed it the most and you needed it the least. Without you, I would not be here. I am in your debt forever."

"We have all faced death several times, lived in its shadow for a long time, you longer than I. To me, this day is a miracle. You are all part of that miracle, and you all made it happen. God bless you all."

"*Mademoiselle*," Mattare piped up. "I think I speak for all of your brothers when I say, truly, it has been our pleasure. We would do it again."

Fleury saw me weeping.

"Gentlemen," he said, "shall we escort our sister the rest of the way?"

Chapter XXI

THE AMERICANS

There had been soldiers, Americans, at the outpost where we first glimpsed freedom. They had been more than willing to allow my friends to pass, especially when they saw the POW cards Fleury and the others had with them. When they saw my tattoo, one of the two who had emerged from the decrepit moving van had lowered his eyes. I, too, was allowed to pass.

It occurred to me as we followed the directions of the soldiers and walked toward Jena that perhaps we had not yet encountered anyone who had the authority to prevent us from going on.

I had plenty of time to think that over in Jena, one of the important cities of southern Germany.

We had camped on the outskirts of the city on the night we reached the threshold of freedom. The next day, we completed the first leg of our journey, moving into Jena and seeking out the headquarters and commander.

We had been directed to a schoolhouse and it was outside that schoolhouse in a public square that I waited for my comrades.

The square was dominated by a large fountain, which was surrounded by a promenade of ancient brick and a few scraggly birch and maple trees planted at regular intervals around the perimeter of the common.

In the center of the fountain was a cherub, my only company

during the long wait for my friends. On one of my circuits around the fountain, I noticed the cherub was missing only a toe. He had come through the war fairly well.

There was a church opposite the school across the square. Its tower clock chimed for the second time since Fleury and his band had entered the schoolhouse to present themselves to the commander.

I wondered how much longer they would be gone, and I would be alone. There were other people in the square, and more passing on the roads surrounding it. In spite of that, I felt very much alone. More alone than I had in the treehouse.

Birds flew in and out of the trees decorating the common. They paid no attention to me, either.

I wondered if there were any Jewish agencies left in Germany that might help me.

Flower beds, long strips of dry ground filling the space between the trees, looked long neglected. What flowers there were, mostly dandelions, struggled to find life in the first peaceful spring in a long time.

I wondered if Fleury and the others would be able to convince whomever they were speaking to that I should be allowed to travel to France. Hungary was out of the question. I vowed I would not return to those who had meant to send me to my death.

And then they burst out, Mattare in the lead, streaming down the steps toward me. They half ran, half trotted to surround me.

Fleury was silent while the others told me how they had all vouched for me, and that everything would be all right. They assured me that they had told the commander, a Major Brown, that they had known me in the labor camp in Tchopau. They requested, and were granted, a hearing for me.

As for them, they were all going to be repatriated. Home was only a train ride away for them, once the war was over. Their POW cards had been enough to get them passage back to France.

Yes, they had been treated well and with respect.

Yes, they felt the Americans had compassion for them.

Yes, they thought I would receive the same careful and caring treatment.

Yes, I would be going to France.

No, I wasn't convinced.

Fleury finally stepped forward. "*Mademoiselle*," he said gently, "they are expecting you. It is time for you to go in and claim your freedom. Talk to Major Brown. He is a good and kind man and will help you. He is also a very important man. He has his own interpreter. He has the power to get you to America. Trust in him. I am certain he will help you."

I smiled and nodded and they moved back, giving me a path toward the steps of the schoolhouse. As I neared the street, I turned back to face them.

"They have given us quarters," Fleury said. "We will wait for you here."

For the first time, I noticed the building itself. It was a large brick structure, two stories high, with prominent arched windows keeping watch over the square. The entrance, up a few steps, was guarded by a pair of soldiers armed with submachine guns and a wrought iron gate. Behind the gate a set of oak double doors stood open, letting in the crisp spring breezes.

I was somehow happy that my soft-soled shoes did not echo in the long gray corridor. I heard remnants of voices behind closed doors, as I made my way down the hall. I examined every door for the right name, though none was to be found. I walked down the shadowy corridor until an armed guard pointed the way.

I wondered if the truth would be good enough.

A curt "come in" answered my timid tap on the door. I didn't know if excitement, fear, concern, or just plain anxiety showed on my face.

There was little to see on the face of Major Brown, who sat behind a huge desk adorned with little more than a nameplate and a few documents he had neatly stacked in front of him. I guessed him about forty. He sat erect in a straight-backed chair and watched me, although it did not feel as though he was staring, as I walked across the wooden floor toward him.

"Please sit down," he said, pointing the pencil he held in one hand benignly toward the only chair on my side of the desk.

As I sat, his cool, blue eyes returned briefly to the papers he again straightened on his desk. Then he adjusted his glasses carefully under his broad forehead and appraised me once more. He held the tip of the pencil in his right hand between thumb and forefinger. He did not tap it. The eraser just rested on the desk near the papers.

"What can I do for you?"

Was there a tinge of compassion in his voice? I could not tell.

It was not a voice you would associate with warmth. It was really quite without emotion of any kind. No inflection, no telltale change of tone that might indicate interest. I was facing a military man. More than that, a military man who was no stranger to making decisions, big or small.

I wondered what the military would do about my life. If the military would have any interest at all. I knew this man could, and would, make a decision about my life in this room, probably at this sitting. I had not expected him to welcome me with open arms so I could not be disappointed in his noncommittal stance.

I was having trouble breathing as I gathered my thoughts to speak. The Major leaned forward slightly, placing his elbows on the desk in front of him. His left hand was out of sight, his right still held the pencil, motionless.

"I've heard of some of your experiences from the French prisoners. You've made quite an impression on them. I'd like to hear your version, in your own words."

I took his offer as a privileged invitation and started at the beginning. I told the major about my mother and how I put her on the ship at the start of the war. I'm afraid I stammered often, searching for the right words in English.

Continuing, I told him about my arrest in Budapest and my incarceration at Auschwitz. I told him about Tchopau and finally my escape from the train to the crematorium.

"How did you know you were going to a crematorium?"

"One of the *Aufseherinnen* insinuated it and the Frenchmen warned us."

"Why would she tell you that? Why would she warn you?"

"I don't know, Major Brown. She seemed to enjoy the telling, though."

He made a notation on a pad and looked up at me. "Go on."

"The rest you have heard from the French," I said.

"I'd like to hear it from you."

I told him the rest, about the hideout in the basement and the treehouse. Even the part about my jumping into the blanket. At that I thought I saw the corners of his eyes crinkle.

"Now I am here," I said, "and I want to go to America and join my mother and brother."

At that, the major's eyebrows rose. He sat back in his chair. I stayed on the edge of mine. It was inconceivable to me that he might keep me from my destiny. If that was so, then why did I feel so cold?

"You have a problem, young lady," he said. "I believe you are who you say you are, but there is no way I can issue a pass for anybody without papers. We have to watch the frontier very carefully and have been cautioned against infiltrators. Even, I am afraid, infiltrators with tattoos."

I stared at the major and his face grew distorted through my tears. So that was it. I had no other choice but to go back to Hungary. All this freedom I had celebrated with Fleury and Mattare and the others was a dying dream.

I blinked rapidly, as though I couldn't allow this man to see me weep. As if it made a difference, especially now. I had lost one life, one world, more than a year ago. The one I had hoped to replace it with had now slipped through my fingers. The truth had not been good enough.

"Why do you want to go to America now? At any rate, you will have to wait for a year or more for a visa. Wouldn't it be better for you to wait in Budapest?"

"I will not return to Hungary" I said fiercely.

The major began tapping his pencil on the desk top.

"On the way to Jena, were you stopped by the border outpost for identification?"

"Oh, yes," I said, wondering where he was taking the conversation. "The French prisoners stood up for me and confirmed my status as a deportee. It was the French who rescued me after I escaped the train. They had been waiting a long time, much longer than I, for this moment. But none more ardently."

There was another long pause, each longer than the last. I was still on the edge of the hard chair. I folded and unfolded my damp hands and wished for something I could hold to keep them still.

The major pulled off his glasses and tossed them onto the desk. He shook his head.

"There is no way to verify your story about who you are and no one to vouch for your past," he said. "My orders are very, very plain. I'm afraid I can't make an exception in your case. I wish I could."

There was a ringing in my ears that I had never known. The major was staring at me, shaking his head slowly. He began to speak, but the ringing kept me from hearing him. I wanted to cover my ears with my hands and I wanted to cry out. I closed my eyes tightly and tried to get control. The level of the ringing eased.

"Please," I begged, not knowing if I had interrupted him or not. "There must be something!"

"I wish there was," he said. "There is nothing."

I thought hard, concentrating more than I ever had in my life. There had to be something I could do to convince this Major Brown. Something that would crack the door again on my future.

"My brother lives in New York City," I blurted. "You could contact him. He will vouch for me."

"Of course, he will, he is your brother," the major said. "That is not much help."

"Do you wish to condemn me to live in Hungary under the thumb of the Russians?" I asked defiantly. (The short-wave radio of the French had kept us informed of territorial changes, occupations and repatriations.)The major produced a pack of cigarettes. He tapped one out, lighted it, and offered them to me. I declined with a shake of my head.

I don't know what moved the major to ask his next question. In fact, I barely heard it.

"What is your brother's name?"

"Erno Dunn," I said, my eyes fixed on him as though I could will him to believe me and make the call to New York, if he had the means to do so.

"Erno Dunn. He had a wholesale fur business before the war. Now, I don't know."

The major's eyebrows, unusually heavy and dark for a man with blue eyes, nearly touched as his forehead wrinkled. He leaned forward. Again I barely heard him.

"Where is his office?"

I was startled.

"It was on West Twenty-Seventh Street," I said, trying hard to recall the exact number. The major waited. "It was two-fifty West Twenty-Seventh Street."

At that, the most amazing thing happened. The major's eyes widened slowly, then squinted into a smile that lit up his rugged face. A truly American face with a strong chin, full lips, proud nose.

And he nodded.

"I had an office at two-fifty West Twenty-Seventh Street in New York," he said. "I never had the pleasure of meeting your brother, but I remember his name from the building directory. I think he will be glad to hear from me."

The major was still smiling, looking at me.

I fell apart. There was nothing more to say. Nothing more to do. I tried to thank the major, tried to regain my composure long enough to express my gratitude. I knew at this point that I again had a chance. My life was once again in front of me. There had been no chance for me at all. Now there was one.

"Sergeant!" the major barked, snapping me back to reality. Another uniformed man came through the door.

"See that Miss Dunn has anything she needs," he said. Then he turned to me. "Is there anything in particular you want? It may take a few days for me to get through to your brother. Is there something we can do for you and your friends?"

"Yes," I said, feeling lightheaded. "There are really only three things: lipstick, orange juice, and a clean shirt. It would be wonderful if I could get these things. Is it too silly a request?"

"Not at all, Miss Dunn," he said. "Sergeant, see to Miss Dunn's needs. Is there anything else?"

"I don't wish to impose," I said, quite sincerely, as I wiped the tears from my cheeks.

"You aren't imposing, Miss Dunn. We are happy to help you."

"In that case, do you think my friends and I could collect what is left from the mess hall after meals?"

"Sergeant, see to it that Miss Dunn and the other French soldiers are granted entrance to the mess hall when everyone else is served and finished. Fetch her a fatigue shirt that she can wear and anything else she thinks of. Is that understood?"

"Absolutely, sir," the sergeant barked through a smile of his own.

"Sergeant, I leave Miss Dunn in your care. Be sure that she doesn't want for anything. It will be a few days before I get an answer on her problem. Until them, see that she has everything she may desire."

"With pleasure, sir."

I was still numb, but my voice continued to work.

"Thank you, Major, for everything," I said as I tried to rise. My legs were still stiff. The sergeant helped me, taking my arm. Before we got to the door, I turned.

"Major Brown, I know it sounds funny, but is there anything

I can do for you? Do you need a translator, by chance?"

The major looked thoughtful for a moment, then he remembered something.

"As a matter of fact, there may be," he said. "A woman was brought in by the Red Cross not too long ago. She was in Dachau. She is in the hospital and they are trying to establish her nationality and her identity. But she is delirious."

The major looked down at his desk.

"They know what happened to her, but they don't know when. And something may be wrong with the treatment. She is very sick. Nobody here can understand what she is saying. Would you be willing to help?"

"Of course," I said. "Anything you want."

"Thank you, Miss Dunn. I'll let you know."

Then he turned to the sergeant. "Escort Miss Dunn and her friends to their quarters and make sure they have whatever they want."

"Yes, sir," the sergeant said.

It was a happy reunion with my friends and even happier when the sergeant showed us to a cluster of commandeered houses close to the schoolhouse. There were serviceable beds, bathrooms, electric lights. One even had a working kitchen. The sergeant gave us directions to the mess hall and told us when we would be permitted to use it. Then he excused himself and left, telling me he would return the next day for our visit to the hospital.

The French had to divide amongst themselves the rooms they would occupy in the half-dozen houses we were allocated. But Mattare made sure I had a room of my own. The others made sure Mattare had a room in the house with the working kitchen.

My room had a bed, what I presumed to be Army issue, twin size and made of iron with thin wire springs, sheets, and a blanket. There were also towels, something I had not seen in a long time.

Not only towels, but an old-fashioned pitcher and bowl for washing sat on a table next to the bed. A way to bathe in peace and quiet and alone.

A bare bulb hung from the ceiling. I pulled the cord and the bulb sent a faint glow around the room. Enough light to see, not enough to read. I didn't complain.

Mattare came by and took the pitcher away to get water. A few minutes later, he returned. When he set the pitcher down, some water sloshed into the bowl. He also put something behind the bowl, then bowed silently and left.

I wanted more than anything to wash. I also wanted to savor the luxury of my own room. My little domain, spartan though it was, was still mine. I looked around it for a long time, seeing no one else there. No one to crowd into the bed, no one to watch me, no one for me to watch or watch out for. I had my privacy. I didn't even need anyone to hold up a blanket for me to bathe. I went to the pitcher of water and found what Mattare had left behind.

It was soap. Not the kind made from the fat of murdered prisoners—real soap—Ivory soap. I held it. There was no package to struggle with. It was just a bar of clean, white soap. I smelled it, turned it over in my hands, traced my finger along the I-V-O-R-Y carved on one side.

At first, I hesitated using it. I didn't want to ruin it. It was so pure and new and clean. I poured some water into the bowl and used the washcloth Mattare had also left to clean my face and neck. Finally, the desire for cleanliness outweighed conservation. I dropped the soap into the bowl and began washing in earnest, delighting in the little bubbles.

A little more than three weeks later, on the first of June, when I left Jena, a sliver of that soap went with me.

We went into the mess hall that afternoon as a group. If the others felt as pensive as I did, it didn't show. The soldiers coming out of the building waved and shouted greetings and the French responded in kind. I walked along silently.

What people perceive as a language barrier disappeared entirely in the mess hall. American soldiers and cooks alike welcomed us with pantomime, laughter, and sign language. I felt as though someone had asked them to treat us kindly and they had taken those orders to heart.

The cooks looked on, somewhat amused, as Mattare and a few of the others turned powdered eggs, milk, Spam, mashed potatoes, cereal—what have you—into their own creations. Eventually, some of the American soldiers tried some of Mattare's concoctions. It became a daily ritual.

There were also stories to be exchanged. At each feast, new soldiers appeared and exchanged their experiences with my friends and me. When I could, I served as an interpreter. Mostly, though, these men made do with their own forms of communication.

It became obvious that the American cooks, who had already been making more food than I could imagine, began preparing even more. There was one message I was glad to pass on, this from the very first.

"Tell the men to take everything they want," one of the cooks said. "Tomorrow there will be more to come."

The Frenchmen, being hearty eaters, needed no more encouragement. For me, it was awhile before I could stomach anything more than cereal, juice, and mashed potatoes. My body was ill-prepared for solid food. It would take time to recover from the damage done in the camps. Fleury, and especially Louis Mattare, worried over me during the long days before I could really join them in their daily feasts. They smiled, though, when they noticed me eating more.

As much a ritual as the feasts were the visits of the French to my room at night. Mattare, Gerard, or Fleury would knock quietly at my door just before lights out. Fleury began the ritual the first night we were in our temporary new homes.

"*Mademoiselle*," he said, after I had beckoned him inside. "I will get you more water for the morning." He left, then returned with another knock.

"Someone will be nearby in case you need anything."

"Thank you," I said.

"Until tomorrow, then. Sleep well."

It was much the same every night. I cherished my friends even more.

Our first full day in the hands of the Americans began early. The sergeant arrived to escort us to the mess hall and me to the quartermaster. The sergeant joined us for breakfast. I managed a few spoonfuls of cereal and some juice. The sergeant, noticing how little I was eating, seemed uncomfortable.

"Do not worry about me," I told him. "I will regain my appetite soon enough. Enjoy your breakfast. You probably have a busy day ahead."

The sergeant, a heavyset man with a crewcut, thinning eyebrows, and a huge nose that seemed to meander all over his face, simply nodded and smiled, then filled and cleaned his plate twice.

Our first stop was at the quartermaster's office in the school building headquarters. The sergeant entered the office, beckoned me in, and presented a slip of paper to another soldier behind a desk.

The man behind the desk read the note, looked at me, and smiled.

"You know where to go, Sergeant. Take the lady and get her fixed up. They'll be expecting you. I'll call them now myself."

"Thank you, sir," the sergeant said, and I rightly assumed our business there was over.

The sergeant guided me to a brick building behind the main headquarters. A sign on the outside, over the door, read *Stadthaus*. We went inside, to a small foyer and a caged office with a window in the screen. A corporal came to the window.

"Good morning, Sergeant Griffin. The lieutenant just called. We need some clothes for the lady?"

"Howdy, ma'am."

"That's right, Corporal. This is Miss Dunn. Miss Dunn, this is Corporal Jackson."

"How do you do," I said, smiling.

He nodded. When he had greeted me, he sounded like Tom Mix.

"What have you got for us?" the sergeant asked.

"Well, 'bout the only thing I can think of is a standard GI shirt. I don't have any women's clothes, I'm afraid. We ain't got much call for them."

The corporal produced a shirt from under the counter and handed it to me. I held it up. It was several sizes too big and actually hung all the way to my ankles. I nodded to the sergeant. It was perfect.

"Thanks, Corporal. It will have to do."

"It's wonderful," I said, already envisioning what I might do to it.

We turned to go and the corporal stopped us.

"Ma'am, um, we found something else that maybe you could use. Leastwise, we heard you wanted it. Here," he said, reaching out to me.

What he handed me was a small lipstick, in a plain silver tube. The color was more pink than red, but it didn't matter. The major had remembered.

"Thank you so much, Corporal Jackson," I said. "I will use this, and the new clothes, proudly."

"It's my pleasure, ma'am," he said, beaming. He couldn't have been more than eighteen.

As we left, the sergeant seemed to be preoccupied.

"Is there something else we have to do?" I asked.

"No, ma'am. Nothing I can think of."

"Has the major heard anything yet?"

The sergeant stopped and faced me.

"Not yet," he said gently. "But I know he's trying. At least, he has someone working on it. We'll let you know when we find out anything."

"Thank you, Sergeant, and forgive me for asking, please?"

"Not at all, ma'am. I understand. Would you like me to escort you back to your quarters?"

"Thank you. That would be nice."

A few of the Frenchmen were sitting outside when we returned. The sergeant bade me goodbye and said he would be back when there was news. I thanked him again and he marched away. I waved to the Frenchmen—they were clustered around the steps of the next house over—and hurried into my room.

They had given me the smallest shirt and it still brushed my ankles. But it was a treasure. I held it to my face, feeling the clean of it. There was no smell of delousing, no itch of repeated washing and fumigating. There was no reminder of the camps in it.

The fact that it was too large actually made it that much better. I cut the bottom off and made a belt, tying it around my waist. The hem now came just below my calf. Before I went back out I also used the lipstick. Though I had no mirror, I was thrilled with my first creation back in the free world.

Before I knew it, Mattare was knocking on the door.

"*Mademoiselle,*" he cried, "it is time for lunch. Will you join us?"

When I came out, they were all packed into the little house and on the steps and outside. The word had gotten out. I wore my new outfit proudly, as I said I would. They followed me out and, when everyone was under the bright, cloudless sky, I made a quick pirouette, showing off my new clothes.

"Bravo," Fleury said, and began to clap. The rest joined in and we laughed all the way to the mess hall.

"Tell me," Fleury said as we entered the mess hall, "how did you make the sash?"

"There was a knife in the kitchen."

"Again, bravo."

There were two more celebrations for us to share, the

Frenchmen and I. One was just among us; the other we shared with the entire camp and most of the world.

The first came three days after we arrived at Jena. On that morning the sergeant arrived early, as usual, at the house I was occupying with several of the others. He didn't ask if I had eaten breakfast, he didn't have to.

"Major Brown wants to see you first thing," he said. I tried to read his face. There was no sign what it all meant. I don't think he knew anything more than I—that my fate was about to be revealed.

"Sit down, Miss Dunn," the major said, after I entered. He had a look of determination behind smiling eyes. I sat.

"I have good news for you. I found your brother, Erno, who joined the U.S. army and is presently in Camp Fannen, Texas. The family name has been changed by the authorities from Dünn to Dunn legally. So from now on you are called Alice Dunn. Your brother was quite happy to hear you are with us. And he was quite persuasive. He described you very accurately."

"So you believe me and you will help me?" I was biting my lip.

"I think so."

I raised my eyebrows.

"Tell me, Miss Dunn, do you enjoy the piano?"

I was curious. I knew it was a test. What did Erno tell him?

"Very much. At least I used to. We had a piano at home in Buda. Erno and I often played together. Did he tell you that? Is this an interrogation?"

"Something like that. Miss Dunn, you understand I need to know more."

"Yes," I said, my heart beginning to pound and what appetite I had nurtured, leaving me. "I understand. Please tell me what you have to know to help me."

"Miss Dunn," he said, staring at me hard, "what kind of piano was it and where was it?"

"It was a Bosendorfer and it was in our home in the hills of Buda."

Long seconds passed as he consulted a pad of paper in front of him.

"Is it a nice instrument?" He didn't look away from the paper.

"It was a very rare piano," I said. "It is the Stradivarius of pianos. It was very hard to come by. We believed it was the only one in all of Budapest."

He turned the pad over and looked at me.

"Where did your family get the piano?"

"My mother got the piano at an estate sale. She gave it to my father as an anniversary present."

The major smiled. I breathed.

"That is what your brother told me. That your mother was the one who bought the piano. I guess you really are Alice Dunn."

I returned his smile. The major looked relieved, but probably not as relieved as I was. The truth had been enough after all. Just enough, though. And more truth than I had imagined.

"Major, you have gone through quite a lot to find out about me."

"Yes, I have. It is fortunate that your brother's office knew he was in the service. It made him easier to find. Thank goodness, he wasn't in the field somewhere. It would have taken much longer."

"Did Erno tell you we used to fight when we played together?"

"No," the major chuckled, "he didn't tell me that part. But I had to know something uncommon that only you would know, you and he."

"I understand."

We fell into silence. I didn't want to prompt him. He looked pleased, somehow. I guess the harder it is to help someone, the greater the reward.

"I think I can help you," he said, finally. "I can get you into France. After that it's up to you."

Again I breathed. It was getting easier.

"I am going to give you a pass to board the Red Cross train to Valenciennes, on the border between France and Belgium. It will be carrying ex-POWs and other refugees. All of them have identification. You do not. You will have to convince the French authorities in Valenciennes to let you into the country. I have an idea that will do so."

Once again, I was on the edge of the hard chair in his office. This time it was in anticipation rather than anxiety.

"To get into France you will have to become a French citizen. Getting into America after that will depend on your family and the governments in Washington and Paris. But you have to get into France as a citizen. Here is the plan."

The major explained that the village of St. Loo, on the coast of France, had been virtually razed in bombardments prior to and after the Normandy Invasion. All documents were lost. There simply were no records. I would have to convince the authorities in Valenciennes that I had been born in St. Loo of Hungarian parents and, despite the fact that they had taken me back to Budapest where I was raised, I was a French citizen by birth. They had no way of refuting the claim. He also admonished me to reveal the truth once I was in France.

I never doubted that I would get through the border.

"Do you think you can convince them?" the major asked.

"I'm sure of it," I said. "After all, what have I got to lose?"

"Good," he said, not mentioning what I had to lose.

"Now, before I go, is there anything I can do to repay you for this kindness and this help? You have worked very hard to help me. I can't thank you enough. Maybe there is something I can do."

"As a matter of fact, there is," he said. "You and your friends might enjoy this."

"Anything you ask."

"There are a great many German families living in the area. I don't have the manpower here to inspect every house adequately and nobody in my command speaks German. I am afraid there may still be items that have been hidden from our initial inspections — guns, ammunition, liquor, gold and silver coins that were stolen and should be confiscated. Would you and your friends be willing to conduct searches with a couple of my men and collect these things?"

"I am quite sure we would be happy to do it."

"If there are any serious problems my men will take care of them. But thank you for your help. When we have space for you on a train I will have the sergeant summon you. There may not be much notice so have your things packed and ready to leave."

I laughed a little and the major gave me a quizzical look.

"I didn't bring much," I explained, "so I shouldn't have much packing to do."

The major looked embarrassed.

"Please," I said. "You have been too kind. When would you like us to start our inspections?"

"Is tomorrow all right?"

"I shall talk to Mr. Fleury and find out. If there is a problem I will let the sergeant know."

"Good," he said. "Thank you."

He stood up and showed me to the door. "Is everything else

satisfactory?"

"It is wonderful, thank you," I said with a smile. The major nodded.

"By the way, Major: What of the girl in the hospital?"

"I've heard nothing further, but I will check again. Thank you for reminding me."

I bade him goodbye and left to join my friends.

That was the next to last thing I said that day without interruption. My last uninterrupted statement came a few minutes later. The Frenchmen were waiting for me outside headquarters near the fountain.

"I am going to France!" I shouted, and the laughter and cheering and crying and questions began.

Chapter XXII

THE PATIENT

There were many discoveries to be made while we helped the Americans at Jena. Most of them were found in the homes of the defeated Germans.

There were also discoveries we each made about ourselves and about each other. And, in one stunning case, a discovery that was no more than the planting of a seed that would not bear fruit, would not be a real discovery, until many months later.

In our inspections, we discovered the German families had been very clever in hiding their contraband. The sergeant was particularly amazed at the ability of the French to uncover these things. More amazed even than the Germans.

Our routine was simple: the sergeant would knock at the door and then stand aside when the owners of the house responded. I told them, simply, that we were there for an inspection and meant no harm. The people we encountered, mostly women and children and a few older men, seemed soothed to hear their native language. But they were no less anxious as they waited outside, and no less crestfallen as the Frenchmen trooped out with the restricted articles.

In one house alone we collected a half dozen weapons. In another a handful of silver candelabras and Persian prayer rugs. Still another yielded gold ceremonial dishes stolen from a Jewish family.

Only once did Sergeant Griffin say that he had inspected a particular house and that we would find nothing. At that house Mattare brought out three classic oil paintings, one of them by a little-known, but treasured, French artist.

Along the way, we also found Russian icons, gold jewelry, sterling silver table settings, and more guns.

The sergeant looked perplexed.

"What is it?" I asked.

"How are they able to find all these things? My men went over these places with a fine-toothed comb."

Fleury seemed to understand and asked me to translate. He whispered in my ear.

"Sergeant," I said, "Mr. Fleury asked me to tell you that the French have been hiding things from others, and themselves, for a very long time. They have had more practice at this than the Americans."

The sergeant smiled.

It was on the way back to the compound one afternoon, just a couple of days after our inspections started, that we came across what both the French and the Americans considered our greatest find. And our most timely discovery.

On the edge of town was a small building, boarded up with great locks on the doors. It looked like a beer hall. Though we had no instructions to enter, Sergeant Griffin and Mr. Fleury decided to have a look.

After forcing the doors open, we entered an empty restaurant with chairs propped on tables in one section and stools leaning against the bar in another.

Mattare found a trap door to a basement under a small rug in the kitchen. In the basement was another locked room. Fleury took care of the lock on that while Mattare held a kerosene lamp he had liberated from the kitchen.

Behind the door was a storehouse of alcohol, a veritable wine cellar that included whiskey, vodka, brandy, and assorted wines and champagne.

"Now," Mattare said triumphantly, "we have found something we can use."

Several jeeps had to be called to carry the contraband back to the compound.

By midnight the next day, most of it was gone. We found the hidden liquor cabinet on May 7, 1945. The following day, the German surrender was official. V-E Day was declared. It had been just one week since we arrived in Jena.

The more discoveries we made, the more times we went searching. The most disturbing of all came a week after the end of the war. We were asked by Major Brown—through Sergeant Griffin—to help with the processing of the prisoners a few miles away. There we discovered that Auschwitz was not the only death camp the Nazis had operated.

The revelation was made three weeks after our arrival in Jena, and just three days before my departure. It was all quite innocent. In fact it was a time for celebration, a double celebration.

Major Brown started it all. I discovered he was true to his word. Sergeant Griffin brought me to him on another bright, warm morning when only a few clouds could join in my happiness.

He was brief.

"Miss Dunn, I have good news," he said as I sat down. "You are going to France this weekend."

I was stunned. I had waited for a long time, longer, it seemed, than three weeks. Now my next step toward rejoining my family could be made.

"Thank you, God," I whispered.

"There will be a Red Cross train leaving on Saturday morning. It is going to Valenciennes with refugees and former French soldiers. There is space for you."

My joy could not have been more obvious than my tears showed. Major Brown smiled. Perhaps, it seemed to me, more than he might have in a while.

"Major Brown," I said, trying to keep my voice steady. "I owe you a great debt of gratitude. Is there anything I can do to repay you?"

The major's smile faded into thought.

"There might be," he said. "I'm not sure. The reason I say that is because I don't know if you can help."

"I'd be more than willing to try—anything."

"Thank you. Do you remember that girl I told you about at the hospital? The one we couldn't identify? The doctors tell me she has fallen back into delirium. We know only that she is Hungarian. We have no one who can communicate adequately with her. She was responding to treatment for awhile and then had a relapse, I guess. I don't know. I'm not a doctor."

"I will try to help," I said.

"As you wish. It is not an order of any kind."

"Of course not. You do me a service by letting me help. Thank you."

"Perhaps this afternoon?"

"As soon as necessary."

"I'll send the sergeant."

We parted on that note. I never saw the major again.

At lunch we celebrated, the French prisoners and I. I had mashed potatoes, as usual, with a little bread and some Spam. My stomach was getting better.

We brought our little party back to our quarters. Empty crates from the mess hall served as tables and chairs outside my house. I would have liked to join the feast more voraciously, but I enjoyed the festiveness just the same. Each of the men, who had not yet received their travel instructions, came to me and congratulated me. They knew how much this meant.

Not long after lunch that Wednesday, the sergeant came by and escorted me to the hospital.

Inside the double door entrance to the brick building, identified by two large Red Cross emblems, Sergeant Griffin asked at the desk for Doctor Schmidt. The nurse picked up a phone, consulted briefly, thanked the person on the other end, and rang off.

"Down at the end of the corridor, then up the stairs," she said crisply, not looking at me. The sergeant nodded at me to go ahead. He followed a couple of steps behind.

It was a typical hospital corridor, snow-white walls and the smell of disinfectant. Everywhere, people were in a hurry. In one corner, a stretcher crew raced into the hall on their way to the entrance. I had not heard the siren, but knew there had been one.

At the top of a flight of stairs, there was less commotion. Doctor Schmidt, a young man with a short blond beard to match his thinning hair and mustache, waited there for us. He nodded to the sergeant. I noticed a little disdain.

"You must be Miss Dunn," he said, extending his hand. He had a gentle grip.

"Yes, I am Alice Dunn."

"I am Doctor Schmidt. There is a young lady in my care who I must know more about."

I looked at him quizzically.

"I can tell you very little, partly because I know very little," he said, turning toward a door a few steps away. "We had to bring her here because she was delirious. She has been hurt very badly and seems frightened. I know what the medical problem is, but that is not enough. She is not responding to our current treatment method. I'd also like to know more about what happened to her and only she can tell me that."

"What do you need from me?"

"I'll be frank, Miss Dunn," he said, stopping within reach of the door. "We have been trying a fairly new drug on this patient, trying to break her fever. However, I don't know if it is the infection, or the drug, that is pushing her away from us. If she is having an allergic reaction to penicillin—that is a very new drug we are experimenting with in our research—then we must discontinue treating her with it and try some other method. But we have to know soon. The tests don't show an allergy, but this medication is so new that we just don't know. She is slipping away, we know that, and she is using up a lot of precious strength in the bargain."

"What do you want me to do?"

"Try to find out who she is, where she's from, things like that. I'll help with the questions once we get started. We also need to know if she has ever been treated with penicillin before. We need to know what she has been treated with, if she knows, and what has worked. In short, we need to know her history. It might help us save her life."

"I will do my best," I said.

"Whatever you can," he said.

"By the way, Miss Dunn," Doctor Schmidt said as he pulled open the door, "please don't be alarmed by what is happening in here. This is a psychiatric ward. We have everyone, including the patient you are to see, heavily sedated. Most of them we can't treat, because their problems aren't physical. But all of the violent ones come here. And this one we can treat, to a certain extent. I want to be able to do my job. Then, if we find out there is something more, well, we'll have passed one hurdle."

"Of course," I said. "Will she be responsive? How do you say . . . coherent?"

"She should be. At least, she will be soon. I had the nurses weaken her sedative this morning because I was told you might come by," he said. I raised my eyebrows. "Major Brown indicated you might be willing to help."

"Is there anything else I need to know?"

"Only be prepared for what you are to see. I don't need to explain to you what went on in the camps. You will understand that part of her condition only too well." His square jaw was tight. "But, in her state of mind she has hurt herself some, and she has been hurt badly by someone else. She is restrained so she can be no harm to you. Are you willing to go through with this?"

I was afraid. I was afraid of what I would see and what it might do to me and my sleep. I pushed aside my selfishness and nodded to the doctor. He pulled the door open the rest of the way and we went in.

Here, too, everything was white—the blankets, walls, window frames, bed frames, nurses' uniforms. The intravenous bottles were clear, with blue seals. Here and there you caught a glimpse of a red cross.

There were two rows of seven beds each. The doctor moved slowly past them. On either side I could see patients sleeping but not resting. Arms pulled against leather restraints strapped to the pulled-up railings. These were not voluntary movements. They were suffering the torture of the mind. They could not escape, not even into sleep.

We moved down the row. Each was like the next. The beds were separated by snow-white partitions, the kind that opened up around the bed for more privacy. Now they stood in a single section between the patients. You could look down a row and see fourteen sets of knees and feet. The partition hid the rest until you got closer and the angle changed.

"She is evidently still sleeping," Doctor Schmidt said, as we neared the last bed on the left. "It may be a few moments before she comes out of it. And then . . ."

He left the possibilities open.

I could see the straps holding down her arms and legs. Tubes went into her nose and her left arm, which was held by an arm board and a leather strap near her shoulder. Her right arm was secured at the wrist.

Her legs were held fast at the ankles, one strapped to the left railing, the other to the right, making them spread slightly. An intravenous bottle hung from a steel support over her left arm and slowly dripped into a clear plastic tube.

"Is there a chair?" I asked, moving around to her left side between the bed and the wall.

The doctor picked up a chair from near a tray table a few steps away and brought it over. He set it down gently beside the bed, close enough to where I could touch the woman's upper arm.

As we had come down the hall, I noticed that this was the only patient concealed by the partition. It was opened so that you could see nothing until you reached the foot of the bed. Now, sitting next to her, I wondered what this woman looked like and if I would be able to help her. I wanted very much for my freedom to mean something to someone other than myself, to be useful. I stared at the back of the woman's head—she was turned away from me—and I prayed I could make her understand.

Her head had been shaved, but not recently, and a black fuzz covered her scalp. Her ears were delicate, as a child's. Her neck was terribly thin and the skin stretched across her jawbone. I wondered how she had done her hair before this nightmare had begun. Was it long and silky? Was it short and boyish? Was it curly? Flowing? What did she look like? I could not yet see.

The doctor stood silently and waited with me. Sergeant Griffin had remained at the door.

It was not long before she stirred, turning her head toward me. Her skin was the first thing I noticed—gaunt cheeks with the gray pallor of the almost dead, hollow eyes, and dark circles, her mouth, full lips pressed tight with a pain that is not only physical. Those lips had been bitten more than once.

And she looked familiar, somehow. I searched my memory,

going back through the camps. Perhaps she had been at one of them and I had seen her? No. That wasn't it.

The doctor motioned to someone I couldn't see and a nurse joined us with a clipboard, standing at the foot of the bed.

From her profile I could tell she was young, very young, barely more than a teenager. Yet her face, sallow and pained, seemed older even as it was young. She had heavy eyebrows that would have been sensuous had they not been wrinkled and twisted by her own private demons.

Her nose was straight, like an eagle's, nearly perfect.

I was certain that I knew her. At least that I had seen her before.

On one of the trains? It would have been too dark.

Tchopau? I doubted it.

Auschwitz?

Csepel? Maybe. Or maybe I just wished it. Wished I had found another survivor whom I could say I knew.

I tried to block out everything else and just think about her face. In the process I didn't see her open her eyes. Didn't see her ravaged lips curl into a tight smile. Didn't see her eyebrows relax. Didn't see the first of the tears, the dampness, begin. Didn't see the doctor's look of surprise. Didn't see her look of recognition.

But I heard her whisper.

"Alice."

My own eyes snapped back into focus and I looked at her. Into the dark eyes that once held a touch of mischief and now held only the strain of betrayal. The eyes that had been gay and bright and deep and were now clouded and vacant and distant.

With all the changes, though, there was no mistaking those eyes—the color, the dark, liquid, resonant black that reminded me of ripe olives.

I should have known from those slender hands.

"Magda."

"Alice," she whispered again, pulling at her restraints.

"Yes, my dear, it is I," I said, half laughing and half crying. I looked up at the doctor.

"Can you untie her?"

"You know her? he asked, incredulous.

"Of course I know her," I said, looking back at the girl who was no longer young and never would be again. "She is a friend of mine. Now untie her at once."

"The doctor nodded to the nurse, who hesitated a moment, then unstrapped Magda's legs. Magda snapped them together and curled her lower body. The nurse moved around to unbind Magda's right arm while I struggled with the left. The doctor finally leaned over to help me free her and to help guide her arm and the tubes as she reached out gently to return my embrace. I could feel the protruding ribs on her back. I felt the heat in her cheek on mine.

It was a short embrace. Magda slipped back and the nurse moved quickly, to support her and allow her to lean back slowly and gently. The doctor again guided her arm to the board. This time he tied it gently, without the leather straps.

I reached over and held her hand and she smiled a very tiny smile. Her eyes closed and then flickered open again.

The doctor asked the questions of me and I asked them of Magda. They came quickly but that is all I remember. As it turned out she was not allergic to the new drug. She was allergic to an old one—the sedative.

In a little while she was asleep again and the doctor tapped me on the shoulder. He said it was time to leave and that I had been of help.

"May I come to see her again?"

"Certainly," he said, smiling, but no longer as confident or presumptuous. "She will be in the regular ward tomorrow. At least I think she will be. Your presence seems to have calmed her a great deal. And taking her off that particular medication should help even more. I'm sorry about that error. Come back as often as you like."

"What happened to her?"

"I'm afraid I can't divulge that information," he said. "Let's just say that now I think she will be all right. Perhaps she will tell you herself when the time comes. But it must be up to her. I can only tell you that she has been brutalized. Probably in more ways than one."

As the doctor said that final word, his face took on a hardened look. Not at all the look of a gentle man of medicine. More the look of someone very bitter. I decided not to press the matter.

My visits to Magda were many and they were brief. The doctor and the nurses didn't need to remind me that Magda was still a very sick young lady. Magda reminded me herself, often falling asleep in mid-sentence.

Still, I felt her cheek each time I came to visit, and each time before I left her side. On Friday morning her face was cool.

She never broached the subject of her illness. We talked about little things, unimportant things. Neither our families nor our pasts were brought up. We talked a great deal about the food the Americans made.

On Friday afternoon, just before they brought Magda's supper, we talked for the first time about the future. And that I would be leaving to join my mother and brother in New York City.

Magda's eyes, brighter and clearer since they had reduced the dosage of morphine they had been giving her for pain, stayed alert while I told her of my impending trip to the French border. I told her the story Major Brown had given me to tell at Valenciennes and his implicit instructions that I tell the real story once I get inside France.

Though her eyes were bright, her face remained impassive. I wondered if I was describing to her a dream that she felt she could never share. She must have read that thought in my own expression.

"Do not worry about me, though I know you will," she said. "You will get to America and be with your mother. When they finally let me out of here perhaps I will also find my way to the United States."

Smiling, she squeezed my hand. Then they brought her dinner tray. Solid food was still a few days, or weeks, away for her.

The nurse said nothing. She just stood by.

"It is time for me to go," I said. "May God keep you safe."

Magda just nodded.

As I reached the door of the ward, much like the room upstairs but without the straps, I looked back. I realized that seeing Magda there helped me. Though I never would have thought I needed more resolve, she had given it to me. I swore to myself that I would never take her place in that bed.

The next morning dawned clear and cloudless. Summer was precisely three weeks away. Only the calendar knew that. The weatherman didn't.

Fleury rapped on the door early that morning.

"Come, *Mademoiselle*," he said through the door. "You can finish your packing after breakfast. Mattare has promised to carry your bags to the train."

"Bags!" I thought. I was still laughing when I opened the door.

We had breakfast together and then they escorted me to the station. Fleury walked on one side, Mattare on the other. The rest, all of them, followed. On the platform I kept looking up and down the tracks, waiting for the train.

"It will be along," Fleury said calmly. I did not share his confidence.

At last I heard the whistle and, for the first time, truly realized that I might be leaving my friends behind. I wanted to express my feelings for them. This time it was up to me to approach each of my comrades. I discovered quickly that I could not speak. Each, in turn, offered his hands.

With Fleury I had to find the words.

"You are the best and finest human beings I ever met," I said in a whisper, as I embraced him. "I had almost given up believing such gentlemen existed. You have helped me live again. I have no words to thank you enough. Please know that all of you will live in my heart forever. I only wish that you were going with me. God bless you!"

Fleury held me gently. Finally, Mattare spoke up.

"If we do not put her on the train," he said in mock gruffness, "ours will have to wait."

I looked at him.

"*Oui, Mademoiselle*," he said, breaking into a grin, "ours is the next train."

"Then I must go quickly," I said, laughing. I hugged Mattare again and stepped up onto the train. "Your loved ones are waiting. They are very lucky. So am I."

"*Bonne chance, Mademoiselle*," Fleury said, and they all echoed his words. I stepped into the car and out of sight.

I stood by the door, waiting. At last the whistle blew and the train lurched forward. I could see first the station, then Jena pass behind us. The wheels turned and the click-clack of the rails came faster.

Only then did I believe I was going to France.

Chapter XXIII

WELCOME TO FRANCE

It was not a pleasure trip, nor was it an unpleasant one. As tangible as my excitement was, my worry was just as evident, and, perhaps, more penetrating.

It was certainly different, although the train itself was similar to the ones I had been on the last few times. It was another dusty, dirty, damp freight car.

Unlike the others, this one had an open door. It was not nearly as crowded as the others had been. And, most of all, it was heading west—toward freedom. It was leaving the past behind. It was joyous; it was expectant. There was, at least, a foreseeable, believable future for the refugees who joined me on this train to France. There was a cause for hope, for curiosity, for anticipation.

Yet, in spite of the boisterous atmosphere, there was a thread of worry. Reality was all around us as we click-clacked across what was left of the *Reich*. We did not wonder that France was still there. We wondered who and what remained.

It was on their faces, these men in their blue overalls and the others in rags, who had spent who knows how long at forced labor for the Nazis. The sweet taste of victory was on everyone's lips, the possible cost in everyone's eyes.

It might have been easier for me. I knew from the start that

France was only a destination. There had never been a promise of a former lover, or family, or friend. I needed only cross the border and take the next step.

That is not to say that doom was not lurking, stalking my feelings of hope from the shadows of my mind. It was. I only mean to say that being denied at a border doesn't hold the shattering finality of coming home to a gravestone.

My hope was built on freedom and a good story to tell at Valenciennes. The others' was built on freedom and the thought of a reunion.

Some would see the banners and the neighbors all agog and the confetti and hear the cheering. More would see wreaths on the doors. Others would discover there was nothing left . . . nothing.

All of them knew the possibilities.

I was the only woman and the only death camp survivor in this particular car. So I was afforded special attention by these men as they celebrated their voyage home and fought heartily to hold reality at bay. As cheese, wine, and bread continued to materialize in front of me, I told my own story several times. I think many of the men simply wanted to hear a story of survival. The kind of story that they could use to compare. One that could make other survivals seem more possible.

Throughout the entire first day, food and wine were passed from mouth to mouth, from victor to victor and to me as well. We toasted each other and we toasted ourselves. Silently, privately, we toasted those behind. Quietly, almost furtively, we toasted those we looked forward to. But only when we dared.

I ate very little. Huddled in a corner near the door, I watched the others, nodded to many, answered a few and smiled carefully at their happiness. Their own grins pushed back the haggard looks and disguised the misery for a while. Their laughter, their boyish enthusiasm, their chest-inflating hoots, and the rubble of Germany as it passed by us was infectious. I remember being offered, of all things, a precious Gauloise, the strong French cigarette that was a primary medium of exchange on the black market. I tossed back my veil, accepted the smoke, inhaled deeply, and dropped like a stone.

That is not what tempered my enthusiasm, what made me a part of them and at the same time separate from them. I felt their joy, shared in it, let it envelop me.

But their laughter was too loud. Their triumph too complete. Their voices a little too high, their animation a little too consistent. It was as though they were celebrating now, a little in fear of what was to come.

So they sat and jostled each other and rejoiced and drank and shared and shouted and dreamed and prayed and hoped. Some of these things I did with them.

I huddled farther into my corner, sinking deeper into my own reservations. A man appeared before me and thrust a hunk of goat cheese and half a loaf of black bread into my arms.

"Eat this, *ma petite*. Join us for lunch. It will lift your morale," he said.

He was a large man, like Louis Mattare, and he bent and patted my face. Then he moved back to his end of the freight car, deftly stepping over and around his exuberant compatriots.

As he left, I felt tears break through. I wondered why I was crying.

"It is good to cry," came a soft voice from nearby. "You will feel better. Don't worry, you are among friends."

Wiping my eyes, I turned to where the voice originated. The light from the open door and the vents above made the shadows even deeper. I could see the outline of a man and was able to focus on his khaki uniform, as tattered and threadbare as the work clothes of the others. Even though he was sitting, I could see the clothes were only hanging on his gaunt frame.

His head was bandaged, but I noticed no telltale stain. The wound must be healing, I thought, and was strangely thankful. A small bundle supported him against the wall of the train.

"It is already a long trip and will be longer," he said. "I wonder when we will reach the Dutch border."

He was staring out through the sliver of doorway visible from where he sat. Had I not said anything, the conversation would have simply ended, no harm done. He allowed me to join it graciously, or decline gracefully.

"I can hardly wait," I said, surprised that I responded at all. "And yet, it scares me. I don't know what scares me and I don't know why."

"We are all frightened a little, *Mademoiselle*. It is better sometimes to talk about it. We are not afraid of the dark until nightfall. And never after sunrise."

I smiled at his analogy and slid a little closer. He sat, his hands folded in his lap, his legs straight out in front of him. The freight car was crowded but not confining.

"Yes." I said, getting settled again. "You are right, of course. Thank you."

The man smiled a greeting.

"My name is Alice Dunn, and I am pleased to meet you."

"I am Jean-Jacques, and the pleasure is mine." He gave me a little nod. "Please do not be afraid to voice what is troubling you. I listen with an open heart. We are all the same, really. We have all been tested. We all have more tests to come."

He looked past me again, somewhere in the middle distance, for his own answers to his own questions. I made no conscious decision to trust him; I just did.

"I am afraid of the border," I said. "I am afraid of what I will find there, or not find. Some French prisoners helped me get to Jena and the military commander there gave me a story that will get me through the border into France. But I am deathly afraid that I won't make it."

Jean-Jacques was thoughtful for a moment.

"You have come a long way to be stopped at the French border," he said. "You do not sound French, at least, your accent is not French. Are you not French?"

"No. I am Hungarian. But I do not want to go back to Budapest. The occupying Russian forces are going to stay in Hungary an undetermined time. I want to join my family in America. You are right; I have come too far to be stopped. I sometimes think that a higher force has brought me to this point. Do you believe, as I do, that our destiny is predetermined?"

"I do," he said firmly. "Ever since a stray bullet nearly killed me on the day our labor camp was liberated. Yes, I believe."

"Is that how you came to be on this train?"

"Yes. A group of prisoners, those of whom were wounded and worked in the mines in Silesia, were picked up by the Red Cross and transported to Jena. That is how I am here with you now."

"And where are you going?"

"That is where my fear lies," he said, smiling wryly. "I am going home. At least, I am going to where my home used to be. I don't know if it is still there. I don't even know if anyone is left. My whole family was with the Resistance . . ." His thoughts trailed off with his voice.

We sat there quietly for some time. More of the *Reich* passed, the rubble drawing cheers from those who sat with their legs dangling out the door of the car.

"Look!" one would cry. "Look how we took care of that town." Others would crane their necks, look out into the waning daylight, and join the cheering and clapping.

"You are right not to go back to Hungary," he said finally. "You will never get out. At best, it would take years before they allowed you to leave and join your family. Once you are through the border, try to contact the Croix Rouge (Red Cross) International in Paris. This organization is assisting war victims from all over Europe in contacting their families and bringing them back together. They are also providing food, shelter, and clothing. Some of these men will end up there, although they don't know it yet."

I nodded.

"Don't give up hope," he continued. "That is all we have left."

"Yes," I agreed absently, "that is all we have. Though I hope it turns out, for all of us, that we have more."

The other men dozed off as we talked. With the last of the wine came night and, for a while, we were alone with the sway of the freight car. I left Jean-Jacques to his private thoughts and he left me with mine.

Abruptly, Jean-Jacques pulled his feet under him and pushed himself up. I looked up at him. I guessed him to be at least six feet tall. I decided to stretch as well and he helped me to my feet. Leaning over, I could see through the open door. The darkness was broken by the glow of nearby fires and distant villages.

"Alice," he said quietly. I turned and saw him pull a necklace and medallion over his head and hold it in his hands in front of me. "I want you to wear this. It will protect you as it did me. I have nothing else I can give you, only this. Please accept it."

He held it out for me. I looked at the silver chain and ornate medallion. I looked into his eyes.

"Jean-Jacques, I cannot take this from you. I am very grateful. I am touched by your expression. But I cannot take something so precious from you. You don't even know me. I am a stranger. How can you give this to me?"

He smiled again.

"I can give this to you because it is mine, and because I want Saint Christopher to watch over you. He is tired of looking after me, and there is no longer any need for him to do so. Please accept this."

Jean-Jacques reached over and placed the chain around my neck.

"You must understand how good it makes me feel to have something left to share. Something to give to someone who might need it more than I do. You have much farther to go. It will help you."

I fingered the medallion hanging down to my chest. Though it was only about the size of a quarter, it was very smooth and felt strong.

"Thank you, Jean-Jacques," I said. "Thank you very much. I will cherish this as long as I live. And I will cherish you just as long."

We sat down again and I turned toward him.

"Jean-Jacques," I said quietly, "will you hold my hand and pray with me?"

He reached out silently.

I awoke to the beginning of a new day. I had my feet tucked under me and was leaning into the corner of the car. Jean-Jacques had placed his bundle behind my head as a pillow. He was in the same sitting position I had seen him in last. His hands were still folded in his lap.

I pulled my GI shirt closer around me against the dawn chill, but I did not shiver. The strange calm I felt was stronger than the cold.

A few of the men were awake and the others were stirring. Clearly, the jubilation was at an end, at least for the moment.

The smell of moist grass and fresh flowers from outside came through the door of the car. One of the men struggled up and pushed the door open wide. The sweet smell became stronger. I stood and looked out at the streaks of orange and purple in the sky and took a few deep breaths. In a moment, the sun peeked over the horizon and I stood and watched it climb.

The train took us north out of Saxony into west-central Germany. Along the way we stopped, picking up more ex-prisoners at more beaten cities behind more splintered signposts. Though I spent most of the trip sitting in my corner, out of sight of the countryside, each village and city was announced. The greater the destruction the greater the joy.

"Look at that!" one would shout. "That is what is left of Düsseldorf. Can you believe it?"

"That would have been Essen, if it had still been there," another laughed.

"Did anyone notice Koln as we went by? Our bombers knew where it was."

When each had settled his own personal score, the car fell silent. In time there was no longer any triumph, any crowing, in their voices. There were no voices at all. There was only awe at the magnitude of destruction.

They cheered, instead, the other survivors who boarded the cars behind us.

At the Dutch border, the train stopped again. Women and children waved happily and rushed to the doors with milk and bread. Fruit and boiled potatoes were among the most popular items that passed from the trucks and handcarts onto the train. As the train chugged through Holland, more food and drink were distributed by more people looking for a familiar face.

While the others ate, I rehearsed my story.

We reached Belgium on the third day, and the passengers with me fell even more somber. There was rubble in the Low Countries as well.

But as we neared the French border, spirits lifted again. Valenciennes was four villages away, then three, then two.

"Last stop before Valenciennes!" a soldier shouted, as another village went by. "Anyone getting off must do so immediately."

This time the laughter was not at all nervous.

In a few minutes, men were hanging out the door of the car, peering ahead expectantly.

Jean-Jacques was among them.

As I felt the train slowing down, the click-clack becoming less frequent, I repeated to myself the story I would tell the border authorities. I wanted to be sure.

The men were strangely silent. There was no cheering and waving. I was standing, but I could not see the small station and platform, nor the sign that said Valenciennes. I just knew it was there.

When the train shuddered to a halt, Jean-Jacques looked back at me, gave me a nod, and smiled. Then, he jumped off the train with the others, each carrying a small bundle. For some, those bundles contained all that was left of life before the war. They didn't know that yet.

I was helped onto the platform by a uniformed man, who was pointing the refugees toward a building at the end of the station. Everyone was headed there; I joined the exodus past the main station, down the steps, and into the building.

Inside was a large hall with several benches, a few windows facing the tracks, and a large table at the other end of the room. Doors behind the table led to separate rooms. There were no windows on the side of the building that would have faced the city.

Lamps hung from the ceiling. On the wall between two windows, a table and coffeepot were set up. There was a long line of men waiting for cups. Two cheerful Red Cross volunteers, their insignia on their sleeves, happily served every comer. I joined the line and, as I got closer, I noticed a draft. The day was almost gone and a chilling breeze made me shiver. That is when I noticed that the windows were broken. Only empty holes remained.

One by one, people were called. I waited and tried in vain to locate a clock. The light was fading out the windows beyond the walls of a building. I looked for Jean-Jacques and could not find him. I wanted to see him again before we were separated forever.

Just before night fell completely, a man in a short, white doctor's coat emerged from one of the rooms behind the large reception table. He spoke briefly to one of two people handling documents at the table, then peered around the room. His eyes fell on mine and he pointed at me. I rose and walked across the hall. I waited for him as he reached the door and saw as he waved me toward him.

I followed him into a small, windowless office. He sat on a round stool and motioned me to a chair next to an x-ray machine.

"What is your name, *Mademoiselle*?"

"Alice Dunn," I replied, watching him make a note on a pad of paper. "I am a French-born citizen who was captured by the Nazis in Budapest. I . . ."

He held up his hand.

"All I am here to do, *Mademoiselle*, is examine you and determine if you are fit and healthy enough to return to France, nothing more."

I nodded and he began a seemingly endless series of questions, prodding, poking, and more questions. Finally, he motioned to a screen.

"I will go behind there while you remove your clothes. We must take an x-ray. Please take off your clothes and stand behind this plate. When you are ready, I will take the picture. Please remain very still while the x-ray is being taken."

He went behind the screen and I removed the Army shirt that I had worn for three weeks. The plate was cold as I leaned against it and I moved back a little.

"Okay," I said, and I heard a click and a buzz.

"That is fine, *Mademoiselle*," he said. "Please put your clothes back on and wait for me here."

He waited a moment, then came and retrieved the square plate on the standing x-ray board and left the room. I wondered, remembering what I had been through, if I would pass the test.

It was an exercise in self-control as I waited for the doctor. After a time I decided to count to one hundred to take my mind off the wait.

I hadn't gotten to sixty when the man appeared in the door.

"We will have to do it again," he said quietly. "There is a shadow on your left lung. We have to make sure that it isn't tuberculosis."

He walked over and put another x-ray plate on the stand.

"Turn sideways this time, your left side toward the plate. Let me know when you are ready."

I shivered at the thought of having T.B. My heart was racing and my legs trembled. This could not be happening to me. It just could not. I had come too far. It must be a mistake. It had to be a mistake. Oh, please, God.

I was unbuttoning my shirt again when I felt the medallion on my chest.

"Look!" I cried out, "Look. It is this chain on my neck. This medal that Jean-Jacques gave me. Nobody told me to remove it and I forgot it was there. That is the shadow."

The doctor came around from behind the screen and looked at the medal. He stood looking at me for a long moment, then he smiled.

"This is unbelievable," he said. "In all my years of practice I have never forgotten to ask a patient to remove his jewelry. It is fortunate for you we realized the shadow was your medallion. That medal has brought you luck."

A Red Cross volunteer was summoned and the doctor told me to follow her into another hall.

Only then could I breathe well again.

The new hall was set up with another large table and more benches, much like the previous one. But in this one, several volunteers busied themselves at the main table, processing others like me who were applying for repatriation. There were a half-dozen volunteers at the table, each of them speaking to a former soldier or prisoner across the table from them. A man standing behind the volunteers was apparently overseeing the work. He motioned me toward the benches.

As more men moved to the tables, each called by name, more came through the door from the first hall and the examining rooms. The processing was taking as much time as the examining by the doctor, so there was a regular flow of people in and a slower flow of people out of the room. Still, the room was not as crowded now as the other had been and it was not very long before my name was called.

I went forward and a bespectacled man in the middle of the table waved me over and pointed to a chair across from him. He had wavy brown hair and a cleft chin. His glasses were perched on the end of his nose.

There were no arms on the chair, so I clutched the seat to

control my fears.

"You are Alice Dunn?" His voice sounded tired.

"That is correct."

"Your questionnaire says that you were in forced labor for thirteen months. Tell me more about yourself."

The man removed his glasses, leaned back in his chair and crossed his arms.

"I was born in St. Loo—la Manche to Hungarian parents on holiday there. They took me back to Hungary as a baby and I was raised there. But my love for France never waned and their guidance nurtured it. I lived in Budapest, was schooled there, and worked there until the Nazis came and imprisoned me. At this point, all I want to do is join my family, now in America, and be free. I do not want to go back to Hungary. The military governor in Jena assured me that my having been born in France would get me permission to enter the country temporarily until immigration to America could be secured. I pray that he was not mistaken."

That was it. The man made a few notes, then got up and left the room, passing through a door at the end of the building behind the table.

I wondered who was making the decision about my future.

I began to hear the pounding of my heart in my ears. I looked to my left, to the door that led from the other large hall, and saw Jean-Jacques come through. He smiled and gave me a victory sign with his fingers, then moved on behind me into the sparse crowd. I hoped that he was right in his prediction.

The man who had taken the notes during my story returned a short while later with another fellow, younger and bearded. The younger man stood across from me while the first sat down. The man who questioned me, and then the younger man, each yawned in turn as they took their places. I wondered if that was a good sign. I concentrated on the younger man, his bow tie and cuff links. He was dressed in a tailored brown suit.

"Do you know anyone in France who you can join while your passage to the United States is being arranged, *Mademoiselle*?" The younger man was obviously in charge. As he asked the questions, his eyes concentrated on a notebook he carried with him.

"Yes," I answered. "I have several cousins living in Paris. At least, they were there before the war. I am sure my mother will try to contact them, if she hasn't already. I only need to reach her in New York to begin that process."

Time stopped. I looked at him. Rather, I looked at his notebook. He had scratched only a couple of notes in it and must have read them a hundred times while I sat there sweating.

I didn't dare get impatient.

Finally, he spoke.

"Yours is a very curious situation," he said. "We have not had this problem yet, though I fear we will see it again before all this is sorted out. At any rate, that is not your problem, is it?"

I shook my head and held my breath.

"No, *Mademoiselle*, that is not your problem at all. Getting to America is your problem. Perhaps the authorities in Paris could help you if you get there. I cannot."

"Does that mean you will not grant me passage to Paris?" I asked, and I held my breath.

"I don't know," he said. "Do you know anyone in St. Loo?"

"I was a child when I left," I said. "A very small child. I know no one. But they must have records there of my birth."

"No, *Mademoiselle*, there are no records there anymore," he said.

I remained silent.

"They cannot help you in St. Loo, and only Paris can help you get to America. What I am empowered to do is clear you through the border or send you back. That is all."

He stared at me for a long time. I held his gaze. It was all I could think of to do.

Finally, he spoke.

"I will let Paris decide what to do with you. That is the best way."

The younger man walked away. The older one, sitting in front of me, smiled weakly.

"Miss Dunn," he said, "welcome to France."

Chapter XXIV

A NEW PARIS

It is true that the great cities of the world have their own special personalities. They are like living beings—some charming, some sultry, some intimidating, some comical, some chaotic, and some controlled.

Paris was certainly no different.

With personality can come moodiness. In this, Paris had become, at least for me, a prime example.

I had already seen two faces of Paris. She had been for me the Queen of the Seine, enchanting, embracing all who came to adore her majesty. As a designer I had been among those who had come to share in the spells she could cast over art, literature, music, and fashion. I had come to win a nod from the vibrant empress who, it seemed, always had a special favor to bestow on the best and the brightest.

I had made my pilgrimage at least twice a year before the war, in hopes of winning a smile from her highness, always arriving in a first-night excitement and always leaving reluctantly, but with an enriching, stimulating new sense of creativity and acceptance.

Her mood had changed quickly in the late summer of 1939. The City of Light then just flickered with a remembered glory. She had tried, at times, to conjure up some of the old potions. Mostly her arms just stayed folded across her bosom. Now an aging courtesan, she had been jilted by her lover and abandoned by those who had convinced her they had her own interests at heart.

She was still the star, still standing on the most beautiful and elaborate set on any stage. Only the story was dismal and those doing the directing had forgotten their own way.

Perhaps she was just lonely, bitterly so.

Not surprisingly, she turned inward and uncaring. Old friends simply became outsiders and were treated as such. Any loyalty left in her was rationed to those few remaining Parisians who stuck by her and with her endured the dogs of war.

Many of her people, the lesser lights and extras of the city, reflected Paris's betrayal. The baker who once had sold his bread to anyone who would enter his shop, now closed his doors to all foreigners. A room with a bed for the night cost a gold watch and a ring.

And in the air raid shelters only the French wore the masks.

Living in the city had become even more difficult than leaving had once been.

Paris had become cold and disappointed and angry.

I did not know at the time, as the train crossed the French countryside, sometimes rolling for miles before chancing on another razed vestige of the war, that neither Paris I had known was still there.

Perhaps, from that last outpouring of charm that had saved her from the fires, she had finally learned compassion.

In hindsight, the outbreak of hostilities had peeled away the facade of condescending kindness and left only the zealous chauvinism of herself and especially her minions. Now she had started to glow anew. I would find out that she had become impulsive in her caring on the most basic levels. Like everyone else she was confused. She could at once rejoice in her survival and break down and weep at not knowing which broken window to replace first. For the most part she was whole, but she had been gnawed at, blistered, rubbed raw by six years of hatred, and did not know where to start to pick up the pieces.

I would find out, in time, that you could stand naked before her, as never in the past, and she would not snicker. She welcomed without, at last, any need for homage.

The price she paid, and the price those who had admired her paid, was her loss of *joie de vivre* that had made her throw her head back and laugh out loud, even at herself. She had backed away from the sharp edge of excitement, back from the precipice of life's sudden, charming thrills. She had backed away to a mulled-over existence—an existence of dignity without drive. A somber stroll where once there had been dancing. Coffee instead of cognac. A nightshirt instead of a negligee.

Her pulse was weak, her heart not as strong as it once was. She was not as adventurous as she had been. She was not as young. Nor, it seemed, did she want to be. This time she had seen too much. It would take a while for her to forget.

This was not something you noticed immediately. It was something you came to know. Not suddenly, like waking up in the morning and knowing you are in love. Rather, it is like hearing a familiar tune and realizing you are not.

I had no idea which Paris I would find as the train crept into the Gare de l'Est. It was raining, and the outlines of the city were barely visible. More mist than shower, really, the city remained shrouded behind the gossamer veil of the early morning.

A passenger train, unlike any I had known since before the war, had carried us from Valenciennes to Paris. I sat by the window, alone, watching the countryside go by. When it came to a halt in Paris, people heaved their belongings out the windows and crowded into the aisles to leave. I looked for Jean-Jacques in the crowd, wondering if Paris had been his destination or if he had been aboard another train.

When the car was nearly empty, I got up and joined the line heading off the car. I remembered this station as one of welcome, of friends and family, of happy embraces. Today there were no cheerful reunions. There was only the exodus off the train. There was only haste to say goodbye.

No one's name was called in discovery, no one's eyes searched eagerly, no face showed recognition at finding a loved one in the crowd. These men had come to Paris just as I had—with no one waiting. Those who had made friends along the way clapped them on the back and shook hands and didn't say they hoped they would find somebody home.

I stood bewildered as the passengers shuffled around me, finding a direction. What this station had meant in the past, the anticipation, the fancy luggage, the gateway to Paris and its colorful boulevards, had been in another lifetime. It was now just a few barren planks creaking and echoing under the footsteps of its lost sons.

The crowd surged toward the main exit and I moved with it. Off the platform I caught a glimpse of the Red Cross placard. I felt strangely alone among the hundreds of people rushing toward a home only existent in their memory. At least they had that much to go on.

The placard had an arrow pointing toward a large building a few meters from the end of the station.

The Red Cross was not just one building. It was a complex of several. The first, of faded brick, with a few windows, occupied one of Paris's small city blocks. Inside, beneath unshaded hanging lamp bulbs, the huge room was separated into a maze of individual cubicles divided by bare plywood.

And the mice were loose. The only people standing still were the two stolid guards inside the door.

Each cubicle looked the same. One desk, one harried employee trying to decide whether he or she should get up and go somewhere or remain seated to continue with paperwork, one mass of paperwork, one telephone adorned with a row of buttons that ostensibly could connect the person with the answer to any question. Most conspicuous was the map of Paris tacked to the plywood wall of each miniature office—as if you could follow the directions, even with a map in hand.

I wandered over to one of the offices and confronted a youngish man who had been rubbing his eyes with one hand and holding a stack of papers by the top left corner in the other.

He looked up when I came to his desk.

"*Oui, Mademoiselle?*" His voice had a tone of impatience.

"I have just come from Valenciennes and I would like to go to join my family in America. Can you help me?"

"I'm sorry, *Mademoiselle*," he said, and abruptly rose from his desk and turned his back. I was about to speak when he pointed toward another desk down the first aisle closest to the wall.

"Do you see the woman with the dark hair and the blue blouse? She may be able to serve you." He turned back to me.

"Thank you," I said, and he nodded.

I kept my eyes on the woman as I walked past four of the small offices.

"Excuse me," I said. The woman made a mark on the document she was reading and replaced it in a folder. She looked up at me, her mouth smiling but her eyes blank.

"How may I help you?"

"I have just entered France after being a prisoner of the Nazis and I would like to join my mother and brother in America."

"I'm sorry, *Mademoiselle*. I cannot help you. But I think I know who can." She stood, just as the first worker had, and searched the room. She walked out from behind her desk and stood beside me. She was a full head taller that I was and stood on tiptoes as she looked around the room.

"There," she said, almost a shout. She took my arm and pulled me closer to her. It surprised me a little that she touched me at all. She bent over a little to point out what she had found.

"There, three rows over. Do you see?" she said, turning toward me. I stretched myself as tall as I could get.

"Where?"

"Number seven. Do you see? The lady with the short blond hair? The curly-haired one there?"

"Yes. I see her," I said, echoing the girl's excitement.

"I think she can help you. I hope so."

She looked at me, closely, for the first time. This time her eyes smiled as well.

"Thank you," I said.

"*Bonne chance.*"

I went three rows over and two desks left and came to number seven. The girl, a Kewpie doll of a young woman with flashing eyes, stood up as I entered her cubicle.

"May I be of service to you, *Mademoiselle*?" she said, smiling.

"I hope so," I replied. "The girl over near the wall said you were the one I should see. I have just arrived in France after being a prisoner and I want to join my family in America."

The girl opened a drawer to her desk, pulled out a

questionnaire, and picked up a pencil. She settled herself in her chair and straightened her back. There was nowhere for me to sit.

"What is your name, *Mademoiselle*?"

"Alice Dunn."

"Do you have any kind of identification at all?"

I couldn't think, so I simply rolled up my left sleeve and showed her the tattoo.

She said nothing. For a long moment she just looked at my arm. A grayness came over face, a cloud that took her somewhere for a moment. Then she looked into my eyes.

"The camps," she said quietly.

I nodded.

The girl got up and went to the next cubicle, for the moment unoccupied. She got the chair from behind the desk and brought it to me. Without a word she set it down next to me. I sat down as she moved back around her desk.

"*Mademoiselle*, my name is Francoise Thomas," she told me. "I am going to help you." There was far more determination in her voice than there was sympathy.

She kept her word.

With the blessing of the Red Cross, I was assigned living quarters in a converted schoolhouse down the avenue from the agency offices. The building was on the Boulevard Raspail, and I shared it with refugees of many nationalities. My bed was near one of the many huge windows in the gymnasium which overlooked an inside courtyard. There were between sixty and eighty beds in rows with clean sheets, pillows and cases, and blankets. There was a small metal closet for every two beds.

To my surprise, Mlle. Thomas also handed me Metro tickets, ration cards to use in designated community kitchens, and a map of Paris. She added to my supplies a special telephone number that I should call in an emergency, small change for the phone box, and five one-franc notes.

Best of all, she gave me the first toothbrush I had seen since Budapest.

"I will phone ahead and tell them you are coming to the gymnasium," she said. "Is there anyone in Paris we can contact for you?"

I thought for a moment.

"I don't know. I probably have some cousins in the city somewhere, but I can't think of any names right now. It would be nice. Perhaps my mother would know of someone."

"Is it possible we could contact your mother?"

"I don't know that either. I hope so. She is in the United States, in New York. She has a place of her own. At least she did when I last heard from her. We lost contact three years ago."

"We shall contact her for you, if you can remember the address. She will be able to help you get to America. There are things she will be better able to do there than we can do here."

It was true and I knew it. I gave her my mother's address and she picked up the phone. She gave instructions to the listener to dispatch a cable to New York to inform my mother that I was safe in Paris.

I was touched by Mlle. Thomas' kindness and assistance. After being rejected by the French at the outbreak of the war, it seemed Fleury and this young woman and all the others were bending over backward in their compassion. I left Mlle. Thomas and arrived at the dormitory with a new feeling of reassurance and the belief that my dream really had gotten a step closer.

The only drawback, if it could be considered one, was that the dorm was crowded. I hoped contact with my mother would find me a relative in Paris. Staying in the dormitory brought back memories. I wanted to put as much distance between myself and those nightmares as I could.

It would be five days before I got out of the dorm.

Chapter XXV

COUSIN ERNA

It was early in the morning and I was in the office of the dormitory to get replacements for some ration tickets that I had lost. There were several desks in the office with a different volunteer at each. As I was thanking one worker for the tickets, I heard my name on the loudspeaker outside. A receptionist at the front of the office was paging me. I approached her and she handed me the telephone.

"Yes," I said, "this is Alice Dunn."

"Hello, *cherie*," came a bubbling voice. It was a cheerful, almost effusive voice and it was entirely unfamiliar.

"*Cherie*, darling, this is your cousin Erna. Erna King. Do you remember me?"

I didn't. She was married to mother's cousin.

"Of course I do. How could I forget you? Are you still as beautiful as you were before?"

"Not quite," she laughed. "But don't tell anyone. Are you all right?"

"Yes, now I am. I am overwhelmed that you called. Where are you? How did you find me?"

"Your mother phoned late last night and asked me to contact the Red Cross. Isn't it a miracle? I am so happy that you are alive. I am coming to get you now and you will stay with me."

"Why, you must be in Paris," I said, trying to suppress a shout.

"Of course I am, darling. I am alive and well and living in the City of Light. And you are going to come live with me until we can get you to America. Now let me talk to someone and iron out the formalities."

I held on to the phone for a moment, trying to let it all sink in. The woman at the desk just stared at me, her eyebrows raised. We had been speaking French, so she undoubtedly heard enough to know what was going on. Finally, she reached for the phone and I released it.

The girl nodded her head a few times, gave an address that I guessed was our location, and hung up.

"Your cousin will be here in fifteen minutes."

Stunned, I simply nodded and turned toward the door.

"*Mademoiselle* Dunn," she said after me. I stopped and turned.

"Good luck."

Since I had no belongings to pack, I waited in the office next door. I was still startled that everything was happening so fast. Yet it was in no sense a foreboding feeling. On the contrary, I remember a very strong premonition that something good was about to happen.

Erna's fifteen minutes turned into a half-hour. It was the first time in quite a while that I had actually waited for something I felt worth waiting for. Finally, I saw her through the window. She arrived in a cab, and almost ran up the steps to where the door must have been. I noticed first the beige cashmere polo coat, the huge silk scarf, and the alligator handbag. I turned and watched her enter the office. She walked past me to the first desk.

Erna exchanged a few brief words with the girl at the desk and then turned around slowly. I watched the disbelief grow on her face. Her eyes widened, then softened into compassion. She pressed her hands against her cheeks, then reached toward me. I got up and she came slowly toward me. We embraced.

She held me gently then leaned back and looked into my eyes. I saw tears in hers.

"It is all right, Erna darling. I am different. We all are. It only matters that you are here. I am just so happy to finally have someone who wants me. It is the most wondrous thing and the most beautiful feeling. Thank you."

She hugged me again, then she took my arm and led me away. I stopped at the main entrance and looked around. Nobody noticed my leaving. I thought it was just as well.

We made the trip back to her five-room apartment. It was in a baroque building in the *Rue de Fleurus*. Neither of us spoke on the trip over. I just watched as the familiar parts of Paris went by the taxi window and I remembered happier, gentler times. And some not so gentle. Erna held my hand as we rode and glanced at me occasionally, always smiling.

I saw that Paris had indeed been touched by the war. Everywhere people were repairing walls, windows, doors, and their lives—patching things up. I felt eager to join them.

Erna lived on the second floor of the building. We walked up slowly, my cousin in the lead. More slowly than I needed to go and more slowly than I thought she might normally climb the stairs. I smiled inside at her graciousness.

Inside the door she kicked off her shoes as she always did, one shoe barely leaving her foot, the other bouncing across the antechamber and coming to rest at the base of a hat rack. She showed me the living room and pointed out the bedrooms, kitchen, and bathroom.

"Make yourself at home, darling, while I make some tea."

I plopped down on the sofa, an overstuffed, enormous flowered print with plenty of loose pillows. For the first time that I could remember, I, too, kicked off my shoes.

There were Persian rugs everywhere and the rest of the furniture was all Louis XVI. The dining room table was huge, reflecting Erna's passion for food. She also had an obvious passion for Oriental lamps. An end table near the entrance to the antechamber held a tarnished Roman urn. As the tea steeped, Erna scooped her purse off the dining table, fished out her loose change, and walked over and dropped it in the urn.

"My piggy bank," she said, opening her hands and giving a shrug.

She also had walls of mirrors, too many mirrors. Mirrors I could not escape. They were everywhere I looked and I was in all of them at once.

Erna came out of the kitchen with a pot of tea and two cups dangling from a finger. She sat down on the couch next to me and placed the teapot on the marble-top coffee table in front of us. She poured the tea and handed me a cup.

We had been friends since childhood, her visiting Budapest on occasion, and me traveling with my mother to Prague and Karlsbad to visit Erna's family. We had lost touch before the war, so there was a lot of catching up to do.

The first pot of tea was spent remembering times together. Erna reminded me of the paisley shawl that I had covered the piano with in Buda and I reminded her of the beautiful pearl necklace my mother had given Erna on her sixteenth birthday and we went from there.

Candles were lighted and we finally came to the war.

I discovered that Erna had fled Hitler and the Nazis in 1939. She had found a peasant family in southern France that had taken her in. She had wanted to hide but the farmers had other plans.

"They told me to work with them," Erna remembered, almost laughing at the thought. "I was mortified! But they said if I was found, I would have more of a chance of fooling the Nazis if I had the hands of a peasant and not the hands of a stockbroker."

When I finished my story, we were silent for a long time.

Erna spoke first.

"Here it is, dark and supper time, and we didn't even have any lunch," she said, and scurried off to the kitchen. She brought back a platter of finger sandwiches.

"Here is our lunch," she giggled, and we talked into the night. When Erna looked at her watch again, she seemed a little startled.

"It is late, *cherie,*" she said, touching my hand again. "Let me show you to your room."

She rose, still holding my hand, and I stood with her. We crossed the living room and went through an open door. Erna reached to her right and switched on a lamp.

"This is your room, darling," she said. "I hope you will find peace here."

It was a small room with a double bed centered against the far wall. To my right was a large armoire. To the left, under a wide window, was the dressing table and vanity. A small table and lamp were at the head of the bed, also under the window. A rack stood next to me at the door.

"If you need anything, I will be in the next room. All you have to do is call out. I must go to work in the morning. It is a new week. There will be coffee on the stove and pastry in the refrigerator when you get up. The apartment is yours."

I did not know how to thank her, or to put into words what I was feeling. I had been in Paris less than a week and already I had been taken in, and without question. She had opened her house and her heart to me and given me a home. To me that was everything, for I had not had a home in a long time.

For several moments I just stood there and looked around the room. She squeezed my hand and I turned to her. Again we embraced.

"Sleep well, *cherie*," she said. "I hope you feel at home."

I nodded because it was the only form of communication I was capable of. Then she left me and disappeared into her own room.

I heard the sound of hangers on hooks and a drawer opening and closing. Then another. I was still standing in the middle of the room when Erna appeared again.

She handed me a flannel nightgown, pale yellow and very soft.

"Here," she said, "this should fit. I hope it is comfortable. By the way, there are fresh towels in the hall closet. Help yourself."

That night, for the first time in fifteen months, I took a real bath. By the time I donned Erna's proffered nightgown, the water in the tub was cold.

For the first few days that I was with Erna she rarely came home without a little box in her arms. Those boxes contained everything from goat cheese to toilet articles.

"More from *Grandmère*," Erna would announce gleefully, kicking off her shoes, as I would emerge from my bedroom with a skeptical look on my face. I wasn't convinced of *Grandmère*'s existence until the day I watched as Erna kicked open the door and bent to pick up a box left on the threshold. Then I met this *Grandmère*.

She was an old woman—no one knew just how old—who served as the concierge of the building. Her name was Marie, but everyone called her *Grandmère*. She seemed to like that better. Though her face was old, puffed and rumpled as that of a child who had stayed up too late, her smile made her years younger.

Grandmère had made it her vocation to call on the other families of the Rue de Fleurus and inform them that a poor deportee was among them and deserving of their kindness. And kindness they showed me, making *Grandmère* happy.

One gift contained crudely knitted khaki-colored socks, among other things. Another held lavender soap, a hair brush, and crocheted bedroom slippers. Still another brought a bright red woolen muffler. It made Erna laugh. "That will be perfect on these cold summer days," she said.

I was overwhelmed by it all. But after each gift it was Erna who had to deliver my thanks to the *Grandmère*. I stayed in the apartment, most often in bed, waiting for sleep when it would come, wondering what gifts might be next and why.

"*Grandmère* says it is just natural," Erna explained one day. "You live here. You are in need. She asks. They give. That is all."

To me it was much more. I did not try to explain it to Erna. I could not put the words together.

Nor could I explain why it was she who had to thank the *Grandmère*. I rarely ventured out from my room, much less to the door, and not out into the hall for several weeks. I only asked myself what I had done to deserve this outpouring of compassion. I had no answer.

Most of the time I was not presentable anyway. At night, when sleep came at all, it brought with it the nightmares. Peggy's eyes and the Rabbinat, Csepel, Auschwitz, the nozzles in the camp, the bodies.

And me. Running. Hiding. Always pursued by something I could not see. Didn't want to see. Running and hiding in a small room. Hearing the hissing, the gas. Smelling the smoke from the chimneys and waking up with the nightgown soaking wet and me screaming. Erna rushing into the room and holding me.

So I slept in the day when I slept at all. Sleep then was interrupted only by infrequent trips to the kitchen for a drink or to the bathroom for a cold towel to soothe my face.

Erna kept to herself, only once telling me that she would be there when I needed her. My only real evidence of her presence on some days would be a bouquet of flowers on the vanity or the first cherries of the season on a platter on the nightstand.

And the money. Erna would never offer me any money. But I had once found a few francs in a purse that the *Grandmère* had delivered and I knew that Erna was responsible. In that, and in other tiny ways, Erna prodded me back to life. Most of all she was patient. It was what I needed.

Most weekends Erna stayed out late and was careful to be quiet coming in. I usually heard her because I was awake anyway.

But one Saturday night she came home early, at least early for her. I reckoned it was about eleven o'clock.

I heard the front door open and close, and the creak of the rack as she hung up her shawl. I never heard her footsteps.

"Are you awake, *cherie*," I heard her ask softly, barely able to make out the words.

"Yes, dear. Please come in."

The door opened and Erna's head appeared.

"I saw your light on. It is late, after eleven. I thought you would be asleep."

"I slept earlier, some. Right now I am wide awake."

"Well, would you like to be alone or could you stand some tea and cookies and company?"

I smiled. "I would like all three very much. I have some things on my mind. Would it be all right if I shared them with you?"

"Certainly, darling. Let me get the tea and cookies and I will be right back."

"I don't know what to do," I said. I didn't mean to be vague. It just came out that way.

"What do you mean?"

"I mean I don't know what to do. I don't know what to do . . with my life."

Erna looked puzzled.

"For the last sixteen months, Erna, I have fought to live day by day. I have prayed that somehow an end to it would come. At one point I even tried to kill myself—so that I would be the one ending my life instead of the Nazis. I hoped against hope and I counted each day. I held my breath when I escaped and I have been holding my breath ever since. Now I have what I want, or what I thought I wanted, and I am helpless. It panics me to look ahead. It is not something we did—look ahead, I mean. I don't know what I did to deserve getting to this point, and I don't know what I am to do now that I am here. I am just afraid. Afraid of being a burden to you and afraid of being a burden to my family. I feel like I am a hundred years old and when I see myself in one of the mirrors I look a hundred years old. I don't want anything and especially don't want anyone to have to put up with me."

Erna sat quietly as I told her this. Her expression never changed. When I had finished she took a cigarette from an antique silver box, fixed it in a long holder, and lit it with a click of her Dunhill lighter.

"You know your family as well as I do. You know them better, in fact," she said, blowing out a plume of smoke. "You are not going to be a burden to anyone, not me and not them. You know in your heart that they have been praying for you all along. Their greatest thrill was hearing that you were alive and in Paris. I could tell from your mother's telegram to me. You cannot even think of being a burden anymore than you can think of them being a burden if the shoe were on the other foot. Can you think that way? Of course not. You are going to have a happy and productive life in America and be your old self."

"That is just it," I said. "I am not my old self. I have no desires. I have no drive. I tell you I appreciate your kindness, but I don't really feel it. I only feel that you would be happier without me."

"I understand that. It is simply not true. What is true is that you have had a horrifying experience. You must now give yourself time to mend. It is going to take some time. This is only the first step. It is an important one. You must let yourself become you again. It will happen."

"I hope so," I said. "I really do. But I keep thinking about the others who will not be themselves again because they are no more. I wonder why I am here."

"It doesn't matter why you are here. It only matters that you are and that you are going to get better, which will come. Now sleep," she said, and leaned over and kissed my cheek.

It was that way for a month. I knew that because Erna had mentioned, a couple of days earlier, that when I got to America I would have to remember the Fourth of July. It was their Bastille Day, their day of independence, and I would have to celebrate it when I became an American. I barely heard her.

What I did hear was the phonograph, for the first time since I had arrived in her apartment. It was playing Beethoven's *Appassionata*. I listened for a few moments as the sound wafted through my door in the late afternoon, drowning out the noises of the street below.

It reminded me of a different time. It also reminded me of the little girls with their violins at Auschwitz.

I stormed out of my room.

"Turn it off!" I shrieked. "I don't want to hear any music. I can't stand it. Turn off the phonograph this instant!"

Erna, who had been in the kitchen, bolted around the corner and into the living room. She immediately went to the phonograph and lifted the needle off the record. I retreated to my room.

I curled up in my bed and pulled the covers over me. Erna did not come in to rebuke me for my thoughtlessness, my ingratitude for her kindness. I was quite capable of doing that for myself. And seeing the effect of my outburst on Erna made it all the more easy. She had every right to withdraw from me and she did so for a time, perhaps for the rest of the evening. Seeing her the next day carry on as usual made me all the more ashamed of myself.

That weekend she bid me goodbye and said she was going away for a couple of days. She told me there was plenty of food in the apartment and that I was to help myself. She did not put it in a way that suggested I suddenly had to fend for myself or else. It was simply another act of kindness, for which I felt I had no means to repay her.

I suddenly became terrified that such a demand might be the next step. And it would have been justified, considering my disposition. I was ashamed of the way I had acted, the way I had responded to her compassion with my childishness. Moreover, I was distraught at learning that I could hurt someone so dear to me.

I finally realized that something was wrong. I spent a long night after she left lying awake and reliving the days I had spent with

her. I felt my body under the blankets. I had, in a month, become
bloated from retaining the fluids I had consumed. Now, instead of a
skinny pariah, I was a swollen one. I ran my hands through my hair.
It had grown out in patches at first, now it was fuller. Yet it was still
short and gray.

I wanted to do something, but could not decide what to do,
much less what I was capable of doing. And I had no right to do
anything. This was not my house. I fixed simple meals while Erna
was gone, always careful to take as little as possible.

On the night before Erna returned, the nightmares came back,
specifically one nightmare. It was Margit, finding me at the wire and
exacting her punishment. I awoke with my hands and the pillow over
my head and my legs kicking off the blankets.

That morning, just before Erna arrived, I had made a decision.
At the moment I was a little awed that I had made any decision at
all. But I had done so and in fact I reveled a little in it.

"When you return home from work," I said as Erna prepared
to leave again, "could you take me to the proper authorities? I have
to tell them my story."

Erna smiled. "I will be home early."

That afternoon our taxi stopped with a jolt in front of the
Prefecture of Police on the *Ile de la Cité*. This small island in the
Seine is also home to the Cathedral of Notre Dame and that day it
loomed in the afternoon light like a jewel.

We entered an austere building and took the elevator to the
first floor. Heavy, dark red carpeting muffled our steps. A
receptionist facing the elevator motioned us to approach her. Yes,
she told Erna, she had been expecting us.

The Prefect of Police met us at the door to his office. He
bowed graciously over Erna's outstretched hand.

"Thank you, *Mademoiselle*, for your thoughtful gift. What can
I do for you?"

"I would like to introduce you to my cousin, Alice Dunn,"
Erna said, and the prefect shook my hand warmly. "She has a story
to tell you."

He listened to every word, only interrupting to clarify a
particular point. I wondered as I neared the end of my tale why I
had dreaded this meeting so. I finished and the prefect crossed his

hands in front of his chin, fingertips resting just below his full lips. I noted that while he listened he had moved very little.

"*Mademoiselle*," he said, "I appreciate you coming to me with this matter. Your goodwill is manifested in wanting to clear the matter up."

He came out from behind his polished mahogany desk and walked to me, placing his hand on my shoulder.

"We will grant you an unlimited stay in Paris. That is, until you get your visa number from the United States. Then we will grant you an exit visa, immediately, of course. Since Hungary has not yet opened its consulate, the Swiss legation will furnish the necessary papers, I'm sure without problem."

"Thank you," I said, and Erna rose. I stood up as the prefect took a step back.

"Feel free to call on me should any difficulty arise," he added. "I wish you good luck."

He shook my hand again and saw us to the door.

"Thank you, *Mademoiselle*, for your help in this matter," he told Erna. "You are always welcome in this office."

"You are most kind," Erna said.

"What gift?" I asked, as we rode down the elevator.

"A case of Courvoisier," Erna said with a wry grin. "It is his favorite."

The next morning dawned rainy. After Erna left for work, I got out of bed, went to the kitchen, and made some tea. I found some pastries in the refrigerator and took a couple of them on a plate back to the living room. I opened the flowered curtains to let in the gloomy morning light and settled onto the couch, pulling the pillows around me. The apartment was calm and there was no noise from the street. It was onto that street, I thought, I would go next.

Finishing the tea and washing up the dishes I had used, I went to the closet in my room. As I went through the clothes, it occurred to me that Erna had at first put skirts and blouses in there that had been smaller. Yet these were almost large enough for my current condition. She must have changed them as time went by. I smiled.

I found a soft blue silk shirt and slacks that I could squeeze into and a darker blue long raincoat with a matching scarf. Black rubber boots completed the outfit.

On the vanity there was a purse. I checked in it for house keys and found them, as well as a couple of hundred francs. Again I smiled at Erna's thoughtfulness.

I hesitated for a moment at the door and took a deep breath. I felt for the scarf covering my head and realized no one would notice. Both the shirt and the coat had long sleeves, so my forearms would not be seen. I opened the door.

At once I knew the main entrance downstairs had been open because the fresh air came up to me. As I closed the door to the apartment, I took another deep breath, this time to take in the outside world I had denied myself for so long.

As I came down the stairs I noticed *Grandmère* at her own apartment door. She looked at me for a moment—we had met only once—and then she gave me a little wave before she disappeared into her rooms.

When I got to the street I hesitated again. Which way to go? I decided on left, down the *Rue de Fleurus* to the *Parc de Luxembourg*. There was a light rain and I felt it on my face as I strolled in delicious solitude. I felt Mother Nature was welcoming me back and I didn't mind that I would get soaked before long. I knew it had rained hard earlier because the gutters were still flowing with water rushing to the sewers at the end of the street.

Reaching the park I walked through the gate I had known since long before the war. This park had been my friend. It had been my only place of peace in 1939 when I had waited to go back to Budapest.

Here I was, waiting again, this time for a dream quite different from the one six years ago. I had been denied America then. Now I was a step nearer.

I found a bench near the center of the small park and sat down. The only other person in the park was the caretaker. I watched him make his rounds with a small pull cart, collecting leaves and dead branches and stuffing them into the square wooden box on the cart. The drizzle subsided altogether and the sun made an effort to break through the clouds.

"Not on this day," I said to the bright spot in the overcast sky. "Perhaps another."

With the rain gone the birds came out. At least their voices did. First one song, then another and another. I didn't know whether they were answering each other or just enjoying themselves. Down the sidewalk from me, one of the birds, a robin I think, found a puddle and happily hopped through it, back and forth. As the caretaker came by, the bird hopped out of his way for a few seconds and then spread its wings and flew off into one of the trees.

The caretaker nodded at me as he passed and I followed his progress to a large mesh receptacle near the pond. The pond, now brimming with rain water, rippled only slightly in the gentle breeze blowing toward me.

Though many of the leaves and branches were damp, those in the bottom of the receptacle were older and dry. I watched as the caretaker tried repeatedly to set them afire, picking matches from a box he carried in his coat. Finally a small glow began near the bottom of the receptacle. It grew upward as I watched, first drying the leaves above it and then igniting them. It was a slow process and I knew it would take a long time for all of the leaves to burn.

When the caretaker had his fire burning brightly, he pulled away with his cart.

For me the task was just beginning. But the day was tranquil and I felt my life, now begun anew, might someday flare just as brightly.

I was not watching when the leaves began burning more vigorously. I was aware of it, though. A puff of breeze came past me and with it came the smell of the smoke. The smell made my heart freeze as I remembered the chimneys and the constant odor. I leaped from the bench and ran.

Back at my cousin's building I raced up the stairs and fumbled with the keys. Finally I found the right one and unlocked the door. Erna was home and I bolted past her, sitting on the sofa. I wrenched open the door to my bedroom. My clothes smelled of smoke and I tore them off and threw them out the door. The blouse hit Erna as she came through, startling her even more. While she watched I stripped off my undergarments, jumped into bed and pulled up the blankets.

"*Cherie*," she said, "what happened? You are crying. It is all right. Tell me what has happened."

She sat down on the bed beside me and I tried to control my

sobbing.

"The smoke," I said, breathing hard, trying to find air that was clean. "The smoke from the leaves."

Erna put a hand on my shoulder.

"Everything is going to be all right," she whispered. "I understand. I will make sure those clothes are cleaned thoroughly. There is nothing wrong. You are safe now."

I tried to return her little smile, but all I could see were the chimneys. She sat there until I fell asleep, perhaps until she knew that this time the nightmares would not come back.

On the next night they did. And they continued as long as I wondered whether or not I would ever again be able to enjoy the outside world. In a way, Erna made that decision for me. At least, she led me on the path to it.

A week later, after returning from a seminar, Erna greeted me with an offer. The *Grandmère*, she told me, had arranged a street fair for Sunday. It would be from noon until four in the afternoon. The Rue de Fleurus would be closed to vehicles the entire time and all of the neighbors would participate.

When the day came I looked out the window and saw the tables and chairs arranged haphazardly up and down the street. There was no central location, no area of special importance. It was simply a gathering of neighbors and friends to enjoy the warm sun and each other.

As the preparations continued I saw baskets of fruit, clothes and books, homemade articles of clothing and household goods materialize on the tables. As noon approached I thought that there must be no one left inside their homes except Erna and me. I could see the *Grandmère* making rounds, greeting everyone on the street.

"I will wait until you are ready," Erna said, as she made a cup of tea for each of us and sat down on the couch.

As I dressed I looked out through the slit in the curtains and saw masses of people. The sheer size of the crowd gave me pause. Large groups of people still do.

I walked out into the living room.

"We don't have to go, really," Erna said when she saw the anxious look on my face.

That is why I did.

As we emerged from the apartment building, those who noticed waved and called Erna's name. They added a wave and hello in my direction. *Grandmère* spotted us quickly and came over to us. She took my arm and began making the rounds again.

"This is Alice Dunn," she would say at each table. "She is Erna King's cousin from Budapest." Then she would introduce me to the person to whom she was talking. Most of the time they would welcome me to the neighborhood. At each table they had something they insisted on giving me. Sometimes it was only an apple. At other tables a skirt or apron or another simple gift welcomed me.

I nodded a greeting and a thank you to each person before *Grandmère* led me away. Early on, in our weaving through the crowd, she had swept up a basket. By the time we were finished, it was full.

As we walked and made our way around, I thought how different these people were from the French I had encountered in this very city during the early years of the war. Had these people also been guilty of treating others the way I had been treated back then? I didn't know for I did not want to judge these people. That is what I told myself.

Though Erna and I were only there for about an hour, the giving didn't stop until late afternoon. While I wondered at being afraid of staying on the street with them any longer than I had, the people from the fair continued to parade up the stairs and leave boxes of gifts at Erna's door. She thanked each of them graciously and stacked the boxes in the antechamber until there were too many. Then she began putting them in the kitchen and in the living room.

From the middle of the apartment I thanked each person, one by one, as they came to the door. Inside, though, I felt indifferent. I was grateful for their kindness and at the same time untouched by their giving.

There were so many, I had been afraid on the street. It made me think of what else I might be afraid of.

Even as I peered out the window at those remaining at the fair, I could see *Grandmère* in her element, indeed, in her glory. She had organized the fair—this I knew—and everyone came to congratulate her.

I felt I knew *Grandmère*. So, near the end of the day, I went downstairs and onto the steps and caught her eye.

She scurried over to me.

"*Grandmère*," I said as she embraced me. "I want to thank you for all you have done for me. I am ashamed that I have been such a poor guest. But I want you to know that this day means a great deal to me. It feels as though I have now arrived in France."

"Do not worry, child, your heart will come back to you," she said. "I am glad, we are all glad, that you could join us."

"*Grandmère*," I said, remembering something I had seen in Erna's apartment. "Would you come upstairs this evening and have a glass of Cordon Rouge with us? It would mean a lot to me that I might in some small way try to return your kindness."

As she smiled another ten years left her face.

"It would be an honor," she said, hugging me again.

I nodded and retreated.

Erna had not been pushy as I attempted to find my way. Yet she was not going to let me give up the ground I had made. A couple of days later she approached me as I sipped coffee in the kitchen. She was preparing to leave for work.

"I have an appointment at Antoine's tomorrow to get my hair done," she said. "How would you like to accompany me? Perhaps if I call them they could fit you into their schedule. You know, a little pampering and maybe a change in the color might lift your spirits a little more. It certainly couldn't hurt, could it?"

I almost laughed.

"My darling," I said, "Look at me. With these few inches of hair what could they possibly do to change my looks?"

Erna shrugged. "If they could do something, what color would you like? Haven't you always looked wonderful with auburn hair, your natural color? Imagine. They could just bring that back out and be done with it."

It was my turn to shrug and Erna didn't press the issue further. I ran a hand through my hair. Erna noticed and stared at me.

"Maybe," I said.

"Why not?" she replied gaily.

"Why not," I repeated, and Erna went to the telephone.

I didn't realize at the time that she wasn't gone long enough to really persuade anyone of a second appointment. Now I wonder if she didn't simply call to confirm a previous plan. At the time I just quietly, thanked her for prodding me toward a plan I wouldn't even have thought of on my own.

The next day Erna summoned a taxi and, like Cinderella, we drove off to meet Alexander, the most famous of Parisian hairstylists in the most famous of Parisian salons. I had never been in the shop before and I marveled at the crystal chandeliers, the velvet armchairs in the waiting room, and the plush carpeting that, for a moment, made me think of the Royal Palace in Buda. A marble fountain was the centerpiece of the reception and waiting area and the basin was filled with exotically colored fish.

The hostess recognized Erna immediately and welcomed her warmly. Then she turned to me.

"You must be *Mademoiselle* Dunn," she said, smiling. "I am Greta and I am very pleased to meet you. Thank you for selecting Antoine's."

Before I could reply she led me to a booth with a pink curtain separating it from the rest of the salon. She took a pink taffeta robe off a hook and handed it to me.

"When you have changed, please take a seat here. We will be with you in a moment. What did you have in mind for color and style?"

I looked at the reclining, padded maroon chair and the washing sink.

"I used to have auburn hair, but it has changed. I would like the color back. As to the style, I will leave that up to you."

"Very good," she said, and disappeared through the curtain.

As I changed I heard Erna's voice in the next booth. I could not make out the words, but I heard her laugh often. I removed my blouse and put on the robe, buttoning it to my neck. After a moment I took off the scarf around my head. Barely more than a minute later the hairstylist appeared.

Though my body had responded outwardly to the improvement in my diet, there was still a serious protein deficiency that needed to be corrected. In an hour I found that out.

Had the hairstylist tested the treatment on a small part of my hair, the lesson would not have been so traumatic. She did not. No one took into account the fact that I had spent sixteen months in captivity with little or no protein. Hair is made up of protein.

That lack of protein manifested itself in turning auburn coloring into flaming red hair. I went from an old lady to having the head of a fire truck. Because I was facing the curtain, away from the mirror, as is often the case, I did not know it at first. I sensed something was wrong when the hairstylist stood before me, looking at my hair. Her face showed no expression. Neither did she hand me a mirror, which one might expect from someone who is proud of her work.

For the first time since she had joined me, I spoke.

"Is something wrong?"

She handed me a small mirror, crossed one arm in front of her and took her chin in her hand as though she was puzzled.

When I looked in the mirror I was stunned. I might have physically flinched, I don't know. What I do know, or did know then, was that I had gone from a sympathetic waif to the laughingstock of the neighborhood. I had the hair of a five-franc harlot from the Left Bank. I opened my mouth to say something, to ask why, to chastise the hairstylist, Erna, Alexander, and Antoine. But I could not speak.

As the hairstylist stepped back I stood up and reached for my blouse. The girl left me alone as I changed.

When I came out of the booth, Erna was paying the bill. She turned to speak to me and stopped before any words came out. She simply stood there with her mouth open. I held up a hand, joined her, and we made a dignified but quiet exit.

Dignified, that is, until we reached the street. There were no taxis nearby so we began walking slowly toward the corner. Erna had not taken her eyes off me, not even when she was receiving her change.

Now she was still watching me. I heard her make a small noise, almost like a hiccup. Than a half-sneeze, or something like it. I stopped to look at her. She had a hand across her stomach and she was half bent at the waist. Her lips were pressed tightly together and there were already tears forming in her eyes.

She finally giggled, then erupted into a long, screeching howl that got me started as well. We stood there in the street, her looking at me when she could, me looking in the mirror and occasionally patting my hair in a mock primp, trying hard to breathe and wiping away the tears. Passersby stopped for a moment and watched as the two women, one of them with the remarkable avant-garde hair color, hooted like lunatics. A distinguished-looking couple stopped and I heard through the laughter the woman ask her husband if something was amiss. Erna heard them too and nodded, pointing at my head.

We strolled on, and each new look of amazement from people on the sidewalk brought on another fit of laughter. I could not remember ever having laughed that hard before. Erna fished a handkerchief out of her bag for me and another for herself. Before we got into a cab, and before either of us said anything, I embraced my cousin.

"Thank you," I said. "This is . . . unbelievable."

As we both laughed once again she opened the door of the cab waiting at the corner.

By the time we got home I was exhausted. But it was a different kind of tired, a better kind of tired.

Erna made tea and we were both still smiling when she brought it into the living room and set it on the table.

"Alice," she said, "you have no idea how happy I am and how happy you made the *Grandmère* the other day. She knew as well as I do what an effort it was for you and that made her feel both proud and worthy."

I nodded, still unsure of my ability to speak.

"By the way, I really think the hair is very becoming. No, really. It is a new you. But then, that's what you really are. I hope you don't regret the visit."

"Oh, no," I said, a giggle bubbling in my throat. "On the contrary, it is making me forget the rest of my body. But that is not why I treasure you for helping me make the right decision. It has really helped all of me."

We sat in the living room and passed the afternoon comfortably. Erna read her mail, using the light streaming in the window. I leafed through the July edition of Paris Match. Just before supper she opened the last of her mail. I noticed her, out of the corner of my eye, drop the letter in her lap and stare at it. I could see she was concentrating on something.

"What is it?" I closed the magazine.

"This is a bulletin that might interest you," she replied, smiling brightly. "Ashkenazy is having his first appearance since the end of the war in the Palais Pleyelle next weekend. Why don't we attend?"

I looked into her eyes for a moment, appreciating how thoughtful she was. Again.

"Thank you, darling, it is a wonderful idea. But I just could not sit through a whole evening. Please go and enjoy it. You must not pass it up on account of me."

Erna knew how much music had been a part of my life. She had been disappointed at my outburst over Beethoven on the phonograph, disappointed and hurt. Now she was simply surprised. No more so than I. I was a big fan of Ashkenazy specifically, and classical music in general. Erna knew that.

She did not make me tell her that music was something I was still convinced I had lost forever and that music only represented the horrible experiences I had suffered. She did not make me tell her that I feared, more than music, the idea of being closed in a room with that many people. I didn't want to feel locked in and I didn't want to embarrass my cousin if it happened. How could I run out of the concert hall without attracting attention?

How could I face all the concert-goers in their beautiful gowns with their handsome companions and not feel inadequate and ugly?

I felt I should tell Erna these things.

"Don't worry, *cherie*," she said. "It is no matter. There is time, all the time in the world. There will be other concerts when you are ready. The music will last."

Chapter XXVI

GEORGE

Eventually the music came to me. It came in through the window of my room during the second week of September.

It must have been one of the many Catholic holidays. All over Paris church bells were ringing. People passed beneath my window in a small procession. There were about fifty of them, dressed in colorful ceremonial garb, carrying flowers and religious flags and bearing the picture of the Virgin Mary.

I had watched the procession stroll up the street and suddenly found myself behind them. We turned onto a small cobblestone road and walked another few blocks until they filed into a small church. I went in behind them and stopped just inside the wooden double doors. The only light inside came from the stained glass windows near the rafters and from the candles the acolytes were lighting on the altar.

The organ hummed to life and swept into the strains of a solemn hymn as the boys' choir took up its part. When the singing stopped the organist continued, slipping into a fugue. It was music I had not heard in —much less appreciated—in quite a while. Although I was in a Catholic church, I felt very much at home.

I replayed the music in my mind during the brief Mass. Standing away from the door, I barely noticed the pews emptying and the people leaving. I simply stood there, engrossed in the tunes that lilted through my mind. Even when I noticed I was alone, I didn't want to move. There was magic here that I had denied myself and I didn't want to break the spell. The arpeggio still echoed in my ears and it was holding me gently.

In my mind's eye it slowly became clear what I had been missing. What I had been denying myself. How guarded I had been with my feelings. In that caution I had denied myself one of the things I had considered most precious in my life. Across the alcove was a statue of the Virgin. I walked slowly to her and let my fingers touch the cool marble. She had a mysterious, knowing smile. I knew, felt, that where I touched had been touched by many other hands looking for solace and love.

I left the church and wandered aimlessly. The Left Bank has its own color and personality and I remembered the street corners with their little fountains at the crossings. I greeted them again as though they were old acquaintances that I had inexplicably neglected.

Flower carts were brimming with the blooms of the season, mums, chrysanthemums, violets from the Riviera, sweetheart roses. Long-stemmed roses were on every cart. I stopped to pick up a bouquet for Erna.

As I walked by, the workmen were eating their lunches, laughing and jostling each other on the benches along the sidewalk. Outdoor cafes also were catering to diners, people enjoying their break from work, couples holding hands, sometimes kissing. I still felt like an outsider, but I realized it was all there waiting for me.

"I have to start living again," I said aloud to myself. A couple at a table near me looked up quizzically and I smiled at them. They smiled back before returning to each other.

I looked at the street sign over my head, got my bearings, and headed for home.

"What have you been up to today?" Erna said as she watched me come through the door.

"The usual, my darling," I told her, smiling as I saw another puzzled look. "I am just trying to be positive about the day and believe that tomorrow will be a better one."

I stood there, returning Erna's look and watching her curiosity turn to encouragement.

"I went to see the lovers in the cafés and the workers on the benches and wandered around the Quartier Latin, refreshing my memory of Paris. I looked for a pastry shop I used to go to, but it must have moved. So I settled for some sweet peas for the sweetest girl I know."

Erna took the flowers from me.

"You are so thoughtful," she said, turning to take a vase from the bookshelf. After she had arranged the flowers, she went to the kitchen to put some water in the vase.

"Have you eaten?" she called from the kitchen.

"Do you think I need to?"

Erna came out of the kitchen and placed the flowers on the dining table.

"Just look at me and be truthful," I said. "Do I really need to eat? What I really need is for someone to help me lose these pounds."

Erna just smiled.

"Isn't it incredible," she said, "that not too long ago you could not have said this. No matter. Your problem can be taken care of. I was very successful with my doctor's regimen. Whenever you feel like it, we can make an appointment and he can help you."

"Do you really think I can be helped?" I asked.

"I don't know. I hope so. I really do."

That was all Erna needed. She picked up the phone. Then, after a moment, she spoke.

"This is Erna King. Could you have the doctor call me at his earliest convenience? I would like to make an appointment for Monday for my cousin to see him." She waited for a moment, then: "Yes, ten o'clock would be fine. Thank you. He has the number if there are any problems. *Merci.*"

And she hung up.

"It is all set. Unless I hear from the doctor himself, we have an appointment for the day after tomorrow at ten in the morning. I know you will like him. He is one of the few doctors in the world who still knows how to listen to his patients."

I discovered that Erna's Doctor Goulet was all that she said he was and more. An elderly, bearded gentleman who was extremely serious, but knowledgeable and scholarly as well. What I did not tell him, he asked about. I loved him and trusted him on sight. After an hour I even trusted him with my story, my fears, and my condition.

"This is not unusual," he said. "Many of you have suffered the same type of reaction."

I had almost forgotten that, in the weeks that had passed, he must have seen more refugees.

"You have a hormonal imbalance brought on by your treatment while in the camp and exacerbated by the famine you suffered while in captivity. Please be assured that it is correctable. But it will take time and will take some special medicine."

That medicine was unavailable in France. However, he told me that it was used commonly in the United States. He wrote out a prescription that I was to include in one of the letters I had begun sending my mother. She would need to have the prescription verified and filled in the states and sent to me. Because of the circumstances and the fact that only this medication would work in my case, the doctor felt there would be no problem in obtaining the drug.

And, he assured me, in time I would see improvement.

"My dear child," he said as I put on my coat to leave, "use your own tempo to come back. The day will come. You must trust me. Just be ready to embrace the world. You will know when the time is right. Just be patient."

I trusted him in this as well.

Ten days later the injections began. For the first two weeks—two shots per week—I saw no effect. Finally, I noticed that my weight had come down. Then it became clear that my mood swings were no longer so pronounced. I became less thirsty and the outbursts I had felt well up inside me, but which I had suppressed since shouting at Erna, came less frequently.

And I slept better. The nightmares ceased. The days dawned brighter.

Drop by drop I benefitted from America as she reached across the sea to make me whole again. In turn, I wanted to be ready to greet her when we finally met. And I wanted to greet her with confidence and assurance. Seeing the results from the drug, doubled my hope and helped my physical well being.

In a couple of months I was cut back to one injection per week. In early December the doctor smiled at me and told me there was no more need for treatment.

Call it a coincidence, but it was shortly after that I surprised my cousin. It was on a weekend because she was home earlier than I. She was startled when I came in the door with a letter from my mother.

"What is the matter?" she said, bounding out of her bedroom.

"I am going to America," I said breathlessly. "I am going to America. My visa has been granted. My mother says so right here." I handed her the letter and then snatched it back before she could read it.

"It says here: 'Alice, darling, I have just received word from Washington that you have been granted a visa to join your brother and me in the United States.' Oh, what a wonderful day it is."

"Oh, what a wonderful day it is indeed," Erna echoed, laughing at my joy and sharing in it.

I laughed and cried at the same time. Then I looked at her and she opened her arms, the same way she had at the Red Cross six months ago. I embraced her and began to miss her already.

"It is wonderful, darling," Erna said quietly. "It is the news you have been waiting for. Here, let me get some champagne. This is a wonderful time for you."

She brought out a bottle of *Cordon Rouge* and two glasses. We sat on the couch together the way we had so many times. She opened the bottle slowly, the way it is supposed to be done with champagne or bubbly wine, and poured us each a glass.

My friend, my sister, my mother—she had become all of these to me and more. And here she was toasting my departure.

"Erna," I said, seeing her smile. "I would like to propose a toast."

"To America," she said a little impishly.

"To you, my darling," I said. "I could not have come this far without you. No one would have put up with me the way you did, much less help me as much as you have. It is because of you that I am able to go to America altogether. I love you very much. I want you to know that."

I raised my glass and she clinked hers against mine.

"So be it," she said. "It was my pleasure. I would do it again, gladly!"

I believed her.

It wasn't long before the idea of going to America sank in. Coming with it was the idea of leaving Erna. I knew I would miss her and her sweet ways. I would miss the laughter, the almost slow giggle that I had come to know. As usual, she noticed my melancholy mood.

"What you need is to get away, go south for awhile," she said. "Change your surroundings and have some fun. Then you will really see an improvement in your health and your outlook."

"But darling," I said. "There is nothing wrong with my outlook. I am just troubled by . . ."

"I know," she said. "I am troubled by the same thing. But it is the best thing for you. It will be a while before the prefect processes your exit visa. Why not go to the south for a holiday. It can't do any harm."

It was impossible to say no, so I sat down with Erna after supper and we decided on a location. That location was St. Jean de Luz, near Biarritz, on the southwest coast of France, near the Spanish border.

"It is a beautiful town," Erna said. "Very picturesque. It is surrounded by mountains, right down to the rocky seashore jutting out into the Atlantic. It will be a perfect place for you to bide some time by yourself while you wait for the French government to grant your release."

So it was settled. And it was a splendid idea. For three days I had paced back and forth in my room, in the kitchen, in the living room, waiting for the go-ahead from the French authorities. I had been getting claustrophobic. A change would do me good. I had brought music and art back into my life, slowly, and had become the better for it. But it had made me restless trying to absorb all of it. The Louvre had brought back memories a little at a time and I had controlled them. Now, though, there was more waiting. And I hadn't yet reckoned with waiting in a small room.

It was another train ride, and, for a moment after boarding, I was anxious again. Slowly this train ride became a carefree one. I settled in, near the window, and watched the beautiful countryside pass by. I wondered if it was near here that Erna had hidden from the Nazis. I wondered if that farmhouse in the distance, brought into relief even more by the thin layer of snow covering the ground, was the one that had harbored my cousin and thus indirectly helped save me. Or was it that one on the hill?

The farther south we went, the more patches of green and light brown we saw through windows of the train.

I was far from alone on the ride. The train was filled, mostly with American soldiers headed to Biarritz. They had interrupted their education to serve in the army, and now had a chance to get back to their studies while waiting to be shipped home. The hotels of the city had been turned into colleges of physics, mathematics, history, and literature. Another became the site for a clubhouse.

My home for three weeks was a small two-story pension with Spanish-style balconies looking out over the ocean and toward Biarritz, a city snuggled into the mountains just north of St. Jean de Luz.

I lived in that pension, but I spent most of my time at the hotels in Biarritz. I took the bus daily to view those college classes and the people who attended them. Though I was not permitted in the classrooms, I was allowed to wander around the grounds. Everywhere there were people like me, waiting to go home to America. In a way I was one of them, and as we got acquainted they embraced me as such. We exchanged our own war experiences and our little dreams. Their questions were sincere and their offers of help were gracious. I had loved America before I came to Biarritz and meeting its people did not change that.

In my own way I was able to help them. Many of them had French girlfriends and communicating was often difficult. I became an interpreter and at long last knew the joy again of feeling needed. Sometimes the role of Cupid's messenger became embarrassing, often awkward, but we were all good-natured and often had a good laugh.

It was in Biarritz that the Americans gave me back something I had forgotten entirely. On New Year's Eve the clubhouse was opened to civilians for a dinner dance, and one of the GIs had come to make sure I had a ticket. That much accomplished, they all made sure I did want for dance partners. As we whirled away the old year and rang in the new I tried to remember the last time I had danced.

Everybody's favorite tune was "Sentimental Journey," and I

took one all the way back, past the pain and the nightmares, and finally remembered only the good I had left behind.

Then it was another dance that brought visions of the good I was to know.

I realized, watching them, that not all would be good for them, especially as the time for departure grew near. There would be many broken hearts in Biarritz and some on the trip home.

I must confess that when I wasn't dancing that night, I was lonely. I knew Erna would not be home alone on this night. And I knew that I wasn't, either, not really.

That last realization made me happy. The pending visa probably had a lot to do with it.

Erna kept me informed as to the French government's progress on my visa. She called three times a week and each time ended our conversation by telling me to have a good time. There was no more positive news yet.

So I sat on the rocks, high over the ocean as it pounded against the coast, and gazed across the Atlantic. At times I wished I was a bird. As the waves rolled in, thumping against the rocks and exploding into huge splotches of foam and mist, I wondered what America would really be like.

Paris beckoned before America and I took a last train ride through the French countryside. I began making daily trips to the consulate trying to expedite what had become an exasperating process. I was met with both smiles and shrugs.

January turned gloomy in the City of Light and so did my mood. A letter from Mother was reassuring and stated that a visa number would be at the consulate shortly.

"Just be patient," she wrote, as though reading my mind. "It won't be long now."

"It has already been too long a time," I replied to the walls of Erna's apartment.

There was more to Mother's letters, especially a later one.

"Someone related to a friend I work with at the Red Cross here in New York is going to call you," she wrote. "He is a young man from Hungary who fought in the French Resistance and was wounded and decorated. He is as lonely as you are. You might be able to help each other."

The thought of a man, much less romance, seemed remote. I was not the person I once was, I told Erna. Something had died in me, I insisted. In the old days, maybe. Then, life had an immediacy. The future was that day and we lived it to the fullest. But now . . .

Erna, of course, was having none of this.

"There is nothing like a beautiful love affair to restore belief in yourself," she said. Then she smiled wistfully. "You say this young man is Hungarian. I suppose he will do."

I looked at her for a long time. She just nodded her head knowingly.

I had hardly been back from Biarritz a week when Mother's help and Erna's therapy phoned.

"Hello?"

"Hello. My name is George Lindner. May I speak to Alice Dunn?"

My mother's letter came back to me.

"This is Alice Dunn."

"Hello, Miss Dunn. I have a message from your mother. I know this seems peculiar but she said I should give it to you personally. Please do not think I am being forward. But your mother insisted. So I would like to meet you and relay her message."

He had a pleasant, almost shy voice. And I knew my mother.

"Erna," I said, cupping the phone in my hand, "it is the man about whom Mother wrote."

"Talk to him," she exclaimed. "Or can you tell from his voice that he has leprosy?"

I waved a hand at her and returned to the phone.

"Yes, Mr. Lindner. My mother wrote that you might get in touch with me."

"I would like to call on you and deliver the message. If you don't mind."

"Well, I stammered, "that would be nice. Yes. That would be fine."

I thought I heard him sigh.

"Good," he said. "What day would you be free and where could we meet?"

I thought for a moment and looked over at Erna. She had a magazine open in her lap. I could tell she wasn't reading it. But she wasn't helping me, either.

"Perhaps the day after tomorrow, Friday, we could meet around five o'clock."

"Excellent," he said. "Where would you like to meet?"

"Is the tea salon on the corner of the *Rue de Fleurus* and the *Boulevard Raspail* acceptable?"

"Of course," he said, sounding a little too excited. "I will be looking for you."

"And I you," I said. "Goodbye for now."

I hung up and looked at Erna again. She was still reading the same page.

"How in the world can I make a date with a man I don't even know, have never met, and in my condition?" I asked. "And how can you just sit there and pretend to read that magazine and let me do it?"

She raised her eyebrows as she looked up at me.

"There is nothing wrong with your appearance and there is probably nothing wrong with his. Therefore there is nothing wrong with the two of you meeting and enjoying yourselves."

"Is it that simple?" I was trying to sound annoyed, but it was obvious that I was not meeting with much success.

"It is that simple," she echoed.

"I guess you are right," I said and saw her nod at the magazine. "After all, if I don't like him or he doesn't like me then we can simply spend some time together and then say *au revoir*. Right?"

"Absolutely. *Au revoir. Bientôt.*"

"You are incorrigible," I said.

She nodded again.

I dressed carefully in Erna's tan jersey shirtwaist dress and a beige coat. We had been back to Antoine's together, with more moderate auburn results, so that wasn't a problem. My doubts lingered just the same, even though I told myself repeatedly that this was another step in the right direction. I left the apartment, walked down the street, and entered the tea salon.

He was already there.

George Lindner was a tall, dark-haired man in his early thirties. He stood up to greet me as soon as I came in the door. He was alone in the salon except for one couple. I had spotted him, too, as soon as I entered. I thought only of how handsome he was and how many girlfriends he must have. I caught myself regretting he wasn't homely, so I wouldn't feel so insecure.

"Miss Dunn?" His handclasp was firm.

"How do you do, Mr. Lindner?" I concentrated on not letting my eyes drop.

He reached out and showed me to a chair and then sat down across from me. Then he motioned for the waiter.

"What would you like?" he asked as the waiter approached.

"Just some tea would be nice," I said. "Perhaps a napoleon."

George smiled.

"Napoleon and tea for both of us," he told the waiter, who turned on his heel and went to fetch the drinks.

"Miss Dunn," he said, "thank you for coming. First, I must give you your mother's message. She said that you should be patient and believe that it won't be long before you will join her. That means more to you than it does to me, I hope?"

"Yes, thank you. It does. It is so like my mother." I was still a little nervous, but his easy smile and warm voice were making me feel comfortable.

"I must confess," he said, "that I have heard quite a bit about your remarkable survival, your courage. I am truly fascinated. Would you tell me more about it?"

I hedged at first, until his dancing eyes and his smile chipped all the ice away. We sat there for hours. The waiter came by, lit lamps on all the tables, and brought more tea; asked if we would have supper; seated people near us and took their orders and bid them goodbye. We talked about the past, and we touched for a moment on Hungary itself.

"Do you think you will ever go back?" he asked.

"I left Hungary in a freight car. Left it forever. That is the way they wanted it, and now that is the way I want it to remain. I don't mean to sound severe. That is just the way I feel. I am taking a ship forward, to America."

George nodded. "I shall never return either. I understand you perfectly. It would be wrong to go back."

"You won't return, either?"

"I have lived for years in this country," he said, pausing to take a sip of tea. "I fought for freedom here and I will stay here. They owe me something. I returned after having fought in the Underground. Still, they have not seen fit to grant me citizenship. I am disenchanted by that, but I will fight for my rights."

As it turned out I was wrong about George. Not about him being handsome, but about all the girlfriends I had manufactured for him. He was as unattached as I was and as lonely. He was even more undecided, pondering what direction to take in life. He seemed to be leaning toward a career in engineering.

"Tell me," I said, "I have family waiting in America. Did you leave anyone behind in Hungary?"

"No," he said, and I smiled. "Both my parents came to France before the war and were deported while I was in the Resistance. I found out when I came back home to Paris."

He lowered his eyes for a moment and my smile disappeared.

"My parents and I were very close," he said.

The waiter came by a moment later and broke the silence.

"*Monsieur, Mademoiselle*, I am afraid we are closing. Would you like your bill?"

After that George and I saw each other almost daily. We nurtured our trust in one another. I was comfortable with him and we spoke Hungarian often, went on long walks, and recited poetry. Many of the things I had forgotten, George would pick up in mid-stanza and we would both laugh.

We climbed the Sacre Coeur Basilica and watched the rising sun and picnicked in the Bois de Boulogne. And we laughed. The little girl inside me came back with George and I like to think that the little boy in him, the one not scarred by the war and the loss of his loved ones, emerged.

We became affectionate, but I shied away from any feelings of real love. That commitment would have to wait a little longer, probably longer than I desired and certainly longer than I had realized. At times I thought again of Silbiger Boriska and the man she had predicted for me. Had it been Fleury? Was it George? I think not.

Instead of becoming lovers we became great and dear friends. That suited us better. We talked openly about everything, except of

lovers. Neither of us had one. Everything else pointed to a first
romance and it would have been appropriate. After all, with George
I really did feel reborn. But he did not press the issue and I did
nothing to invite it. I simply looked forward to being with him and
he seemed to accept that restriction, although it was never a real
restriction because the subject was never broached.

And there were times when it might have been. When we fell
asleep in each other's arms on Erna's couch. Even then it didn't
happen and somehow that made our relationship that much stronger
and sweeter.

Had it come down to a confrontation, I would have had to tell
George that I still waited for the day when the mail would bring my
visa and my date of departure. I think he knew all along that the day
would come. It was the only other subject that we never discussed
after the first meeting at the tea salon.

Not until just before the day it came.

"Alice," he said softly to me one evening as we approached
Erna's building. "I don't want you to go to America. I won't let you
go to America. We have found each other, and that happens only
once in a lifetime." I looked up at him and saw the
determination—and hope—in his eyes.

"Dearest George, my darling," I said, looking down at my
shoes. "You know how I feel about you and that what you ask is
unfair. You know this is the greatest dream of my life. My mother,
my family, my whole future is in America. Must you ask me to give
that up?"

He was thoughtful for a moment.

"Maybe you could give yourself some time and if you must go,
visit them and then come back. I want to marry you. I love you. I
want to spend the rest of my life helping to erase all the suffering
you have known"

I smiled, squeezed his hand, and kissed him.

"Don't answer me now," he said, seeing the resolve in my
face. "Sleep on it. Think about it. Please."

I nodded and blew him a kiss as I went up the steps into the
building.

That night Erna and I talked for hours. She questioned me but
gave no advice. She knew that this time she could not help me. It

wasn't that she didn't have an opinion. It was that she knew this decision had to be mine alone.

Finally, my obsession with America and my love for my family came to outweigh the beauty and harmony I had found with George. I could neither tell him I was not going nor tell him I would be back. My only answer was that I was going to America.

I wish I could have given him more because he gave me so much. In retrospect it is obvious that my love for him, and it was quite substantial, was not as great as his love for me. But I still love him today—for his help in making me function as a woman again, in helping me regain my self-confidence, to reach out and enjoy the things around me, in having a plan, a goal, and trying to achieve it. In a way, it was George who helped me get to America. He had made me become whole again.

"Do something," he would say. "Read. Play the piano. Anything. Just don't dwell on the past. You have a beautiful, splendid future."

I will always be grateful to him for giving me that outlook.

He professed that outlook even on the day my visa arrived. It was the last day of February 1946, and I didn't know whether to feel happy or sad. All I could think of was that I didn't want to hurt George. And I was about to.

I have never liked goodbyes. I had to think of the days when Erna and George would no longer be a regular part of my life. I did not want to think of that, but I could not escape.

"Erna," I whispered on the night of March third, when we finally learned that there was space available on a flight out the next day. She called for me to come into her room.

"Erna, before I leave I want to tell you something." Although she smiled, her eyes were somber. "I want you to know that it is because of you I can face my new life. You have given me the foundation to go on. I was lucky not only to have escaped, but that you came and shared your world with me. And made me share it with others. Without you I could never have faced this challenge. God bless you for everything."

Before she could speak I scurried off to my room.

Erna and George together escorted me to the airport the next morning. Little was said on the way, even less in the terminal. There were weak, almost grieving, smiles. At the gate I looked at them both.

"*Au revoir*," I said. I didn't look back.

I boarded a plane full of military personnel and a scattering of war brides. I was not one of them.

Chapter XXVII

INTO MOTHER'S ARMS

I don't remember moving. I just sat there, listening to the stewardesses and their instructions, to the rattle of the engines, to the inarticulate shouts of frightened passengers, to the captain's voice over the public address system, and to the hum in my ears.

My life did not pass before my eyes. It was my future I saw. The dream that had evolved into hope and eventually into realistic expectations, crumbled and sifted away like sand in an hourglass.

On the short hop from Orly Airport to Shannon, Ireland, I barely had time to think about George and Erna. Now I began wishing desperately that I had stayed in Paris.

We had hardly lifted off from Shannon when it started. The plane, a TWA Constellation, abruptly tilted sharply to the left, pushing me into the man in the window seat. Overhead compartments popped open and carry-on baggage fell into the aisle. Before anyone could react, the plane began to shudder and shake violently. I held tightly to the armrests while the plane righted itself. But the machine never stopped trembling.

Shannon was behind us, blanketed in dense fog and a driving rain. Ahead of us was the Atlantic, ahead of us and beneath us.

"Please remain calm and follow the instructions of your stewardesses," the captain's cool voice advised.

"I can't believe this is happening to me," I answered aloud.

I had escaped Auschwitz, escaped the ovens at Nurnberg, escaped dying as an enemy of the Third *Reich*, and now I was going to die in a broken plane at sea, alone.

It had been my decision to go to America. I had made the choice, to test myself, to prove that I alone was master of my own destiny now. I was discovering that I had made the wrong choice.

While one of the stewardesses addressed us over the loudspeaker, pointing out the various exits, the others moved up and down the aisle, first pulling the life jackets from under the seats and then giving personal instructions as to their use.

The man next to me, disheveled before he came on board and now showing a large drop of spittle from the corner of his mouth, was more realistic. He produced a flask from his hip pocket. He unscrewed the cap and put the neck to his wet lips. I thought he must be going to empty the bottle in one draft. He did not. Instead, he stopped, wiped his mouth with his sleeve, and thrust the flask into my hands.

Although I found the stranger somewhat repulsive, I found the brandy warm and welcome. I felt a little more calm.

"What they should do," I said under my breath, "is come around with drinks instead of those unmanageable life preservers."

I handed the flask back to the man next to me and nodded a thank you.

The calm from the liquor didn't last long. I started to hear the voices around me.

"Mary, mother of God, please help us," a woman across the aisle said as she fingered her rosary.

"Let me through! Please! I have to get closer to the exit!"

"Someone help me. Help me! My head is stuck in this thing. Please help me!"

As we banked slowly for a return to Shannon, the lights dimmed. Babies cried unceasingly. The passengers defied orders to remain in their seats, many of them crowding toward the lavatories.

It was only a half-hour, a long half-hour. And the last few minutes were the longest. We were instructed to fasten our safety belts as tightly as possible and bend over, putting our heads between our knees. The captain explained that we would touch down with a single landing gear. At that, I noticed, the cabin became much more silent than I would have expected.

One of the stewardesses crossed herself.

A moment later the plane touched the ground.

When the bumping and screeching and scraping and screaming was over, a few would recall seeing the sparks that sprayed away from the plane. Many more took notice of the many flashing lights from the emergency vehicles lined up on the tarmac.

Miraculously the plane did not catch fire. Nor did it break up. The same was true of the passengers. We all came through unscathed. The bruises were minor.

We became guests of TWA at an old inn near the airport and toasted our good luck with Scotch and hot barley soup. Under normal conditions it would have been much too early for the Scotch. Despite that, the night was a sleepless one for many. The sheets were damp and the old-fashioned copper bed warmers did not help. That was the excuse everybody used.

Those of us who could, passed the crossing the next day in fits of sleep, awake only when food was served. It was a long crossing, but I did not notice. I didn't awaken until we were circling Idlewild Airport.

I peered out the window past my seatmate, whose only sound during the trip had been snoring and slurping. Low-lying clouds shrouded the view. I was looking at an enormous gray curtain, a veil that kept my dream a mystery a little longer.

As we circled, the light from the sun, more a faint glow in the clouds than anything brighter, alternately lightened first one side of the plane and then the other. It wasn't even strong enough to keep people from having to squint to see what was behind and beneath those clouds.

And I was not the only one trying to catch a glimpse.

As I watched, I thought about reaching my goal. There would be more waiting. Now, though, I wondered what I had actually achieved. I wondered what New York would be like. For the first time I wondered if I would find anything worthwhile there for me. I wondered especially if I would find anything resembling what I had left behind. The thought of my mother waiting for me made the unknown less frightening.

Out of the plane and into the terminal we followed the arrows that would lead us to Customs. We marched single file through a narrow passageway—some of us by training and some of us through necessity—to a room set up with long tables for luggage inspection.

Inspectors looked tired, and sometimes unpleasant, as we filed past them. The line slowed down when we arrived at Passport Control. There, the atmosphere took on the feeling of a police line-up. There was much grunting and harrumphing as uniformed officers leafed through each passport. I looked around at the passengers who waited for their luggage to be inspected and their passports to be approved. I had traveled across the entire Atlantic Ocean with these people and did not recognize a single face.

I had only my gift from Erna, a lovely burgundy Hermés handbag of genuine leather, a bottle of Guerlaine perfume, and a bottle of Courvoisier brandy, which had somehow survived the Shannon experience. I took a mental inventory of my belongings as I approached the inspection table and presumed I had nothing to declare.

Suddenly I spotted a familiar face. My mother was there waiting for me at the other end of the hall. Though the others were stopped in front of me, I moved around them and walked quickly past the table toward her.

"Stop. You can't leave. You haven't been processed," said a voice from behind the table. It was a coincidence, though they could not know it. Their statement came at the very time my mother's presence had overwhelmed me. I broke into a run.

They chased me, of course, but I was unaware of it. All I knew was that my mother, and all my dreams, were at the end of that hall. I ran until I was in her arms. Her voice calling my name was all that I heard.

We hugged each other tightly. Enough for seven lost years. Until we couldn't hold on any longer. She held me at arm's length and looked directly at me. In her face I saw sadness. And old age.

I realized that one of the things I had missed most since we parted in Le Havre that day was the sparkle in her eyes. It was not there now, either.

"You are so thin," she finally said after hugging me again. "At least you are finally here. Thank God for that. I can hardly believe it. We must get you something to eat."

The customs official, who had alternately leaned on one foot and then the other while he waited, broke the reverie.

"Everyone must be processed through customs and immigration," he said curtly.

We were led back to the table together arm in arm and proceeded through the paperwork.

I had nothing to declare. And, when the customs agent had grunted his last permission, we left.

"Mother," I said as we walked down the hallway, still arm in arm, "I did not see the Statue of Liberty. Where is she? Did you see her when you arrived? Do you remember how we talked about seeing her?"

"Yes. I saw her from the ship. She is on an island in the harbor. We'll go visit her."

The airport was busy that afternoon. Thousands of people, millions it seemed, were pushing carts, rushing to make connections, meeting families. I heard snatches of every language known to man.

My first impression of the New World was of utter confusion and impatience.

People scampered everywhere. They moved quickly to get out of the terminal and into the afternoon breeze, crisp and clear. They jammed the exits and then dashed for taxis. Once within the mass moving toward the doors, we were caught up in the stampeding herd.

"Just hold onto me," Mother said, a hint of anxiety in her voice. The crowd gave me pause, but I obeyed.

"Where is everybody rushing to?" I said when we finally hailed a cab and settled in. It seemed as if everyone was in a panic.

Mother just smiled. "That's New York."

Through the window of the cab, silhouetted against the haze, the Manhattan skyline slowly became visible. I tried to keep my eyes on it as we passed over the many connecting bridges and the web of turnpikes that swallowed up trucks, cars—all types of vehicles. Giant high-rises were first visible, then the smaller buildings they dwarfed. The closer we got, the more Manhattan became a forbidding maze.

It took an hour of honking horns and screeching tires to reach our destination. I could not watch as the taxi swerved in and out of traffic, barely avoiding the other cars. By then fallen speechless,

Mother was clutching both my hands in hers. I closed my eyes and rested my head against the back of the rattling car seat.

The shriek of the brakes and a lurch forward brought me back to reality. We were stopped in front of a six-story residential hotel on Central Park West. My mother led me to a modestly furnished two-bedroom apartment on the top floor. Long French windows opened onto the lush green park, bringing the beauty of nature into the apartment.

"Mother, this is lovely. It is a precious view. I know I will be happy here," I said, embracing her. I wasn't sure I was telling the truth, but her eyes looked at me longingly and she deserved reassurance.

I sank into a deep armchair and could barely touch the homemade cookies she produced. In a little while I was sleeping.

When I awoke it was dark. Nothing around me seemed familiar. I didn't know where I was. I sat up, startled, and then saw my mother in a chair next to me. Wrapped in a worn silk robe, she was staring at me, a half-smile on her face.

I smiled back.

Sometimes it takes so little to be happy. Just sitting there, looking at her once-lost child, must have been all she wanted at that moment. And that half-smile certainly meant all the world to me. It wiped the sadness off her face. The sparkle in her eyes had returned.

I removed the light blanket she had put over me and got up, walking to the window.

The lights nearby, twinkling in the night, gave way to the soft glow of the city in the distance. The stars had to compete to be seen and only the brightest penetrated the luminescence of New York. I stood there and gazed at the glistening towers of Manhattan, sparkling in the darkness. I felt safe, knowing that I could reach out to this teeming city when I wished, without fear, getting to know it on my own terms. Yet it seemed so vast! There was so much of it. I knew I would need time. I suddenly felt quite inadequate.

But at least I was there. It had taken longer than I had wanted, much longer. And it would take more time to become integrated into this new life. That I would reckon with later.

"Mother," I said, "this is my new birthday, a new beginning. I will never forget March 6th, 1946."

I turned back to my mother and smiled. She said nothing. I walked back to where I had been sitting and leaned close to her.

"Do you remember when I wrote to you about breaking up with George and how difficult that was?" She nodded. "He wanted me to return after visiting you and marry him. But I feel it's all over."

She smiled again. That was her only response.

"I still miss him, though."

"I understand," she said, and her look did not belie her statement.

We did more remembering than we did catching up. There was little worth remembering, and even less that could be repeated, about the recent past. What had occurred since the war began was a subject she seemed reluctant to broach because most likely she felt personally responsible. That is how my mother was. It was a subject I was not comfortable with for obvious reasons.

She did ask me about the shop, about the apartment, about our home in Buda.

"What became of Peggy?"

I remember those eyes.

"She was shot when they came for me," I said, looking past my mother and seeing my dog.

We fell silent for a while.

"I tried to help you," she said finally. "A few weeks after the Japanese attacked Pearl Harbor, all my letters to you started coming back unopened. Hungary was declared an enemy of the Allies and communication was cut off.

"Someone told me, though, that the Red Cross might be able to help me get in touch. I worked there four days a week and I knew the people, so I thought they might help. But," she said, shrugging her shoulders, "there was nothing that could be done."

"I understand."

"That is not all, not everything. I took up fasting twice a week as penance and finally cousin Max told me about all our relatives being deported from Austria. I was terribly frightened, almost frantic. That is what spurred me on.

"I tried the Red Cross again and a friend there gave me the name of an agency that provided false documents for Jewish people in countries occupied by the Nazis. They even had a contact in Budapest, a Swedish businessman. He became a hero to our people because he saved so many lives. He brought them to the Swedish embassy for shelter. His name was Raoul Wallenberg and he was risking his life for the Jews. Can you believe that? It's true. In early January of 1944 I was instructed to send him a document with your name on it. So, even though I didn't hear from you, I hoped you were safe."

"Mother, what happened to our Hungarian relatives?"

She paused for a long moment.

"They are all gone."

I remembered them, each in turn. Then I remembered my name being called over the loudspeaker at Csepel. I wondered if it was Mr. Wallenberg trying to save me from the death camps. I had saved myself from the ovens. But I wondered whose name had to be left out so that he might call mine.

"Mother, I think he called for me."

"Who called for you?" She leaned forward in her chair.

"Mr. Wallenberg. Before I left Budapest for the camps, we were in Csepel. My name was called. I was afraid and didn't go to the camp office. I didn't trust them. I thought they might have leveled some accusation against me and then killed me. I'm very sorry."

"It is nothing, child," she said. "Do not worry. You are safe now."

I nodded feebly.

Dawn came and we finally stopped talking. Mother rose wearily, came to me for a hug, and then helped me stand. She showed me to the little bedroom that would be my home. I thanked her as she turned down the bed.

When she had gone I crawled under the covers and remembered all my uncles and aunts and cousins. I had a roof over my head now. I was cared for and protected. I should have been happy. But the ones who had been left behind kept crying for help. I had wasted my chance. They had never gotten one.

Chapter XXVIII

NEW YORK'S MANY FACES

Breakfast was at night and supper arrived as the city awakened. The long plane ride had its effect on me, and getting my body used to the difference in time zones took awhile.

Mother was patient as I adjusted. Whenever I woke up she fed me breakfast, and whenever the day was over, sometimes late at night for the first few days, there was a semblance of supper.

Staying up most of the night on my arrival hadn't helped, and it took me that much longer to get my bearings.

When my inner clock was sufficiently corrected, near the end of my first week in New York, I decided to venture out onto the street. I wandered up and down the sidewalk, never far from the entrance to my mother's building. I was getting used to the hustle and bustle of the city, one block at a time.

It was difficult for me. I was unaccustomed to people rushing by, bumping into me, and then just racing off as I murmured an "excuse me" over my shoulder.

I eventually found a friend right in front of the building. He was a grinning black man named George and the name reminded me of other times. But he did not let my mind wander too far back.

"So you are Miss Dunn," he said. "Well, well, well. Welcome to America. You gonna be happy here. Your mama said you was coming. I work as a handyman in the house, so if there be anything you need, you just give a holler. George'll come running."

His toothless smile lighted his face.

I surmised that this was what they called a middle-class neighborhood. The buildings, with their costly architecture, fancy balconies, and detailed stone carvings, stood behind intricate wrought iron fences and iron lanterns. I had learned that they were built in the early twenties. They had not remained unscathed through the years and undoubtedly had seen many owners. The upkeep had become costly and they were now being turned into residential hotels. Eventually, they would be refurbished and sold as co-ops.

But many still had their doormen, their elegant lobbies.

These were all in contrast to the trash cans lining the streets as I walked north across from Central Park. What surprised me most were the items being thrown away. It seemed sinful to me that people would discardsuch foodstuffs in such great quantity. I could not bear to see it.

"What is the matter with these people?" I asked Mother. "Can they afford to throw out so many things?"

"I know what you mean," she replied, smiling. "I guess I don't notice it anymore. It surprised me at first. You will notice more of it before you stop seeing it. Even on the East Side, in the best of neighborhoods, the sidewalks are littered with cast-off possessions once a week. It is not unusual. You will get used to it."

Mother sounded certain; I was not so sure.

The garbage was just one of the things I learned about those first few weeks in the city. I also learned that taxicabs were as much a menace to pedestrians as they were to their customers. They hurtled around the streets at a dizzying pace, cutting in and out of traffic, and defying any sense of conformity. They seemed to be a half-step in front of the hectic pace of the city.

The cabs were just the vanguard of the rest of the traffic; cars and trucks streaked by, forcing people to run across the street to reach the relative safety of the other side. It was certainly something I could not become accustomed to. I would never be able to challenge the screaming traffic of this city.

That became clear to me as I stood on the corner nearest my mother's house, a block away from the newsstand. Apparently, I stood there long enough to seem bewildered, because suddenly a man touched my elbow.

"May I help you cross?" he asked gently. I was wearing sunglasses and the thought occurred to me that he might think me sightless. It was easier to play along than it was to tell him that I was just petrified.

I took his elbow, and when the light changed, he warned me to step down off the curb. We moved briskly across the street. He held up his free hand and motioned traffic to stop. On the other side he warned me of the curb, slowed down, and made sure I didn't lose my footing.

"Thank you," I said, half-turning toward him.

"It's quite all right. Are you okay now?"

"Yes. I'm fine."

"So long, then."

I knew that there would not always be a kind man to help me, and I felt the city overpowering me. I also wondered if I would ever make it back across the street. There was everything a person could want in New York, my mother had assured me of that. But it was not all on my street corner. I had to look for it, and if I found that getting to the other corner was impossible, I would never succeed.

I watched the changing traffic light, and timed the cars. It looked as though the yellow came up every minute or so. Then the green coming the other way. There seemed enough time to reach the other side. It was time to try.

When the light turned green I started out. I had scrambled halfway across when a truck screeched its brakes, and skidded into the crosswalk. I froze in the middle of the street, unable to move.

The driver of the truck, and several other motorists, were patient only until their green light came up. Then the shouting began. Those who could went around me, barely missing me, while the truck driver continued screaming his obscenities.

I turned around, looking back the way I had come. Cars raced by, their horns honking. It was too far to attempt going back. But when I turned in the direction I had started out, it seemed even farther. I had nowhere to go. I felt my eyes begin stinging.

Before the panic could boil over, someone grabbed my arm and led me to safety. Trembling, trying to control myself, I didn't get a chance to thank the person before he was gone.

No one else even seemed to notice.

I had tried and I had failed. I knew it. Part of me tried to be reassuring and remind myself that it would take time to learn to cope with the city. The other half of me said there was more to it. It was vague and indecisive. All it knew for sure was that the future was dark.

Based on what I had just discovered, I could not argue. I spoke the language, but nobody understood me. My accent was quick to draw sidelong looks. At least from those who stopped long enough to listen.

Yet I could not give up. I had sacrificed too much and tried too hard to get here. In the days it took me to contemplate my fate and my future, I remembered something from Budapest.

I could learn about New York from my own street. If it beckoned to me, I would go beyond. I would confront that when the time came. But for now I would try to learn more about it. I would reach out to it with the love I had nurtured within me after seeing those old movies.

There was George at the door and the newsstand on the corner. They held the key. I made it my daily routine each morning to go to the corner and get a copy of the *New York Times*.

Each day George would greet me with the same smile and the sightless vendor at the newsstand would tell me the same joke.

"Good morning, Miss Dunn," he would say. "Nice to see you again."

The *Times* became my textbook and I spent every morning with it. I followed a pattern according to my interests. Politics, world news, and editorials followed in that order.

Next came information about the theater, the arts, new books, exhibits in town, and literature. There was always something interesting happening. The allure of the city began to reach out to me.

Fashion, and everyone connected with it, were amply covered. It was refreshing to sit in the little apartment and wait for the paper to bring the latest in Paris fashions to me. I read about the famous designers, names like Balenciaga, Schiaparelli, Lanvin, who had made it through the German occupation and were once again enriching the world with their creations.

The *Times* transported me in my dreams to the Broadway shows I could never afford to attend. I tasted the cuisine in the restaurants I would never enter. I learned about the tastes of the rich and powerful, and their lifestyles and favorite charities.

The throbbing force of the city was getting through to me in my seclusion. I felt as though I were pressing my nose against the window of a delicatessen, seeing those delicacies, and yet unable to get them in my grasp.

I noticed the advertisements of art schools to attract students and the announcements of free concerts and museum exhibits. Once again, it was the music that lured me.

The concerts began with the warming of April and I forgot how afraid I had been to cross the street. I went to a band music concert, nearby in Central Park, featuring Hungarian folk music. The performance drew a thunderous applause from the audience.

It was reassuring that the music had no ill effect on me. Not once did I feel homesick for the country that had been my home.

The diversity of the city was reflected in the classified ads. The different offerings were mind-boggling. The more I read, the more interested I became. And often the more intimidated. There were occupations listed I had never heard of. So I concentrated on the garment industry ads. Most of them, though, carried the admonition "experience necessary." It saved me the pain of a rejection in person.

Later that month I was forced to try. An opening for a stock girl was listed, and no experience was required.

When I left the apartment, directions in hand, I felt little fear. It grew only as I moved down the street and was reinforced as I boarded the bus. The bus was crowded and I stayed by the front door during the trip downtown. Those getting on after me were forced to walk around a woman, frozen by fear, who was blocking their way. The driver just ignored me. I ignored everyone, almost everyone.

I held onto the handlebar tightly after the first screech of brakes sent me perilously close to the windshield. It was not long before I heard the people in the first seat whispering.

"Look at that girl. Do you see her arm? You know what she

is? She must be an escapee from one of those European camps. Why don't they go back where they came from? We've got enough rationing and price controls without them. We've got enough unemployment of our own."

At the very next stop, I stumbled off the bus. My throat was tight and my eyes burned. If the tattoo on my arm and the pain in my heart was so easy to see, why would they want to rub salt in my wounds? I tried hard not to believe that the opinions I had heard were those of the majority of Americans.

I turned toward home, forgetting my mission, breathing in the fresh air. I felt incapable of getting on another bus so I walked the distance back home, trying to stay within the flow of the masses on the sidewalk.

Finally I reached my newsstand and was sure of where I was.

"Hello," I said to the vendor. "I believe I owe you for yesterday's paper."

He smiled as I reached into my coat pocket. I realized then that my money was missing. There must have been a pickpocket on the bus. I apologetically explained it to the vendor and slowly walked the rest of the way home.

Chapter XXIX

UNEXPECTED DISCOVERY

After the incident on the bus, the apartment once again became my cocoon. There seemed to be no butterfly left in me.

Mother smiled often, laughed a little too gaily, and treated me as though there was nothing wrong—just a coincidence that I never went out. As if she didn't notice. When she was unaware that I was watching, I saw the truth, the worry in her eyes, and the tears.

I observed the approach of summer from the window. Sweaters started to come off and strollers were in to shirt-sleeves. A little while later shorts and T-shirts became more comfortable.

The city never left. It stood there, waiting for me. Mother, bless her heart, kept bringing the newspaper. I rarely got to the stoop downstairs and George's front-door office, much less to the corner.

Something finally caught my eye, and made me want to extend my wings again. Ironically, it was something of the past.

In the east eighties, the Hungarian community was planning a street fair. The notices promised many colorful costumes, native dishes and old music, and a lot of fun. It was an easy decision for me.

Mother forgot her worries about me but stopped short of encouraging me to go. The location of the street fair was a long walk into the city. She never mentioned buses—neither did I. Once she decided that I was truly prepared to take this hike, she blurted out the directions, making me copy them down clearly on a piece of paper she provided.

My route took me through Central Park and that alone made my decision a glorious one. I had wanted to visit this patch of green since my arrival in New York, but my own fears had kept me from it. Now, in the midst of all the trees and grass and water and children, there was no more fear, not for the moment.

I was drawn to the children in the playgrounds, areas surrounded by statues of fairy tale characters and surrounding manmade lakes that served as oceans for the many little boats the youngsters turned into mighty armadas. I was led by intuition through the trees and slowly the noises of the city faded into the past. I felt the kind of serenity you know only in the forest. I wondered at the concept of this oasis, located as it was in the shadow of all those skyscrapers. This park, I told myself, was to become my home away from home. And it would become my friend.

On the other side of the park I began to discover the hidden rewards of New York—the ethnic flavor of the neighborhoods that could not be seen by cab, train, or plane. Only on foot does one discover the elusive charms of the city.

Driving down a street you might notice the elegant, turn-of-the-century brownstone buildings, still privately owned and standing side by side to review the passing parade of pedestrians. But walking, you see the trees, saplings really, lining those streets. Saplings that the homeowners had planted as part of a concerted effort to humanize Manhattan.

In a cab you might notice the beautifully carved oak doors and heavy wrought iron gates of the buildings. You would also notice the plain walls that hid the opulent decor inside. But you would have to be on foot to see the hidden gardens behind those townhouses. Summer had brought everything into bloom and just a glimpse of that splash of color made the air taste sweeter.

As I walked, I passed an embassy—I don't remember the flag—and was almost overcome by the colors. From the balconies of the two-story building hung baskets of petunias and geraniums. A little farther I found carriage houses converted into dwellings.

Another block and the high-rises again began competing for space with the buildings that would have looked more appropriate with a carriage out in front. The charm of the old world, or a more innocent one, balanced the acceleration of the new.

It was in the changing flavor of the scenery and the subtle beauty that I learned to love New York. I made sure to try to explore only the quiet little streets and avoid the busier, more bustling locations. On these streets I discovered the shops that featured copper utensils from Great Britain and porcelain from France, and a place that cried "We Buy Junk and Sell Antiques." Tiny restaurants with blooming backyards catered to the younger crowd and galleries displaying precious paintings were wedged next to Chinese laundries.

I found a struggle at East Forty-Seventh Street. A two-story building, tiny by comparison, squared its shoulders against a pair of skyscrapers, the tops of which you could not see in the haze, walking or driving. The little guy was holding out. So far he had not been intimidated.

As I said, these were the streets. They ran east and west. The avenues ran north and south and they carried the bulk of the traffic. When I reached Third Avenue, with its buses and trucks and cars and cabs all ignoring the traffic lights that I thought were my only ally, my resolve to find the street fair dissolved completely. Painfully, I elected to turn back. At least my return would take me through the park. Perhaps another day I could try to defy the traffic more bravely. I would have to wait and see.

I continued my east-west walks. I fell into a routine of breakfast, morning with the paper, lunch, and a walk until before supper time. It was becoming a warm summer—even though it was not quite summer officially—and the days were comfortable.

The city was allowing me to grow, to catch up to it, and the past was fading into a shadowy memory of loose planks on a bridge over oblivion. New York was allowing me to rebuild my confidence on my own terms. The city was being patient—something I had never been very good at—and some of that was rubbing off on me.

It did so until I came upon the YMCA on Lexington Avenue.

I had wandered there alone on the narrow streets of the east nineties. It was on the corner of Ninetieth Street and Lexington

Avenue. In the windows and on the walls were posters announcing upcoming events, including concerts and lectures and exhibits of new artists. The brightly colored placards lured me across the busy avenue and I scampered over to see what was coming and what had been. One of the coming attractions astounded me.

A simple poster with blue letters on a gold background proclaimed the future recital of a young European pianist, a Hungarian girl, who had been a child prodigy before the war tore everything apart.

The bold letters proclaimed her name as Magda Fugazy.

At first I was hurt. She had come to New York, without making any attempt to find me. I distinctly remembered telling her about my trip to the States in the hospital. Perhaps she had been sicker than I thought and just didn't remember.

Then I was glad for her. Glad that she had come through and was able to function. Especially glad that she was able to continue her ambition as a pianist. Then again, she was lucky and had displayed the ability to make the right friends, even when it came to the right designer for a gown.

I was also impressed. When I thought of how involved the preparations for a recital must be, I guessed that she must have recovered quickly and retained a great deal of her prewar training. She would never go on stage unprepared, so evidently she must have put in a great deal of preparation time.

Perhaps I also felt some envy. For her to accomplish all this meant that she had to have a sponsor, someone influential in the music world. Someone who was looking out for her and looking after her.

I envisioned her accomplishments and then compared them to my own. I concluded that I had a long way to go. Creativity, much less coping with the outside world, takes a whole person, someone confident enough to look for a challenge and face up to it. I had done little of either.

I remembered Magda. She had been lucky and she had been shrewd. She had obtained an invitation to the Archduchess's benefit and had arranged for me to design a gown for her to wear. She had made the right friends and had been successful, as successful as she or anyone else could have been in that political climate. And she had done so without seeming manipulative. She had been charming and disarming and people became fond of her and wanted to help her. I had been one of them.

Lost in my thoughts, I wandered back toward Central Park. There was an empty bench in front of the newly trimmed hedges. I sat there and tried to reckon with the gladness that had become sadness. I wondered how the mere sight of Magda's placard had brought on such introspection, almost resentment. I was ashamed of myself again. Did I envy what she had achieved or her ability to do it? Here I had been barely able to cross a street, and Magda was on the verge of another triumph.

I determined that I would find out if she could do it. And if she did, how.

It must be her youth, I thought. That was how she was able to endure and to discard the suffering we had both experienced. She was apparently more resilient than I and had been able to put her incarceration and illness behind her. That was probably what I envied most. Then again, she had the discipline of music to concentrate on. I had only ghosts.

At one time I had symbolized success and talent to Magda. Now the reverse was true. Yes, I would get tickets to the recital. And I would see if she remembered me.

It was dusk when I stepped out of the taxi in front of the YMCA. I stood outside for a time and watched the concert-goers, trying to imagine their preferences. Some were neat, attractive, younger people in casual clothes, keeping cool on the warm mid-June evening. Others were meticulously formal couples enjoying the benefits of middle age. There were several young boys and girls, probably music students, no more than two to a chaperon.

Once inside many of them, especially the more carefully dressed, seemed out of place in the Y, even uncomfortable. They certainly would have looked more at home at Carnegie Hall.

The playbill showed a carefully selected program of Mozart, Chopin, Schubert, and Dohnányi. They were established, popular works. I knew them all. I had studied them all myself. None of them was too demanding.

I smoothed my silk shirtwaist dress as I sat down and waited for the concert to begin. As I looked around, I fingered the diamond pin my mother had lent me for the occasion.

The lights dimmed and I began to remember the friend I had last seen lying in a hospital bed just a day away from delirium. The people around me in the hall, filled almost to capacity, did not know the story behind the stunning, willowy creature who stood proudly next to the grand piano and graciously bowed to their polite applause.

I was near the front and I could see that her mouth still turned up in a piquant fashion. The same full eyebrows arched over her pale face. The grace of her young girl's body had not changed; even after suffering horrors, it had returned to its harmonious proportions. She moved to the bench with an inner rhythm, holding her head high. Her hair was done in the latest style, parted in the middle and pulled back into a chignon. She was obviously older, but not as old as she seemed when I last saw her.

Magda played well. Her technique was flawless, though somewhat mechanical. Her command of the keyboard was complete, yet her inspiration seemed inconsistent.

A short intermission halfway through the program gave me the opportunity to go backstage. I was stopped and asked to return after the performance.

That performance lasted two encores as Magda was called back by the enthusiastic ovations. She played Debussy and then Bartók before a tuxedoed emcee brought the flowers and Magda blew kisses to the audience.

She had her back to the door when I arrived at her dressing room. The room was small and crowded with people, the women admiring the red roses Magda still held and the men admiring Magda, some of them openly. I made my way in and could see her face in the mirrored wall she was facing. I watched her try to answer all the questions, always maintaining her grace and her smile.

For a moment her eyes darted to the mirror for a look around and I thought they fell on me. A second later she looked up again and caught my eye. She had been speaking to someone I could not see, but now her mouth simply hung open. I could see past her to the two men in front of her and I watched as they sensed something and moved back. Magda turned slowly when I returned my gaze to the face in the mirror. Her eyes remained locked on mine until she was looking over her right shoulder at the mirror. Then she turned to face me.

We stared at each other while the well-wishers in the room rubbed their chins and whispered to each other. Slowly Magda held out her arms to me and I took the three steps and embraced her.

"I have to be dreaming. This can't be true! My darling, what a miracle," Magda whispered in my ear. We stepped back from our embrace and I could see that the composed artist from a few minutes ago was weeping openly. I took a handkerchief out of my pocket and dabbed at the mascara now streaking down her cheek.

Magda reached up and took over the mopping up.

"Wait for me," she said, almost pleading. "I will be with you in a minute. Just as soon as I can get free of these people."

She turned away. Then, as if remembering something, faced me again.

"Alice, I would like you to meet someone." She pulled me to her side and beckoned to two men.

"Alice, I would like you to meet Arthur Adler, my attorney, and his cousin Jerry. Would you three keep each other company while I fix myself up?" Then she waded through the crowd to her dressing table.

I struck up a conversation with the two men. It seemed that Magda's attorney had come for the concert and at the last minute Jerry had decided to come along also. As several people recognized and approached Arthur Adler, Jerry and I were left to while away the time.

We chatted pleasantly and I discovered him to be a man of depth, also an attorney, who had been personally involved in the war crimes trials in Japan following the war. In New York, though, he was relatively unknown and still trying to find his way.

Magda, meanwhile, had managed to dab at her cheeks while at the same time trying to thank everyone individually. I watched as a young girl tugged at Magda's navy blue gown and presented her with a bouquet. Magda, in turn, rewarded the pinafored youngster with a kiss on both cheeks.

"Have you been in New York long?" I heard Jerry say.

"Not very. I came here only a few months ago from France. I am still getting used to the city."

"It takes time," he agreed. "You'll get used to it. What do you do?"

"Oh, I'm a dress designer. I'm out of work at the moment. One of these days maybe I'll find a job."

"There are plenty to be had," he said. "You just have to be ready to work. There's always something."

I looked at him for a moment and thought how presumptuous he sounded. I decided not to give his remarks much thought.

"Yes, something will turn up," I agreed, superficially.

Magda hastily repaired her makeup, while constantly turning and thanking the last few stragglers. In a flash she looked herself over in the mirror, nodded quickly, and then rejoined us.

"Do you mind terribly if Alice and I go out alone?" This she said to Arthur Adler. Jerry had a surprised look on his face.

"Not at all," Arthur Adler replied with a smile. "You are obviously old friends and have some catching up to do. Have a good time. I'll call you on Monday."

"Thank you both," she said, and steered me through the exit, still nodding at more fans, her face flushed with success.

"Did you see how Jerry was looking at you?" Magda asked as we got into a cab.

I told her I had not. It was true. I didn't know that one day soon, and many times after that, I would also notice the look she was alluding to.

We took a table in a small café nearby that catered to the after-show crowd. Magda was greeted with warm applause from a scattering of patrons, while the others craned their necks and huddled and wondered who the striking raven-haired beauty was. We sat for a time and just looked at each other. She had become captivating where she had been only charming before. Thousands of question bubbled in my head. A waiter came by and Magda ordered a glass of sherry. I decided on a cup of tea.

I looked into the eyes I had known so well and saw a hidden sadness. I also saw a genuine delight and then more tears. The memories I saw in her eyes made me feel tense and I sensed the same in Magda. It didn't stop me. "To see you like this fills me with happiness, darling," I said. "You were wonderful and will be even more wonderful."

"Thank you," she said. "What makes me happiest is seeing you. I thought we would never meet again after you left."

The waiter brought the drinks and I poured some tea.

"I didn't think I would ever see you again, either. I'm so glad you made it to America. When did you arrive? Why haven't you called?"

"I arrived last February," she said. "I didn't know if you were here or not. I'm just so happy to see you and see you looking so well. You know, I only barely remember seeing you in the hospital."

She fingered her sherry glass but did not drink from it.

"Here," I said, raising my cup but feeling somehow uncomfortable. "To you. I feel so proud of you and happy that you were such a success tonight. You have come a long way and there is still so much ahead of you."

Magda smiled and nodded at me demurely as she clinked her glass against my cup and took a small sip.

"Alice, my dear, if you only knew what it means to me to see you again. I was such a wreck in the hospital. It took them weeks to release me. I wondered if I would ever get out of there. Playing again was the farthest thing from my mind."

"How did you come to America?"

"Another miracle," she said, with a short laugh. "They were very kind at the hospital to contact a Jewish agency and they, in turn, found a sponsor for me. He is a born Hungarian and was willing to be a guarantor and bring me to this country. When I began to recover he insisted on my resuming my career."

I thought how fortunate she was.

"It was very strange to arrive in a new country, even with someone to care for you. I was completely dependent on others. But my sponsor found me a place to live and a piano to practice with and here I am. He has been to me what your mother and brother must be to you."

"You must be very grateful to this man," I said. "You are very lucky to have such support. It is important to have someone to lean on and someone who can help you further your career."

"Mr. Singer has been truly wonderful, as your mother no doubt has been with you. It is fantastic to see you looking so well. I asked him to find you but he was unsuccessful."

She shrugged.

"I understand," I said and felt as though I was lying. "My mother was there for me to lean on, too."

The waiter came by with another pot of tea and Magda waved off his offer of another sherry.

"Was your Mr. Singer at the recital? It would have been nice to meet him."

Magda smiled. "No, he was out of town on business. It is that way often. I think he sends Arthur out to look after me. When you meet him, and I know it will be soon, you will realize how wonderful he is. He is like my father. I am not his only charge, though. Many immigrants have been supported through Mr. Singer. Sometimes I wonder how he can handle it all. He even adopted a young boy who lives with him. It must be very hectic keeping up with that youngster and all his business interests."

"He must be a very special man."

"Oh, yes. He is. Do you know what he always says? America gave me so much. I want to give something back."

"What became of your parents?"

She looked hard at me for the first time.

"They did not survive the war."

I looked at Magda. Before I could apologize, she took another sip of sherry and nodded and smiled to another fan. I thought of her misfortune and how lucky she was to have her future assured. Her only worries were reaching her career goals. Nothing to drain her emotionally, no constraints. The loss of her parents seemed to have had no effect on her whatsoever.

"Enough of me," Magda said. "It is you we should talk about. There is so much I simply must know. How is your family? What is your life like? Who are your friends? I am sure you have made many since you've been here. Where are you living? I will probably forget half of the things I want to ask you but now we have all the time in the world to catch up."

"Mother is well," I said, once Magda fixed her eyes on me and waited for an answer. "We get along beautifully. She is more a sister to me than a mother. We understand each other perfectly. My brother Erno is still in the army in Texas."

"Mr. Singer and I are like your mother and you," Magda said.

"But tell me, what are your plans professionally? Are you still designing clothes? You should do well in New York with your personality and talent. And people don't have to buy a ticket to enjoy your talents, only an outfit."

Again she laughed. Then she looked at me brightly.

"You really do look wonderful. Just as I remembered you."

I finished my tea.

"You have had a big day, darling, and must be exhausted," I said. "It is very late. Why don't we see each other again soon?"

"I am really not tired. But you're right. I will be. And it has been a big day. We absolutely must see each other again, and very soon. You have not told me a thing about yourself. Why don't we get together next week?"

"Let me have your number," I said. "I will come and see you, or we can meet somewhere. My life so far is filled only with the day to day discoveries of a new world. It's great."

"I'm glad," she said.

Magda produced a pen and wrote her telephone number on the cocktail napkin under her sherry glass. After handing it to me with a smile she fished a five-dollar bill out of her clutch purse and placed it on the table. Then she reached behind her and plucked her shawl off the back of the chair. We stood together and I followed her out.

Magda let me have the first cab and blew me a kiss as I rode away. Perhaps I was overly sentimental, I don't know. But she just didn't seem like the Magda I had known before. Still, I was happy for her. She was successful and on her way. I was nothing. Magda had stretched her wings while mine remained folded. She had put the horrors of war behind her and I was still looking for what "me" there might be left.

In a way it was good for me to meet her again. It had helped me to take an honest look at myself. And it had helped me to see that it could be done. I just wished I also had so willing a sponsor.

Chapter XXX

NO. A.135.000

Central Park unfolded beneath me as the sky brightened in the east. It was just a matter of seconds now before the sun peaked over the false horizon of East Manhattan. I counted five ticks at a time. Not yet. I guessed that Long Island was already in sunlight and Coney Island was getting a peek. It couldn't be much longer now. One, two, three, four, five. Not yet. I listened for other signs of life, but the giant was still asleep. The usual city noises, an occasional car horn, the rattle of buses, and the wail of emergency vehicles were few and far between. It was early, and it was Sunday. Maybe the Big Apple would be a little more peaceful today.

One, two, three, four, five. Not yet.

I was at my favorite window, alone, waiting to see if the sun would pop up on a hazy day or a clear one. I sat crosswise on the couch in my nightgown, my legs stretched out in front of me. Central Park was over my right shoulder, growing greener and greener as the sky opened itself to the sun.

One, two, three, four, five. Not yet.

The sun was not the only thing missing from this day. I was missing. At least there was something missing in me. I fit in only with my window, with the pillows I leaned on, and the slippers on my feet.

The city was out there, somewhere else, through the window and down six stories. It was there in the beauty of the park and the charm of the neighborhoods. It was far less alone than I, and infinitely more useful. In a few minutes it would be full of life and hope and expectations. I was as drained as it was brimming. A body without heart, a spirit without a soul. All that the city had to offer was passing me by, and I stood behind my window and allowed it to happen.

No job offers were scooted under my door, no lovers serenaded beneath the window, no hope sprang eternal. No sponsor waited to shepherd me back to life.

I wasn't even alive enough to be ashamed of myself.

One, two, three, four, five. Almost. It must be there soon.

I thought of Magda's remarkable recovery and accomplishment. Remembering last night served only to erode what little self-esteem I had left. She had recovered, come back, and done what she had set out to do, unlike myself. I had my dream waiting for me and would not even hazard a shot at the merry-go-round. I rationalized that trying to do a job without confidence, no matter what that job might be, would be a wasted effort, so why bother? I would have to remain my mother's charge until my confidence returned.

How could I? I might as well be an invalid, or worse. I did not relish that thought. Yet it was the one I was living, the role I had chosen for myself. Resignation was easier than perseverance, especially when there is nothing to try again and no way to accomplish the task.

Even more so, the idea of my being here at all was simply blind good fortune. There was really no reason for me to be in America, no reason why I shouldn't have been left behind by this life I no longer participated in.

One, two, there! There it was! A sliver of orange pulling itself up over the East Side and the city. A city whose people were often gracious enough to smile and tell you to give yourself time to discover its charms, and then bold enough when you agreed to demand from yourself the same kind of fierce loyalty they bore on their shoulders.

It was no wonder that they demanded your patience and then

your affirmation—unless you had no concept of how to belong.

The sun was up now and losing its orange hue, taking on the bright yellow glow it would carry for most of the day. It would be a fairly clear day. Out there somewhere was a breeze blowing away the smoke and fog that even in those days made the sky a milky color.

I heard Mother stir, but I did not turn away from the window when her door opened. She must not have noticed me there because she said nothing, just went to the kitchen and drew water into the teapot. It clanked ever so faintly when she set it on the stove. She was being careful not to wake me.

When she came out of the kitchen, no doubt more used to the morning light, she saw me.

"Alice, darling, you are already up? I thought you were still asleep."

"No, Mother," I said, returning her smile. It was a smile of irony. I really was asleep in a way. "I have been awake for awhile and I just thought I would watch the sunrise."

"Isn't it a little bright?"

"I suppose it is now. I think I'll draw the curtains."

She nodded and I swung my feet off the couch.

"There is tea on the stove if you want some," she said, and padded back into her room.

When the teapot whistled, I went to the kitchen and poured myself a cup and went back to the couch. Mother emerged for long enough to get some tea and then went back to draw her bath.

I took a sip of the tea and examined the cup. It was nothing like the plain white china I had held the night before with Magda. This one was from Johnson's, a blue willow china cup. I set it on the saucer I had brought and placed on the coffee table.

I was startled when I saw Mother again, dressed and carrying a suitcase and overnight bag. She must have seen my puzzlement.

"Don't you remember, darling? I am going to visit Ruth today. I'll only be gone a few days. Are you sure you won't come along?"

"Oh, yes. Now I remember." I laughed. "No, thank you. I'll stay home this time."

Mother nodded as she carried the suitcase to the door and set it down.

"Would you be a dear and call a cab for me, then?"

"Certainly."

I rang for a cab as mother disappeared back into her room and then brought out the teacup she had used. I heard her rinse the cup in the sink.

"Is there anything you will need?" she called from the kitchen.

I smiled. So like my mother. She couldn't know.

"I'll be fine," I said. "Don't worry about a thing. I'm a big girl now; I think I can handle myself."

Mother was laughing as she came out of the kitchen. I suddenly realized that I still hadn't dressed and a cab was on its way. I could never just bid my mother goodbye at the door. I had to see her to the taxi.

Hurriedly, I threw on a cotton skirt and blouse. As I came out of my room, Mother was picking up her bags.

"Let me take one," I said, and she handed me the overnight case.

She chattered at me as we rode down in the elevator, reminding me where all the foodstuffs and medicines and towels and phone numbers were, in case I got confused or hungry or sick during the three days that she would be gone.

At the curb George took the bags and placed them gently in the trunk of the cab. The driver was behind the wheel. George slammed the trunk and then scampered over to pull the door open for my mother. She tipped George, as she always did.

Before she got in she hugged me and then gave me a long, searching look.

"Go on," I said, chuckling. "Give my best to Ruth and have a good time. Stay out of trouble."

"You are going now to get a newspaper?" It was more of a reminder. Until that moment I hadn't thought about it.

"Yes. That's an idea. Now be on your way."

She blew me a kiss and she was gone.

The *Times*, as usual, had plenty of exciting news. For me, the best news was the theater and music section. There, on the fourth page, under a one-column headline, was the review of Magda's recital. It was brief but complimentary, a commenting on her somewhat mannered touch, a touch that somehow, according to this particular critic, did not give enough. It also mentioned a brief background of Magda Fugazy, noting her studies as a child in Budapest before the war. It pointed out that where she studied, the Royal Academy of Music, was an institution made famous by the likes of Bartók, Kodály, Dohnány, and others. Finally, it called, in a subtle way, for another recital in the future from this "promising young artist still new to the United States."

I read and reread the article and reflected on what it meant. I thought of how thrilled Magda must be at her achievement. She was now instantly known throughout the city. I got up from the sofa and walked to the phone. After several busy signals I finally got through. Magda answered on the third ring.

"Hello, darling," I said. "How are you? How does it feel to be written up in the *New York Times*? You must be very proud."

"Oh, Alice. How are you? Yes, it is thrilling. We have come a long way from that Red Cross hospital, haven't we?"

"Yes, we have, indeed," I laughed. "At least you have. You have every right to be proud of yourself. I had to call you once I read the review. Tell me, is your sponsor as proud of you?"

"Oh, yes, definitely. He called me this morning too. In fact, I just got off the phone with him. He told me he knew I wouldn't let him down."

"And you haven't."

"No," she said. "And there's more to come."

"You must tell me about it."

"I will. I will."

"You know, Magda, last night I was just too emotional to sleep. I remembered how we were both looking forward to your concert in Budapest. Do you remember?"

"I certainly do. But I'd like to forget. Those times are behind us now. We can't go on if we're constantly looking back."

"You're right, of course. Incidentally, since we are talking now, why don't we set up a date to meet again. I am dying to get to know the new Magda Fugazy."

She laughed. "I want very much to see you again. But you will be disappointed. There is no new Magda. The young girl you remember being so anxious to meet the famous designer is now a young woman of twenty. That is the only difference between the girl you knew and the one you will get to know. I am still a musician and music is still my life. That's about all there is to it."

"Well, I'd still like to talk."

"Absolutely. As would I. I'm just trying to think of a quiet place where we won't be tempted to eat too much and we can catch up with each other. Is it all right if I pick you up, let's see, how about Wednesday?"

"That would be perfect. Fine," I said.

"Noon?"

"Fine."

"I'll be in front of your building. By the way, has Jerry called? I gave Arthur your number to give to him. I think he'll be getting in touch with you."

I wasn't ready for a man in my life.

"You mean Jerry Adler?"

"Yes. He is going to call you, I think."

"Oh, Magda, that's very sweet . . ."

"Just be nice to him. If he's half as nice as his cousin, he'll turn out to be a very sweet man. I've really got to go now. I'll see you on Wednesday."

We rang off.

Magda was right. Jerry did call. We saw each other on occasion, mostly walks in the park and a movie now and then. Nothing very regular, certainly nothing serious, at least for the meantime.

I marveled at Magda's self-assurance. Her decisions were quick, her conduct almost perfect, her approach unhesitating. She had learned fast. She had always struck me as being intelligent and eager to grow and she was proving that. I also wondered at how easy it had been to make a date with her.

Wednesday came up fast, cool for the season and cloudy. It looked like rain so I dressed in a gray, tailored flannel suit. I loved tailored styles for their timelessness. Fashion would change by the season, but fine tailoring lived on. Besides, I was in no position to change wardrobes to fit the season. The wise investment was in something that would last. Gimbel's basement was a great source.

I selected a bright pink silk blouse and matching scarf to round out the outfit.

As George greeted me and pushed open the door, precisely at

noon, Magda was pulling up in a taxi. I got in next to her, again with George holding the door, and we exchanged kisses on each cheek.

"How about a quiet little restaurant on the East Side? I had thought of a less tempting place, until I remembered the duck there. You must try it. The service is also professional enough that they won't disturb us unduly."

"Great," I replied. "Overeager waiters make me nervous. And we really do have a lot to talk about. I've got a million questions."

Magda nodded and gave the driver the name of the restaurant.

Twenty minutes later the cab pulled up outside the tiny establishment. Because it was a workday it wasn't too busy, but I could see people at the window down the few steps to the entrance. It was a charming Czech place on one of those tree-lined streets I loved in the east seventies.

Magda handed the cab driver a bill and waved away the change. When we went inside, I realized I was wrong about the size. There was a fountain in the middle of the room and more people were sitting around it sipping drinks and munching on salads and sandwiches. In the back we found a lovely courtyard that must have been a favorite for after-work cocktails.

We sat down at a table in the back overlooking the courtyard and wondered how I would ask all the questions milling around in my head. Where did Magda live? What was her home like? Did she have many friends? Were they nice people? What else did she do besides practice? How was she coping with the new world around her? Who was her confidante?

And what had brought her to the hospital in that awful condition?

"Well, congratulations," I said as we got comfortable. "I am sitting with a friend, an artist, who has been written up in the *New York Times* and is soon to be a celebrity. You have become an artistic part of the city. You belong here now. It is simply wonderful. I am very happy for you."

"Thank you," she said, chuckling. "Now the problem is, how do I stay a part of the artistic scene?"

"Oh, you will do fine, just as you did on stage," I said. "By the way, you handled yourself very well. Weren't you the least bit nervous?"

"Terribly," she admitted, glancing past me at the other patrons of the restaurant. "Only toward the end of the Dohnány did I relax a bit. Then I was nervous again with the encores. I hadn't planned them at all. I think it went over well, though. At least, the audience seemed to like it."

"Well, this member of the audience certainly did. I've waited a long time to hear you play."

"Yes, you have. And I've waited a long time to play for you."

"Tell me," I said, and she looked up at me, "Doesn't it frighten you sometimes to think of the dangerous roads we have traveled leading from Budapest to New York? And then our meeting, as if our paths were destined to cross?"

"Alice, darling, you have expressed my innermost thoughts. I don't believe things happen accidentally. Sometimes, though, it takes awhile before we get to know their meaning."

The waiter came over.

"Alice," she said, "you must sample the sliced duck. It is the house specialty and it is the best in New York."

The waiter raised his eyebrows and I nodded. Magda also selected the duck.

"Anything to drink?" he said.

"I'll have some white wine, the house wine will do," I said. Magda ordered a beer.

There were no other tables occupied near us. Magda took a package of cigarettes from her purse, tapped one out casually and put it in her mouth. She found a lighter in her bag and lit the cigarette, inhaling deeply.

"Tell me what happened to you," I said.

"We were shifted between two camps in Germany," she started. "It was hell, as you well know. The cold was constant and the air raids frightening. We worked on the railroad tracks and that took its toll. I watched people simply topple over and die right there on the rails. No one helped them. Women aren't fit to do that kind of work, but that is all there was. Often, their bodies were just left on the rails. The next day they were gone, most of them anyway. One day, after a snow, we were working and I tripped over something. As I got up I noticed that I had fallen over a snow-covered body, a young woman who had been alive the day before."

Magda shook her head as if trying to clear it.

"By a stroke of luck I was transferred and got to unload trains in the last camp. That and do the labor in the barracks. The hours were endless. But that is not what we want to discuss with such a beautiful lunch coming, is it?"

"I only vaguely remember being in the hospital. I had taken ill in the camp in the spring and everything after that is a blur. My name found its way onto a list at one of the Jewish relief agencies and, with their help, Mr. Singer found me and brought me to America. He helped me put my life together again."

"It is a good life, I can see that."

"Yes. At the moment, it is."

The waiter brought the wine and beer and the duck.

"To us," Magda said, raising her glass.

"To us," I agreed.

Along with the duck was some sautéed cabbage and home-fried potatoes. We both tried the duck first. Magda was right.

"There are not too many people who go out of their way to help the less fortunate," I said. "Your Mr. Singer has to be an unusual human being. You must feel very indebted to him. I had my mother, thank God, to help me with the papers. Without a sponsor we might both be back in Budapest today."

"I know that," she said. "You should have heard Mr. Singer welcoming me to New York. He said 'You are a fine pianist, you are going to work hard, and you are going to get even better. I know you will live up to my expectations and reward me with music to a degree far beyond what I will ever do for you.' Then he kissed my cheek and wished me well. There was no preaching and no advice. And there was no ulterior motive. There was only humanity and warmth. He is a wonderful man. I am very, very lucky."

"You are that," I agreed.

We enjoyed the rest of our meal in silence. There would be a time, I thought, for questions. Now was the time to be absorbed in the sliced duck. What Magda was willing to reveal would come out later.

Something occurred to me as the waiter took our plates away. "Magda, I don't know how to put this. I think about you a lot and I am concerned that you have someone really close to you with whom you can share your feelings. Do you have a romance going? You are very beautiful, too beautiful to spend all your days working on a career."

Magda took a sip of beer and smiled.

"You probably won't believe this, but I rarely have time to think about romance. Perhaps I miss it, I don't know. But most of my days are spent practicing. To be the best takes work, hard work. Oh, I have an occasional date—at least I've had a few since coming to New York—but nothing serious. It only serves to make me feel guilty about being away from the piano. I've had the good fortune to have a second life with the piano, and I don't want to waste it."

She paused for a moment, then reached over and touched my wrist.

"That is not to say that if the right man comes around, I will shut him out of my life."

We laughed.

"Magda," I said, "you have become a very well-adjusted young woman and are to be complimented. From what I hear, I don't believe even the right man could separate you from your music. He might inspire you to give more depth to your performance. As for taking you away from the piano? I think not. You are a woman who knows what she wants and goes after it."

"And gets it," she said, not at all jokingly.

"You are also very level-headed. I don't think matters of the heart would stand in the way of your career decisions."

"Experiencing pain, persecution, and fear were a high price to pay for growing up. Maybe I am different now. Perhaps you are right. I think that difference consists mainly of being more careful. It is definitely the result of what I, and you, went through."

I looked at Magda for a moment and assessed her. She was something. Her dreamy air, that innocent face, and behind them a strongbox for a heart. She acted almost too self-assured. Her demeanor gave the impression of tremendous self-control. Just meeting her one would never guess at all the trauma in her past. Even I was puzzled. Could this Mr. Singer have had such a great influence?

Magda answered the unspoken questions.

"The truth is, there is someone else in my life now. He is not a young man in that context, though. He is a lifelong friend of Mr. Singer. He is a psychiatrist and his name is Doctor Lovas. Mr. Singer introduced me to him not long after I arrived in New York and we had a long talk. I have been seeing him regularly ever since. On a professional basis, I should add."

"Go on."

"Well," she said, looking down and smoothing her turquoise skirt. "I knew I needed help. At times my fingers simply gave up and would not play. I would get hysterically fearful that I would never play again and that I would disappoint Mr. Singer. Doctor Lovas helped me put the pieces back together again. And they fit. He gave me back my fingers. He made me believe in myself."

"How often do you see him now?"

"At first I was seeing him twice a week. Once he came to my apartment because I called him. That was at eleven-thirty one night. My hands felt as though they were paralyzed. Now I only see him once every two weeks."

The waiter came by with coffee. We each had a cup.

I contemplated what Magda had told me. Her success had to be due in part to her therapy. It was the result of a caring, professional doctor. She had bridged her emotional difficulties, the ones I was still experiencing. He had erased her doubts and sent her moving forward again. It helped that he was a friend of Mr. Singer and was available at all times. That help, in particular, was immeasurable. And Magda seemed forthright about the treatment. The results spoke for themselves. She had put the pieces together well enough to go on stage.

The whole thing convinced me even more that I wasn't improving, that the heavy weight I was feeling was not lifting. It was only growing heavier, wearing me down. I was an emotional invalid compared to Magda. Her disclosure opened up a new possibility for me.

Our coffee cups were refilled.

"Waiter, do you have that raspberry tart today? Perhaps we could share one with our coffees. Alice, I can't eat it all by myself. Please share it with me?"

I nodded agreement.

"Our little lunch was a feast fit for the Archduchess, and it is all because of you. So how can I say no?"

"Why on earth would you want to?" she asked. "Wait until you taste this."

When the waiter returned, he had already sliced the tart in half. He put a tiny plate in front of each of us. I saw Magda give him a bright, alluring smile. He paused for a moment before moving away.

"What is next in your blossoming career?" I asked, taking a bite of the tart. "Oh, this is delicious."

Magda nodded with another bright smile.

"Well," she said, swallowing, "there is a project we are working on, or at least Mr. Singer is working on, for an all-Hungarian composer's night. It would fill a whole evening and will be exciting. That is as far as we've gotten. I don't think I'm ready for a tour as yet. Mr. Singer agrees. He handles all the engagements. I wouldn't know how to go about it. It is the same with finances. I have a special account to draw money from for my needs, but all the financial and career decisions are made by him."

Again I marveled at the extent to which Magda was being helped.

We finished our lunch amid much yumming and grinning.

Against my objection Magda picked up the check.

"Please, it is my pleasure," she said, and left an overly generous tip.

"We sat there so long," she said. "We want the waiter to remember us fondly. Not like the parties he might have had. He'll be happy to see us again."

Magda led the way out and hailed a cab. When the first one sped by she placed a hand on her hip and her face showed exasperation. The next one stopped.

"Thank you for lunch," I said as the cab pulled up in front of my building and George came to get the door. "It was tremendous. The food, the friendship—everything was just lovely. You should let me return the favor, and soon. If your weekend is free we could do it then. Perhaps Mr. Singer could join us."

"Oh, I don't know when I will see Paul. But it would be delightful. I have told him about you. I'll call and let you know."

We kissed each other on both cheeks again and I got out of the cab. Magda did not glance back as she pulled away.

Going up the stairs to the apartment, I was overcome by a disturbing thought: I could never afford a psychiatrist. And the uncertain result could make the therapy drag on for years. It seemed to have worked wonders for Magda. Would it do the same for me? I didn't know. I did know that there was a benefit in being able to get help, day or night. And the simple truth is that the only promise of tomorrow comes with trying. I decided to make an appointment for the following Wednesday.

Doctor Lovas smoked a pipe. And he paced, back and forth, in the small office that overlooked a neglected garden. I could see that the diplomas, in contrast, was well kept and framed in glass. The case itself was spotless. There was a layer of dust on the one abstract painting that adorned the otherwise bare walls.

In the backyard some scrawny trees held up a child's swing. There was more dirt than grass. The random flower beds looked unattended. It was a forgotten area.

Oddly enough I don't think I ever met his eyes. And that is something I invariably do with gentlemen and ladies alike, in conversation. Not him. He remained a stranger to me. He didn't help me. He told me to sit down and that was his way of greeting me.

Doctor Lovas held his pipe in his mouth, giving him a pinched expression. He was about sixty, I guessed, dark and thin. He wore a tweed jacket and gray flannel pants. He looked more like a country gentleman than a doctor. In our brief relationship I never saw him in other clothes.

I sat on his brown leather couch, he in a matching armchair across the room.

It is very difficult, even today, for me to open up to strangers. It is embarrassing. I need someone I trust to tell my secrets to. So it was a while before I told him about my problems in getting acclimated and oriented to New York. I finally told him about my lack of confidence in getting a job. I told him about my dependence on my mother. I told him of my concern about finances, and asked if he would be willing to take me on as a patient. He eventually spoke, suggesting a down payment and whatever I could afford as we went along.

On my second visit, like the first, I opened up a little more. I told him about some of my experiences during the war and my work in the camps. I told my story of escape and my coming to America. I told him about my first feeble attempt to find work and the fear of harassment over my tattoo.

As with the first meeting, the doctor kept his input minimal. He greeted me by asking me to sit down and, after thirty minutes, told me we were out of time and asked if I would like to set up another appointment. I did.

My third session was exactly a week after I first set foot in the reticent doctor's office. When I came through the door, I was determined to wait until he addressed me. I sat, busying myself by looking at the abstract painting. I examined the brooding work in detail. It seemed even more remote because only a Tiffany lamp lighted the room. I could see only the painting, hear nothing, feel the leather of the couch, taste nothing, and smell only stale smoke.

The doctor, who had begun pacing shortly after I sat down, suddenly stopped in front of me.

"You told me that the remarks of people regarding your tattoo hurt you, right?"

"Yes."

"Well. I think you are using it. You like that tattoo. You like to bring it to their attention. You like it to win sympathy. You feel the world should be reminded of your suffering. You must be honest with yourself about this. You really like that tattoo."

When I leaped off the couch, the doctor took a step back and took the pipe out of his mouth. I spoke through clenched teeth.

"You are trying to manipulate me and it won't work. How dare you accuse me of being such a phony! You have no right and you are dead wrong. Dead wrong! The one thing I hate most in this world is pity. I don't desire that sort of attention. You have absolutely no understanding of the pain I carry constantly."

"Perhaps not, but the truth remains . . ."

"What truth! What truth!" By now I was shouting. "You don't know anything about truth. You simply sit there in your chair, smoking your pipe, and tell me that what I want is sympathy. Nothing could be farther from the truth. And nothing could be further from helping me than sitting here talking to you!"

I slammed the door as I went out.

Down on the street, on the spur of the moment, I decided I would pay the doctor one final visit. And I knew why.

I found a phone booth and called Mrs. Ferguson at the Red Cross. I had been introduced to her by my mother and had been assured I could call anytime if I needed medical help. Now I did. I told her what I wanted and she did not try to talk me out of it. That was to her credit and her prudence. Credit for not giving unwanted advice; prudence for not trying to stop me from trying the impossible. By the time I got home, the phone was ringing. Mrs. Ferguson had arranged an appointment for me with Doctor Orntreich.

Mother did not have to know what was going on and I did not tell her. I was confident Mrs. Ferguson would not reveal my plans to her. The next morning, at eight-fifteen, I was at 12 East 72nd Street.

I filled out the survey for new patients and was led into a spacious treatment room with a table in the center and the usual counter full of swabs and bandages and other tools of the physician. A nurse came in and said hello. A few minutes later the doctor came in.

He asked what I wanted and I told him. I also told him I would be unable to pay.

"That is quite all right," he said. "It is a small service I can perform for someone as courageous as you. It will be my pleasure."

In soothing tones Doctor Orntreich told me how the procedure would work and what was involved. He only asked once if I was sure I wanted to go through with it. I assured him I did. He left, and a few moments later, a nurse walked in and gave me a numbing injection in my forearm. Then, when the doctor returned, they both donned surgeon's gloves.

It was a mess.

Removing a tattoo in those days was something akin to using a scouring pad to remove several layers of grease on an old baking pan. The difference was that the tattoo took longer, and it bled and bled. Before the doctor was done, the local anesthetic they had given me had already started to wear off. The Germans had done an almost everlasting job of marking me. I was in the doctor's office for two hours.

When it was over the doctor and nurse wrapped my arm with

first a compression bandage and then a cloth wrap.

"Good luck," the doctor said, as he left the treatment room.

The pain of my arm began to rival the humiliation I had felt when the Nazis first marked me. At the time I was convinced the mark would last forever. Now, when I looked down at the white bandage, the pain seemed to ease. It was replaced by the discomfort of the here and now. I told myself that the pain would go away. This time I believed it.

Dizzy but victorious I hailed a cab. A half-hour later I was throwing open the door to Doctor Lovas's inner office. He was in front of his desk with his back to the door. He turned slowly as I approached. When he saw who it was, he seemed surprised.

Slowly, calmly, I raised my arm and held it by his face.

"Do you see this?" I spoke carefully. "Do you see this?"

He nodded.

"You thought you would be clever and manipulate me. Is that your method? To manipulate people? Are you a doctor of manipulation? If you are, then you have failed. For me, I think you are despicable. You are inhuman. You are not unlike those who put this mark on me in the first place. Well, now it's gone. And so are you. I don't need your sympathy and I don't need anyone else's. I brought myself back from hell and I won't let you push me back in there.

"In a way you did help me. Not the way you should have. Doctors like you make patients dependent on them for life. You had no intention of helping me. You just hoped I would be able to pay you in perpetuity. Tell me, doctor, how long would you have treated me if I failed to make the payments? Not long, I imagine. Well, you won't have to worry about it. I am no longer one of your patients."

The doctor was still standing there, his pipe halfway to his mouth, when I walked out.

I made it a point to slam the door on his so-called help.

Chapter XXXI

ALICE DUNN—NEW YORK

Need I say that my mother was not thrilled with what I had done? She did not rant and rave. On the contrary, she merely shook her head and lowered her eyes, giving me a slightly reproachful look like never before.

She was the stereotypical Jewish mother. Everyone who came through the door was offered food. She doted on everyone who was either sick or grieving. And she ignored anyone she thought had been foolish.

For three days she paid no attention to me whatsoever, except when politeness was absolutely required.

Finally, Monday morning, she went so far as to ask me where I had gotten the notion to have the tattoo removed.

"I had it done on impulse, Mother," I said. "It was just something that came over me suddenly."

"How did you know to whom to go, darling?"

"Uh-oh." I thought to myself.

"A friend, who shall remain nameless, recommended a doctor of dermatology, and he took the case free of charge."

The reproachful looks were back.

At least she had already made enough coffee for two.

The coffee, the July sunshine coming in the French window,

and the lessening pain boosted my energy level. The pain had been screaming for three days. Now, it had settled into a dull throbbing that sent a tingling sensation into my elbow every fourth beat of my heart. I didn't look forward to the coming Wednesday, when the doctor would change the bandages. But that was still two days away, and there was work that needed to be done, or to be found.

After half a cup of coffee I threw a raincoat over my house dress and went to the corner to pick up a copy of the *Times*. Mother had some muffins waiting for me when I got back and she served them with the first look of understanding I had seen since the weekend.

"What will Jerry say when he finds out?" she asked.

"It is none of Jerry's business. And who is going to tell him?"

"I thought you two were getting along."

"We've only seen each other a couple of times, Mother. We are certainly not engaged."

Mother fell silent again.

I scanned the classifieds, looking for something that didn't include the words "experienced only" in the notice. There was nothing. Just before my enthusiasm, flagged the phone rang. It was Magda.

"What a surprise!" I said when I recognized her voice. "I didn't expect to hear from you."

"And why not?" she said in mock hurt. "We are friends. I wanted to see how you were doing. How is your mother?"

"She is fine. And I am much better."

"Oh?"

"Yes. I visited with your Doctor Lovas and found him an ogre. No, darling, don't apologize. We just had a difference of opinion. But some good came out of it. I had the tattoo removed."

Magda did not know how to respond.

"Are you still there?" I asked.

"Yes," she said, sounding breathless. "Why? Why, Alice? Why didn't you confide in me? I would have gone with you, been with you. Wasn't it painful?"

"Yes. And it still is. Thank you for your kindness. It is something I needed to do alone. Even if you had known, I would not have let you come along. It was very spontaneous, anyway, and it was done in a hurry."

"Are you in a lot of pain still?"

"Not really. The pain is mostly gone. It is nothing I can't live with and I know this particular pain will go away. The other wasn't likely to disappear for awhile."

"I understand," she said, sounding sincere.

"I know you do, and I thank you for your concern. Really I do. Everything worked out for the best. It always does."

"Well, I'm glad you are okay and, if you think it is the best thing, then I am sure it is."

"For me, I think so," I said.

"Well, we must get together and talk some more and we must make it soon," she offered.

"I am sure you are busy, but whenever you can find the time I would be thrilled to take the famous pianist out to lunch."

Magda giggled. "Famous pianist, indeed," she said. "So you owe me a lunch. Let me call you and we will set a date. You are right: At the moment it is a busy time. I promise I will get in touch with you again soon."

"Splendid," I said. "Thank you so much for calling. Now get back to the keyboard and practice."

"Oh, you sound so like Mr. Singer," she said. "I promise I will practice. Goodbye."

"Goodbye."

It was almost a month after the concert and Magda still sounded as though she was walking on air. What a thrill it must be to be successful in the New World. I wondered if I would ever know that feeling.

Seated on the couch I could feel the day outside warming toward noon. The sky was cloudless and a hot day seemed imminent.

I was undaunted. There were new avenues to explore out there, and it had not been too hot a summer so far. Perhaps a walk in the fresh air, blowing the smog out to sea, would lead me in a new direction. It might at least take my mind off the throbbing in my forearm.

An hour later I had put on my make-up and a navy blue linen dress with a bolero and was out the door, my mother's farewell floating down the hall behind me.

Before I left I jotted down the names of a few department stores and their addresses. I thought on my walk that I might do a little window shopping and refresh my memory as to the current styles.

I was not disappointed. The creations of the world's most distinguished designers were displayed in the luxurious department stores of New York. Bonwit Teller, Bergdorf Goodman, Saks, and Bloomingdale's each exhibited samples of the latest looks in their windows, along with the promise of more inside. The windows had lives all their own. Scenes were created for each outfit. A mannequin in a fall cocktail dress stood by a bar. A businessman hailed a cab. You wondered if the mannequins really were lifeless. I went from window to window and made mental notes about the way a display should appear.

Strolling down West Fifty-Seventh Street, I came across a display at Jay Thorpe, a prestigious specialty shop at the time. I wandered onto the main floor and browsed. Near the front was a display of belts and a beautiful purple snakeskin caught my attention. The solid gold buckle glittered in the brightly lighted showroom. The eighty-five dollar price tag glared at me. I turned my attention the shoes and eventually moved on to lingerie and costume jewelry. Most of the items, I discovered, were equivalent in cost to what we paid for a month's rent in our apartment.

I made my way to the elevator and perused a rack of sweaters nearby. A salesgirl came over and stood a few paces away, gracious enough not to stare.

"Could you tell me where the personnel office is?" I heard my voice ask.

"Do you have an appointment?"

"No," I said firmly. "But I would like to talk to the manager for a few minutes."

The girl gave me a noncommittal look. "Of course, it's just up the elevator on the fifth floor. They will be able to help you there. When you come out of the elevator there will be a desk. Talk to the woman seated there."

She pushed the call button and in a flash the elevator door opened. It must have been waiting for me.

As I got off I faced a desk on the opposite side of a small foyer with hallways leading away to the left and right. There were fresh flowers in a bowl on the desk, irises that complemented the pastel decor. The wallpaper and carpeting had the same soothing shade of bluish grey, the doors were polished oak and so were the arms of the red leather-backed chairs scattered around the waiting area.

A girl, in a charcoal business suit over a white blouse with a ruffle at the throat, looked up pleasantly. "How do you do? How may I help you?"

"I would like to see the manager in charge of employment, please." I realized I was clutching my bag very tightly and I tried to relax.

"Is she expecting you?"

"No, she isn't. But if she has a moment I would like to see her."

The girl's smile never faded. She reached in a drawer and pulled out a piece of paper and a pencil and held them out to me.

"If you would, please, fill out the application and I will pass it along to her with the message that you are here."

"Thank you," I said, taking the paper and pencil and turning to take a seat

Before the receptionist had returned from speaking to the personnel director, my application was back on her desk. She picked it up, glanced at the form, gave me a long look, and then got up again. She took the application to a room down the hall. I waited, wondering if I had done the right thing. I thought I saw the receptionist grin slightly when she returned.

I watched the traffic in the administration headquarters of Jay Thorpe. People emerged from the elevator and nodded to the receptionist on their way to offices down every hall. Their steps were muffled by the carpeting, but one could feel their urgency. Telephones rang incessantly, though never more than two or three rings. I wondered if I would enjoy working here, given the chance.

"Miss Dunn?"

A tall lady in her mid-thirties was standing in the doorway of an office down the hall to my right. She was wearing a stylish pink tweed. I stood up and walked down the hall. As I approached, the lady extended her hand to me.

"Miss Dunn," she smiled, "I am Jane Allison. Please come

in."

She led me into an office dominated by a large oak desk that was remarkably free of paperwork.

"Please sit down," she motioned to the only available chair in the room, a cushioned armchair that stood away from her desk.

"Miss Dunn," she said, "I must admit I am curious, even amused. Let me put it bluntly, if you don't already know: Why on earth did you put only your name and address on the application?"

She had a bemused, yet puzzled, look on her face. It was a pleasant puzzlement. I took a deep breath.

"Miss Allison, first let me thank you for seeing me. I know you didn't have to."

She nodded and gave a quick wave of her hand.

"To answer your question, it is because I wanted you to hear my story personally, rather than read it on a piece of plain white paper. There is more to it that I could put on an application form."

Miss Allison sat motionless. Then she made a decision.

"Go on."

"Miss Allison, before the war I owned one of the most fashionable boutiques in Budapest. I designed all my own creations and made the selection of all of the materials to be used in the gowns and dresses. I did all my own publicity and all my own displays. I visited Paris and Vienna three or four times a year and bought some original samples. My clientele was diverse. I learned and mastered four languages so I was able to help them with their purchases. One of my clients was the Archduchess Katherine. What I am looking for is some type of employment in this field. I am hoping you have an opening."

"Well, Miss Dunn, you are overqualified, but you may have just created a job for yourself."

I must have been beaming.

"The board had a meeting just today and has decided to try precisely what you had in mind. Or precisely what you used to do and can help us with. We, too, have a lot of foreign visitors and not a few problems at times with communication. We think that a lot of sales are lost simply due to the lack of adequate communication. The board is willing to find out if that is really the case. I know this is out of the ordinary, Miss Dunn, but can you stay now? We will give you a trial run and a salary based on a commission. Let's give it a couple of weeks and see if we can enhance our sales."

By the time the other employees had started their lunch breaks, Miss Allison had taken me around the first floor and the administrative offices and introduced me to the people I needed to know. Then I was left to my own devices on the main floor to acquaint myself with the merchandise there. It would be awhile before I got off that floor—the ground floor.

At the end of the day I was still stunned that my brave, some would say, foolhardy, approach had landed me the job. As I was leaving it all came back to me. Prior to that I had been too busy to notice that I had actually secured a position with the company.

I had been concerned, as Miss Allison had shown me around, about whether I would be able to handle the job, or my fellow workers. These doubts stayed hidden while I studied the layout of the floor and its treasures and the seemingly sincere welcomes of my coworkers, when I encountered them.

By the end of that day, although I had worked only half of it, I was dead on my feet. Standing an entire afternoon was not something I was used to. I drew sympathetic looks from the others as we pushed through the doors onto the street. Searching my bag I found just enough money for cab fare home.

Over the next months it would not be cab fare I was paying out; it would be bus fare. After that first encounter I had dreaded getting back on the bus. At thirty-five dollars a week, though, you don't have much choice. And there was no way I was going to walk. If that first day taught me anything, it was that I was not used to being on my feet. The second and third days, and every one thereafter, reaffirmed that conclusion. Perhaps I had worn myself out with all the standing at the camps. No matter. All it meant was that I would collapse when I returned home each night.

Magda slipped out of my life again. She called now and then, sometimes when I was asleep in the evening, and when we talked we contemplated getting together. Yet it never happened. One of us was always busy.

So we missed seeing the leaves change together and feeling the oppressive heat of summer fade into the fresh, crisp coming of autumn.

Jerry and I did see each other, though not often. Almost casually, Mother would mention that he was coming over for dinner. She had invited him. He was beginning to carve out a niche for himself in the New York law community and was always as busy as I was.

In time I grew to like him and his occasional luncheon visits, when he would surprise me at Jay Thorpe. Gradually we closed the distance between us, the distance we both had put there at first, a little at a time.

The rest of the time I did my job as interpreter and helper in communication situations. Slowly I began to drift into opportunities where I could make my own sales rather than simply acting as a translator. Most of the time it happened when the other employees were too busy. For these sales I received a commission. Before long I discovered that commissions were a terrific supplement to my meager salary. Still I trod softly. Nothing had happened when the probation period had expired, but I still wanted to be careful.

I wandered about the entire first floor, looking for the undecided customer. Often I would approach someone and discover that she really was just shopping and spoke perfect English. The longer I worked, though, the fewer times I made that mistake. Most often, I simply made myself available to the other salespeople who encountered non-English-speaking patrons.

The first floor was the one with the most diverse clientele and the most traffic. It was there that the more modestly priced perfumes, colognes, jewelry, shoes, millinery, and lingerie were displayed. The expensive articles, from furs to genuine leather articles to evening gowns, were on the upper floors.

My chats with Magda dwindled to once a week, then once a month. It was mid-November before I remembered that I had now known her for more than two years.

Between Thanksgiving and Christmas Magda called and let me invite her out to lunch. We made a date to meet during my lunch hour, but she never appeared. Two weeks later she called to apologize—she had been caught up in planning something and had been unable to get to a phone. I was disappointed. Still, I agreed that we should meet after the holidays.

"I promise," Magda said.

It was a surprise when she kept that promise barely a week into the new year. She called not too long before the end of the business day, and offered to drive me home from work. We stopped for coffee at a café down the street from Jay Thorpe before finding a cab.

I felt somehow uneasy with Magda, and unlike with my other friends, I didn't feel comfortable telling her. I simply sat, sipping coffee and wishing I could take off my shoes. Magda, meanwhile, lit one cigarette after another, and stared vacantly into the distance.

"I really feel badly about us not getting together more often," she said, smiling weakly. "I know how tired you must be after work and that is the only time I really can get away from the piano. We must find more time for each other."

I took a stab at it. "I am not working this weekend," I said. "Perhaps we can do something then. Go to the park or something. Wait. Are you interested in a drive in the country? I know a friend who might take us."

Magda's eyes went blank for a moment.

"We'll see," she said. "I'll have to call you. It is only Tuesday. I will have to arrange my schedule."

"Whatever is comfortable for you," I replied, feeling defeated.

She smiled and lit a cigarette from the stub of another.

"Is something bothering you?" I finally asked when she waved off a second cup of coffee. "Is there something I can help you with? You know I'll be happy to try."

Magda laughed. "There is nothing, really," she said. "I'm, um, planning something, yes. There is someone I want you to meet. It is time we got out and 'recreated.' We are both working too hard, especially you. I will come up with something for us and someone for you."

"Of course," I said, trying to sound sincere. "But I need no one else. I have Jerry, and he is enough for me at present. Though I do appreciate the thought."

"Do you mean Jerry Adler?"

"Yes," I said, and suddenly I realized what I had said. "He is the one I thought might drive us to the country. No matter. If you are too busy we can make it another time."

Magda looked puzzled for a moment, then shrugged. We got

up and she made good on her promise to take me home. We made the trip in silence.

"Don't forget," she said as I stepped out of the taxi. "I will call you."

"I know you will. Please call me this week."

Magda smiled and waved.

I was puzzled. Mother even noticed it when I walked in. She gave me a searching look and I just shook my head. I could have been doing so in reaction to my meeting with Magda.

She had been as impersonal face to face as she had been over the telephone. Something, sometime, somewhere? A glazing over of what was and what was to be. She always asked how my work was and how my life was and finished each sentence with how busy I must be and how busy she was. I worried that she was working too hard.

Seeing Magda for the first time since the summer had taken me aback somewhat. She had appeared pale and wan. Perhaps it was the damp winter that was taking its toll on her. Had she always been so frail? I could not remember. There certainly could be no reason for it now. She was young and successful and her problems were behind her. There had to be something troubling her. Or I was seeing things that had no realistic foundation.

Again I found solace in my work. Mother was pleased that I had discovered a niche into which I felt I could fit. She had never doubted me and I knew that. She never presumed to say so. She was also happy that I was seeing more of Jerry. That she did mention on occasion.

Even with the small commissions I made, I could save little money. I began splitting the rent with my mother and used what was left to enhance my wardrobe and renurture my love of shoes. Actually, saving money was more than difficult. It was folly to try. And when sales were down, there was nowhere to start.

So I used the first floor at Jay Thorpe as a jumping-off point. I just didn't know where I would be jumping off to. Ironically, it was Jay Thorpe that provided me with the impetus to take the next leap. Success and failure came the same day.

It was a bright afternoon in late January and business was picking up again after the post-holiday lull. Six floors up it was really booming. Or it would have been, had they been able to find someone to interpret what an increasingly hostile Argentine couple was saying.

When I was summoned up to the land of Jay Thorpe Furs, I reckoned that my future with the store was sealed. In a way I was right.

An hour after I arrived on the sixth floor the couple had left with fifteen thousand dollars worth of sealskin, Russian lynx, and wild mink wraps. The entire staff on the floor seemed very excited, congratulating me and each other. For an unknown reason I kept silent about the commission I had earned. I didn't even tell my mother.

It is a good thing I didn't get her hopes up because, when payday came, my check was no larger than usual. I asked why I hadn't received a commission since I had salvaged a comatose sale. I was told that they were considering me solely an interpreter and that the person who originated the contact was receiving the commission.

Naturally, I was furious. I contended to Miss Allison a few moments later that without me there would have been no sale. The sale had been dead in the water when I arrived.

"I'm very sorry, Alice," she said. "But this is store policy and we cannot change it."

It was then that I decided on a change.

It was a coincidence that Magda appeared out of nowhere the next day. She seemed in a hurry this time, as well as being distracted. I thought at first I could get a suggestion or two out of her.

Magda had appeared on the first floor, where I still worked, and had looked wildly about before catching my eye. When she saw me, she walked briskly to where I was straightening some handbags on a display rack.

"Please have lunch with me, I have to see you before I leave," she blurted.

"Slow down," I said, trying to lighten the situation. "Of course, I will have lunch with you. Meet me at noon at Antoine's"

Magda looked at her watch.

"It is eleven-thirty now," she said. "You are sure you can make it at twelve sharp?"

I felt a twinge of annoyance at her tone.

"I will be there at twelve," I said. "Have you ever known me to be late?"

"I'm sorry," she replied. "I know you will be there. I'll see you there." She squeezed my arm and nearly ran out the door. Her pace caught the attention of another salesperson, who shot a quizzical glance in my direction. I shrugged my shoulders.

A half-hour later I pulled on my overcoat and wrapped a scarf around my neck against the early February chill. I jaywalked across the street, dodging traffic and looking for a sign of Magda at Antoine's. It was a small, crowded French restaurant where several of the patrons often took their lunch at the bar. I didn't spot Magda until I was well inside and waiting for the harried hostess to return. Magda appeared out of the crowd and came toward me beaming. She kissed my cheek and seemed to relax. It was obvious she had been there long enough to find a place for her coat. She was wearing only a simple white sweater and a brown leather skirt.

"There is a short wait only for the smaller dining area in the back," she said. I noticed the dark circles under her eyes. "The hostess told me we could be seated soon after you arrived. We could have had a table a few minutes ago but they had to give it to someone else. I didn't want to sit alone."

"I understand," I said, refusing the bait.

As we stood aside to let a young couple out of the door, the hostess beckoned us. We were seated and we both ordered the special of the day: *omelette aux champignons*.

Magda smoked constantly until the meal came and stubbed her cigarette out impatiently when the food arrived.

Only after the waiter was gone did she speak.

"I have to leave town," she said. I noticed how she met my gaze only briefly, then looked away. "There is an important meeting I have to attend. It is very important to my future."

"It must be, as nervous as you are. You look very pale, very tense. Are you worried about something? Is Mr. Singer all right?"

Magda gave me a long look. "Mr. Singer is fine," she said. "Everything is fine. It is just that we are getting ready for the big Hungarian gala I told you about and things are coming to a head. I am worn to a frazzle."

"It must be difficult, but I know how you have been looking forward to this night. When will it be? I'd like to go."

"Oh, Alice, I don't know if I can get you tickets or not. We haven't even secured a hall—that is one of the things that makes the planning so disjointed—but if you insist I will try."

"Magda, darling, that is not what I meant at all. I will buy my own tickets. I am just wondering when the concert will be."

"When? Well, we have two dates that we are looking at and two different sites. Both are in March. I will have to let you know when a date is set."

I wondered that there wasn't a firm date since the tentative event was barely more than a month away. I said nothing.

"Isn't the omelette wonderful?" she said brightly. "So light and yet so rich."

I smiled. "What pieces will you play at the concert?"

"I haven't narrowed down the selections yet," she said. "I am trying several different selections and will make my choice from them. I will have to make a decision soon. But not just yet."

"It is good that you are practicing."

"Oh, yes. More and more all the time. I fear that I may be practicing too much. Getting too mechanical. I will have to start concentrating on those pieces that I will showcase in the concert."

She pushed her plate away, the omelette she claimed to enjoy, only half-eaten.

"I am not really very hungry. But the food was delicious."

"Yes, it is. I'm glad we finally had a chance to get together."

"I'm glad, too. We may not get another chance soon," she said. "What with all the plans that have to be made, I don't know when I'll have another chance to relax. I really can't tell you any more about the concert because what I've told you is all that I know. Mr. Singer is handling the details."

"Well, let me know the dates so I can be sure to mark them on my calendar."

"I will, of course."

The waiter brought coffee. Magda glanced at her watch.

"How are you doing with your job?" she asked. "Have you gotten used to all the standing around?"

"As a matter of fact, I wanted to talk to you about my plans and see if you can offer advice."

Magda barked a laugh. "Me, offer you advice? Well, I will try.
But I doubt I can."

I wondered to myself if she really wanted to know.

"I am planning to go out on my own," I said. "Working for
someone is just not what I envisioned. I only really did it to get my
feet wet in the States and to earn some money. Now the store has
cheated me out of a commission and I am determined to leave. It is
just a matter of time. If you could help me in any way, if I could
count on you, it would be great. If you can't, don't feel obligated. I'll
understand."

"Of course you can count on me," Magda said. "I'll help in
any way you ask. You really should be on your own. With all your
talent New York will be at your feet before you know it."

"Thank you," I said, finishing my coffee. "I don't know what
I am going to do just yet, but knowing that you will help is a great
comfort to me."

"Anything," she repeated. Then, "Alice, darling, look at the
time. I really must go. I will get in touch with you when I return."

The waiter brought the check as Magda reached back to get
her coat off the chair. She eyed the bill as I picked it up. She was
gone before I could rise.

I paid the waiter and left a modest tip—Magda would have
been more generous, I thought. As I ran back across the street, I
wondered about my old friend and her urgent meeting. I also
wondered if she had heard anything I had said. I guessed that she
had thrown herself completely into the organizing of this
concert—doing more than she admitted—and was simply too busy to
pay attention to anything else. It would have been like Magda, the
Magda I had known, to do that. She rarely did anything halfway.

That did not keep me from being sad at her not really offering
her help. She merely acknowledged her willingness to cheer me on.
Before work ended that day, I decided that Alice Dunn was the only
person I could count on in this venture. It was as it had always been.
Nothing had changed.

The days had been growing longer. After work that day I
would have another hour or so of daylight before I would have to be
home. So I walked toward the East Side, the patches of blue sky

above the monolithic skyscrapers keeping me company.

I knew what I was looking for and was oblivious to the people rushing by. I thought of how ludicrous my plan was. I had no money, no connections, and no place to work. All I had was the feeling that an opportunity existed somewhere. Finding it was the main problem.

A few brave leaves were emerging on some of the trees on the street where I found myself. I wandered along the sidewalk, examining the turn-of-the-century architecture and the ornate wrought iron gates. One of the buildings, for the most part quite mundane, caught my eye. What was intriguing was the small sign posted in one of the French windows. It read: "Furnished Studio for Rent."

I stared for a moment, then shook my head and laughed out loud and continued walking up the street.

Two steps later I stopped and turned around to look at the sign again.

I retraced my steps and spied a sign in the hall pointing toward the caretaker's apartment.

As I went to knock on the door, it opened, revealing a small woman, similar in build to me, carrying a bundle of laundry. She was old enough to be my grandmother—from the number of wrinkles on her face—and I took her to be the caretaker. She had a handful of keys perched atop the laundry in the basket, all of them strung together on a long chain. When she smiled her wrinkles deepened but her face and features lost ten years. It was a radiant smile.

"Hello," she said, not at all startled. "I hope you are looking for the caretaker's wife. If you are, then she can put down this laundry for a moment and help you. I am Mrs. Stern."

I returned her smile. "I am Alice Dunn," I said. "I am, in fact, looking for the caretaker and I am pleased that I am able to relieve you of your burden for a few moments."

We both laughed and she turned to go back into her apartment.

"Come in," she said.

I followed her in and she placed the basket on the floor in the foyer. Then she tugged at the sleeve of my tweed coat and led me into the living room. I could smell coffee and could see the Bronx Provincial furnishings of someone who had come close to making it, but had probably been too nice.

"Let me get you some coffee," she said. "I just made a fresh pot and was going to have some myself. How do you take it?"

"Black, thank you."

She brought the coffee, motioned me toward an overstuffed armchair, and relaxed into a rocker.

"Now," she said, still smiling, "what can I do for you?"

"I am a fashion designer from Budapest and I noticed you have studio space. It is what I need to get back into business. I would like to inquire about it."

"Right to the point," she said cheerfully. "One sip of coffee and we already know our intentions. I like that. More women should be as decisive and less coquettish."

"Is it available for such a purpose?"

"Indeed it is," she said. "How is the coffee?"

"Excellent, thank you. It is wonderful and it takes the chill away. You are most kind."

"Think nothing of it. The whole building drinks my coffee. Some say I have a special blend. But it is just plain coffee."

"Perhaps it is in the way it is served," I said.

She looked puzzled.

"With such friendliness."

I wouldn't have thought that radiant smile could grow.

"You are Hungarian. I have a sister-in-law who is Hungarian. She is almost as charming as you are. I am going to enjoy becoming friends with you."

"I'd like that, no matter what happens with the studio."

"Good," she said. "The studio is in the front of the building. There is a window overlooking the street. It might serve for a small display of some kind. Who knows? We will take a look at it together."

"How much is it?"

"It is eighty-five dollars a month. We require a month's rent for security and would like references. Now that the finances are over with, let's take our coffee and look at it."

I nodded.

Stooping slightly—I thought at first it had been the laundry—she led me to the studio I could never hope to afford. She flipped through the keys on her ring briefly and came to the right one.

She pushed open the door and let me pass into a spacious oblong studio with a tufted couch, matching armchairs and a Chinese lacquered table. A faux marble fireplace took up most of what would be the west wall. The tones throughout were blue and gray, right down to the carpeting. Two long French windows on the south wall faced out onto Fiftieth Street. The windows were separated by the most important part of the decor—a floor-length mirror. There was a phone in the corner near the door. Away from the fireplace and French windows was a space large enough for a bed and another chair or two. There would be a screen there instead, and a workroom behind it. Suspended from the ceiling was a lovely antique chandelier that caught my eye.

"That is a lovely piece," I told Mrs. Stern. "Does the management furnish this?"

"No," she answered, her smile taking on a wry turn. "It belonged to the last tenant. He was in arrears when he left, quite suddenly, and we kept it as his last payment. I think we made a good deal. What do you think?"

"I have to agree, of course. It is beautiful."

"When would you like possession of the studio?"

I glanced at her, then looked around the room again, making some mental notes.

"If I was to rent I would have to have a few more pieces of furniture. For instance, I would need a small table for my sketching, another for cutting, and definitely more light and more chairs. Do you think that is possible?"

"Leave it to me," she said.

"By the way, Mrs. Stern, what are the dimensions of the room again?"

It didn't matter. We both knew it was mine.

"It is sixty by thirty-five feet, approximately. And it looks even bigger, wouldn't you agree?"

"Yes. It seems quite large. It's lovely."

She led the way back to her apartment for another cup of coffee.

"Tell me more about yourself," she said, both of us now sitting on the couch. "You said you were a fashion designer?"

"Yes. In Budapest," I said. "That was before the war. I had my own boutique. I designed and made my own clothes and would like to do the same here, though I'd probably start with taking in alterations. Tell me, do you think the management would allow me to put a small sign outside the building?"

"That would be no problem at all, dear," she said. "I'm sure a discreet shingle would meet with no objection whatsoever. Leave that to me as well."

"Wonderful."

"You know, it is really going to be nice having you here. And this will be a good spot for you too. The Waldorf Astoria is just around the corner and the people from there often walk down our street. It is an excellent location to start a business."

Everything pointed to my going ahead with the transaction. Everything but the eighty-five dollars and the security, an additional eighty-five dollars. We finished our coffee in silence.

"Mrs. Stern," I said as I put down my cup, "let me think this over. I just happened to walk up the street and this is all very sudden. I just need a little time to think and decide. Do you mind terribly if I call you later in the day, or perhaps tomorrow?"

"Take all the time you need," she said. "In fact, let me have your number in case someone else is interested."

She handed me a piece of notepaper and a pen and I wrote down my name and phone number. All the while I was thinking that I must get back to her before someone else stole my studio.

I walked down the street, noting the number of people who shared the sidewalk. There were many, and most were well dressed. I guessed many of them to be the patrons of the hotels on Park Avenue that Mrs. Stern had mentioned. It would indeed be a prime location, and I would not have to depend on my friends to get me started in business. It would start itself.

Mother listened to my plans and ideas patiently, and slowly became as excited as I was. She supported me wholeheartedly. In fact, she helped me select the jewels that I would need to sell in order to raise the rent money.

A day later, with a small loan from a cousin and the money from the jewelry, I paid the rent and located a small table for five dollars. The table was the only area in which Mrs. Stern had been unable to keep her promise. She decided instead to become my first customer. With her business and my studio, my table, and my mother's sewing machine, I was ready to start my new venture. Another day, and Jerry presented me with the sign that would go up on the outside of the building. It read, simply, "Alice Dunn —Alterations, Designing, Consultation." Mrs. Stern had pointed out a nail in the wall on my side of the front door to hang the sign. It was a shiny, silver nail.

I was open for business.

Chapter XXXII

REBORN CONFIDENCE

The small studio was a world away from my shop in Budapest. Then again, so was my newly found life.

That one room meant a lot to me. Especially on that first Monday, my official opening, when the excitement was still strong enough to ward off the trepidation. With excitement and pride I arranged white daisies and baby's breath in a vase on the mantlepiece over the fireplace. Mrs. Stern had shown me where the logs were kept in the back and two were now crackling in the hearth.

A friend in a thrift shop had taken time on Sunday afternoon to lend me a dressmaker's dummy and it now stood between the mirror and the entrance door. I draped some colorful fabric on her to give the studio a more businesslike appearance. Then I added several strings of beads. After all, she was a girl.

I had arranged to get some fabric samples from the stores in the area on consignment and spread them out with what sketches I had on my little table. Just before eight o'clock I stood at my door and inspected my new boutique. A world away, yes, but functional. I went outside to wipe off my sign with an old dust cloth I had borrowed from my mother. Then I went down the three steps to the street to give it a final inspection. Satisfied and excited, yet still filled with anxiety, I started back up the stairs.

"Are you open for business?" a voice stopped me in mid-step. I looked to my right and saw a distinguished looking lady, with a poodle on a leash, smiling at me.

"Yes, I am," I said grinning. "Please come in."

The small-boned lady with the chiseled features scooped up her dog and followed me into the building and into my studio. She was elegantly dressed in the timeless, reassured simplicity of the very wealthy. The only remotely ostentatious part of her outfit was a printed silk scarf that was tied over her left shoulder. Her pale blonde hair was pulled back to a knot at her neck. A hint of Arpège followed her.

"I am Alice Dunn," I said. "What can I do for you?"

"Pleased to meet you," she replied. "I love your accent. Are you Hungarian, by chance?"

"Yes, as a matter of fact, I am. How did you guess?"

"Our night concierge is Hungarian and he sounds just like you. I thought I'd take a guess. How long have you been in this country?"

"Not too long, really. Less than a year. I have only just opened my business."

"Yes," she said. "I have never noticed it before. That does not mean it hasn't been here. How long have you been open?"

"To tell the truth, it is only a matter of minutes. You are my very first client."

"That is wonderful," she said. "It is really a coincidence, and a happy one. I have some work that I'm sure you can do. By the way, how did you come to open this shop?"

"I was a designer in Budapest before the war. Now I want to begin again in New York. I am hoping to work for a private, fairly exclusive clientele. I know it will take time and, until I catch the tempo, I will have to plod along. Your visit is certainly most welcome."

"Perhaps I'll bring you good luck," she said, still smiling. "I hope so."

"So do I, Mrs. . . . I'm sorry, I didn't get your name."

"I'm terribly sorry," she said, meaning it. "Where are my manners? I am Nina Pulliam, Mrs. Eugene Pulliam. And I do apologize."

"Think nothing of it," I replied, taking her outstretched hand.

"And who is this darling creature?"

"This," she said, scratching the dog's neck, "is Ninette."

"Hello, Ninette," I said. "Do you have any little outfits I can make to fit you better?"

"I'm afraid she is not the slave to fashion that I am. But then, we have never taken her shopping. Perhaps she would be. Eugene would have a fit."

We laughed again. Hers was something between a giggle and a chuckle. Light, like a giggle, but from deep inside.

"Miss Dunn," she said, "it is fortunate for me that you are here. I have lost some weight and several outfits that I bought in California now need adjustment. I just don't feel comfortable in them anymore. Could you do some alterations for me? Do you have the time? I won't be in town long and I would like them before I leave."

"As I told you before, I have only just opened the shop this morning and you are my very first customer. I certainly have the time. But I need to see what must be done. And I need a fitting. Then I will know how long it will take. But it shouldn't be long in any case."

"Splendid," she said. "My chauffeur will drop the outfits off later and I will come in tomorrow for a fitting. For now, though, I must be on my way."

I thanked her at the entrance to the building and found once again that her handshake was firm.

As I watched her walk down the sidewalk toward Lexington Avenue, my elation grew. So did the doubt. I really wasn't sure whether she would send her clothes to me, or if she had just come by and looked the place over. Perhaps I had given too modest an impression. After all, she looked like someone accustomed to more luxurious salons.

Those thoughts haunted me throughout the day as my door stayed closed. The minutes and hours ticked by slowly. I worked on some sketches that I wanted to frame and hang over the fireplace. All the while I suspected that Mrs. Pulliam's chauffeur would not be coming.

"Excuse me, mum," a voice said. I had been concentrating so hard on the sketches that I had not even heard the door open. "Where shall I put these?"

A liveried chauffeur was holding more than a dozen outfits. I dropped my pencil and looked around frantically for a place for the clothes. The back of the sofa looked like a good spot.

"Lay them over the couch and I will hang them up immediately," I said, scampering over to help with the load. We folded the outfits, each in its own plastic covering, over the back of the couch.

"Will you be needing a receipt?"

"No, mum," he said. "I was not instructed to get a receipt. I am sure Mrs. Pulliam will take care of that herself. She instructed me to tell you that she will stop by in the morning. This afternoon she is very busy. Is there anything else, mum?"

"Mrs. Pulliam suggested to me that she will be leaving town soon. Does she live in New York?"

"No, mum. She lives in Indianapolis. We are rarely there, though. Business takes us to New York and to Phoenix regularly."

"What type of business is that?"

The chauffeur raised a single eyebrow, as though either puzzled that I didn't know, or wondering if he should answer.

"The publishing business, mum. Mr. Pulliam is the publisher of the *Indianapolis Star*. He also has several more media concerns in the Phoenix area. Is there anything else, mum?"

There was, but this was not the time to ask.

"No, thank you."

"Very good, mum. Good day," he said, and disappeared.

I looked at the dresses, suits, coats, and blouses, all bearing the Adrian label. I recognized it from the *Times*. Adrian was one of the most popular designers in Hollywood. It was not the only designer or merchandiser represented. I. Magnin, Galanos, and Estaves were also on the couch. It looked as though he had brought the woman's entire wardrobe for alteration.

"Mrs. Pulliam," I said to the shop, "just how long will you be in town?"

I didn't dare guess. She had said she lost weight. I would have to look at the outfits and see where they could be taken up. For the moment, though, I just reveled in the beautiful clothes and styles. I touched a red cashmere coat, the blouses, and the gowns. All of them except the coat were in muted, pastel shades. The fabrics, from silk to wool, were cut with a precise, stylish workmanship I hadn't seen since . . . other times. It would make the alterations easier. Even at that, it would take several days to finish it all on my own. The work would last well into next week if I did it all myself. I guessed that I didn't have that much time. It was still early enough in the afternoon. I went to see Mrs. Stern to ask if she had a copy of the newspaper.

She handed me the paper without a word and I opened it to the classified section. By the time I had found the ad I was looking for, Mrs. Stern had brought me a cup of coffee. I took the paper and the coffee back to my shop and picked up the phone.

It rang three times.

"Hall, hallow? You wish to talk to me? Here is Carmen Lopez."

"Yes," I said. "I saw your ad in the *Times* and I would like for you, or whoever placed the ad, to come and see me as soon as possible. Can you do that?"

"You should like for me to bring work?"

I began to wonder if she understood what I said.

"Listen carefully, Miss Lopez. Do you have a pencil? Please write this down. Come to 320 East Fiftieth Street. Can you find that?"

"Yes. Me come and bring work."

"Can you be here in an hour?"

"Yes. Me come and bring much work."

"Good. Good. My name is Alice Dunn. Come right in when you get here. I'll expect you about four-thirty."

"Yes. Me come. Bring work and friend to help. *Gracias. Muchas gracias.*"

As she rang off I wondered if she would find her way.

Mrs. Stern was standing in the doorway. "Congratulations," she said. "You must have had a pretty exciting start to your business. Don't worry about the girl. She'll be here."

I nodded a thank you to her and she disappeared.

As five o'clock approached I was fairly certain that Mrs. Stern had been wrong. But a moment later two Spanish-looking women peered in the door.

"Come in," I said, leaping off the couch. "Come in. Are you

Miss Lopez? Which one of you is Miss Lopez?"

"She is," said the taller of the two young women, both of whom had to be in their early twenties. The smaller of the two had a dress draped over her arm. "I am Miss Garcia. She wanted you to see the dress so that you can judge her work."

Miss Garcia turned and spoke to Miss Lopez briefly, and Miss Lopez held the dress out to me, smiling.

What I examined was the most intricate hand-finished garment I had seen in quite awhile. The workmanship spoke for itself. It was lace applique needlework on fine white batiste and it was flawless. I knew that Spanish women were renowned for their abilities in tailoring, but I was startled to find such talent in one so young.

"She did this?"

"Yes," said Miss Garcia, in English far better than mine. "She did all of the work."

Miss Lopez tugged at her friend's sleeve. Miss Garcia turned to her and again spoke very briefly. Miss Lopez answered with a smile. I answered in turn with a handshake.

Miss Lopez and I went over the details, including wages, and Miss Garcia translated for both of us. In a few minutes, at the end of my first day in business, I had a happy employee, and hope for the future. The number of times we both said *muy bien* told it all.

Carmen was waiting on the steps of the building when I got to the studio the next morning, shivering in a threadbare woolen waistcoat. I showed her where the logs were, helped her carry a few in, and let her take her time building a warm fire. She lingered only a little and then came and stood in front of the table where I worked. I put her to work tracing patterns on muslin. I did the first, then handed her the material. She nodded vigorously and smiled. I went back to my sketches.

At mid-morning the phone rang. It was the concierge at the Waldorf telling me that Mrs. Pulliam was on her way. I had hung the clothes in the walk-in closet built into the north wall of the studio. I opened the doors to the closet and again looked over the outfits. In another moment Mrs. Pulliam was at the door, but not before I made up my mind to visit both the daytime and the night concierge at the hotel.

It was nearly noon before Mrs. Pulliam and I finished going

through the wardrobe. I made notes on a legal pad of all the details, from darts to making a slimmer fit, to the removal of buttons to sleeves cut shorter so that the cuffs of a blouse might show. In one outfit we agreed to simply remove the shoulder pads and take up the slack. In another I talked her into leaving the shoulder pads in and taking the outfit with her.

"Now I suppose I should try them on so that you can get a better look at what you need to do," she said pleasantly.

"That would be awfully tiring for you, Mrs. Pulliam," I said. "I can see you are a six, and most of these things are eights. Why don't I just take your precise measurements and work from them? It will be much easier on you."

She never hesitated.

"That would be a tremendous idea. At Adrian's they have my figurine and sometimes I just call my order in ahead of time. It would indeed be much easier for me to do it that way."

I took her measurements and then draped the tape measure around my neck.

"It may seem silly to you—in fact it does to me—but I just have to be able to feel my clothes," she said. "And these seem to hang off me now."

"We will make them right," I said.

"I know you will," she replied. "Will you need me to come back for anything?"

"I don't think so," I said. "Those are very minor details that we have to take care of. If anything comes up, I can contact you at the hotel?"

"Of course."

"The only question remaining then is when you want them."

"If possible, I would like them by this weekend. Friday if you can. I know it is only three days away, but we are leaving on Sunday and I need time to pack. If you must, you can bring them over on Saturday."

I hesitated only a moment. "Friday afternoon will be fine," I said.

"Good. I'll tell you what: Call me when you are finished and if you can deliver them yourself, we can have a drink."

"How very nice of you," I said as she slipped into her

overcoat. "I would be delighted. I will call before I come to make sure it is convenient for you."

I saw her out onto the sidewalk and when she reached the end of the street she turned around and waved to me. Until then I hadn't noticed that she was without dog or chauffeur.

What I could not explain to Miss Lopez, I showed her in a sketch. She caught on quickly and my faith in her grew. For that first day we charged ahead with our mission. At the end of the day, though, I knew that Friday would come much too soon.

"Is okay," Miss Lopez said. "In morning I bring Maria, cousin, to help. Is okay?"

"Yes, *si*," I said. "Cousin Maria."

I sketched instructions for both of them. A buttonhole with the thread looping in and out of the small cut in the fabric. Or a scissor trimming fringes. Or hands holding the lace binding to the hem of a garment.

The drawings worked like magic. Carmen and Maria were like children caught up in a new and exciting game. They worked quickly when they caught on and followed my instructions to the letter. I was touched by their childlike innocence and their remarkable willingness to work. Carmen knew very little English, Maria none at all. The language of the cloth and the sketches were all the communication we needed.

It was a real salvation that Maria had arrived because I was able to do little of the work. Throughout the week people from the street stopped in and inquired about certain alterations they needed, and what prices we charged. It occurred to me that the question of money had never arisen between Mrs. Pulliam and me. I wondered how we would handle that.

While Carmen and Maria worked on Mrs. Pulliam's clothes, I met the people. Many of them already had material and wanted it transformed into an outfit. A lady in the building across the street wanted to have a dress finished. A dress she had crocheted. I felt myself settling into the neighborhood.

At the end of each day, I inspected the work that Maria and Carmen had done on Mrs. Pulliam's clothes. And at the end of each day I complimented them on an outstanding performance. Only then did they begin chattering away as they left the shop and bounced out onto the street.

Friday was no different. In the early part of the afternoon Carmen and Maria approached me together. Hands clasped in front of them, eyes lowered, they came up to my table.

"Maria finished now," Carmen said. "She go now?"

"Just a moment," I said. I got up and went to look at what they had finished. Everything was perfect. There was no way to tell that the garments had ever been modified. I went back to the table and sat down. Carmen and Maria trailed after me.

"Do you have another job, Maria?" I asked. "Does she have another job?"

"No. She no work. She no find work."

"Good," I said. Then I spoke, slowly, to Maria. "Can you stay and work for me?"

She looked puzzled for a moment.

"You, me, Carmen. Together," I said, pointing at each of us and then at the table. "We work here. All three of us. Okay?"

Carmen understood and gave a quick shout. Maria was still puzzled until Carmen chattered a translation. It must have been the right one, I thought, as they both raced around the table and hugged me. I set them to work on another alternation that had come in that morning and called Mrs. Pulliam. We made a date for six o'clock that evening.

The Waldorf Astoria stretches between Forty-Ninth and Fiftieth streets on the east side of Manhattan. The front entrance is on Park and the secondary entrance on Lexington Avenue. The Waldorf Towers on Fiftieth were just a half-block from my studio. Lexington, with its devilish traffic, had to be crossed to get to the hotel entrance, and with the help of the girls, we got all of the clothes across the street and into the lobby. The concierge escorted us to the elevator and pushed the button for the penthouse. When the doors opened, the butler took all the clothes and the girls, overwhelmed, backed into the elevator.

"Miss Dunn, won't you come in," Mrs. Pulliam chimed as the elevator doors closed behind me. She was standing at a door halfway down the immense foyer that ended with a window looking out onto Manhattan. She came forward and took my hands. The butler had disappeared.

"Come with me to the drawing room and have a glass of sherry. I know it has been a busy week for you. I hope even more that I predicted."

"Yes, thank you. It has."

Mrs. Pulliam received me as an honored guest. She led me into the drawing room and to an opulent beige and gold couch on which we both seated ourselves.

"Let's sit here so we can chat comfortably. Oh, I promised you some sherry. Excuse me a moment while I pour us each a glass."

She walked to the bar in the corner of the room and produced glasses and ice.

"Will sherry be all right?"

"Sherry will be fine," I said. Before she opened the bottle, the view from the windows beckoned me. I got up and walked over to see what turned out to be a breathtaking view of the city. In a moment Mrs. Pulliam joined me at the window.

"It is absolutely spectacular," I said. "I can't believe it. I live on the sixth floor and the view of the park is wonderful. But this is overwhelming."

"I must confess that after all these years it still does something for me, too," she said. "It is a unique panorama. I imagine there is nothing like it in the world."

"Do you ever tire of it?"

She handed me the drink. "Never."

I believed her.

We slowly moved back to the sofa in the center of the room. Flowers of the season were everywhere. I admired the earthy streak that had to be in this woman.

"Aren't you going to inspect the clothes?" I asked.

"Do I need to?"

"No."

"There you have it. Now we can relax." She tipped her glass to me.

"Tell me," Mrs. Pulliam said after sipping her sherry. "How did you come to America?"

"I spent the war years in Europe," I said, remembering. "My mother escaped before the war and I wanted to join her. She sent me the papers to emigrate and after the fighting was over I came to New

York. I had always dreamed of living in the United States."

"Did you do all of your studying in Budapest? I imagine you must have worked hard to have been, and to now be so successful."

"Not all of it was in Budapest," I said. "I studied in Vienna and Paris as well, and worked as an apprentice in my parents' shop in Budapest. Fashion really runs in our family."

"But Budapest is your home."

"It was."

"It is a beautiful city. We have been there and it was lovely, the people, the food, the mood. It was very romantic and the music never stopped. What a vibrant city. Would you care for another drink?"

"Thank you, no. I must be on my way. It has been a long day and, thanks to you, a wonderful week. It was kind of you to invite me up. I will remember the New York I have seen from your window."

"Well, in that case, I must have you back. Memories fade, you know."

"I'd be delighted," I said, trying not to sound too eager.

"Before you go I must have your bill," she reminded me, smiling.

I took it out of my purse. Every alteration, no matter how slight, was itemized, right down to the buttonholes and the cost of all the materials. She barely glanced at it before writing me a check. I put it in my pocket and she reached out to shake my hand.

"I want to thank you for getting the work done so quickly. I promise that the next time I will give you more warning and more of a chance to work without such urgency. For now, though, good luck in your business. I'm sure you will do well."

She saw me to the elevator. As I stepped through the open doors, she smiled.

"I will let you know when we get back. I'm sure that there will be more to do. And we need to get to know each other better."

"I look forward to it," I said. "Have a safe trip. And thank you again."

"You are quite welcome. Thank you," she said.

As the elevator eased down toward the ground floor, I marveled at Mrs. Pulliam's grace and demeanor. I was engrossed in the contrast between her and Magda. On one side was Nina Pulliam, thoughtful enough to invite a stranger into her home for a drink on the basis of a job well done. And showing a genuine interest in someone who was trying to make it in this world. On the other hand was Magda Fugazy, a friend, who had never in her life asked me to her house, who had virtually avoided me and prevented me from having any contact with her or those around her. Perhaps she was not comfortable with the good fortune and the luxury in which she found herself. Perhaps she was comfortable only with her work. Whatever the case, she had made herself scarce and we had met only in public places and at her convenience. I realized, as I stepped out onto the sidewalk, that Magda and I did not have much of a friendship. I wondered if I simply reminded her too much of the past and the concerts she had missed.

It was two more weeks, just after Valentine's Day, before I thought of Magda again. After glancing through the *Times* for any announcement of a fashion show, I decided to give her a call. Before I picked up the phone, the door to the studio opened and there she stood. Seeing me at my table, Magda rushed in and hugged me.

"How are you?" she asked. "Your mother said you were working and I could hardly believe my ears. But I knew you would put yourself together. You have always been so strong."

"Yes," I said. "And how are you? How was your trip? Is everything all right?"

"It's fine," she said, glancing briefly around the studio. "Not like Budapest, is it? Yes, the trip was fine. And the concert is coming up in the middle of March. It's just around the corner. I'll be doing five different major pieces. The reason I have been trying to reach you is that I want a different gown for each selection. After all, shouldn't the audience get something more for its money?"

"I suppose so," I said. "Here, why don't we sit down on the couch?"

"Oh, no," she said, pulling a cigarette out of her purse. "I can't stay. I just wanted to talk to you about helping your business." She lit the cigarette with a gold lighter.

"Look," she said, smiling mysteriously. "I want you to design one of the gowns to be a frame for this."

Magda reached into the alligator bag and lifted out a red velvet case. She opened the case to reveal a magnificent antique necklace. Rubies, emeralds, and diamonds were scattered with genuine pearls along a strand of white gold, fashioned by a silversmith in the timeless style of the old country. It was one of the real treasures of Hungary, a reminder of times when true craftsmen and artists used their talent and imagination to practice their craft.

"My God," I gasped. "Where did you get this treasure? Is this what that out-of-town meeting was all about?"

"Mr. Singer gave it to me," she said proudly. "It is more than one hundred years old. Isn't it fantastic?"

Of course she didn't expect an answer. And for a moment she even forgot her cigarettes. That didn't last. When the necklace was tucked back in its case and in her purse, Magda became fidgety again.

"Well, I really must be going. I have to get back to the keyboard."

"Magda, wait," I said, almost shouting. "You have to let me know how many changes you want. I have to select and buy material. To do that I will need money. And schedules for fittings have to be made. Come to think of it, I'll need measurements. You are not the same girl you used to be."

"Perhaps I am not," she said brightly, "but I can't talk now. I have a splitting headache. Just to outline it, I'll need six outfits. One for each piece and one for after the concert. I will leave the choice of fabrics to you. Call me when you need something and I'll come back. There is no hurry. It is still a month away."

"I will work on them this weekend. Come back and see me Monday morning. I want to do a good job for you and you will have to help," I said firmly. Magda looked at me, a wrinkle in her brow.

"Monday, then," she said, and her smile returned. Then she gave a little wave and was out the door.

There was no indication that she understood that she would have to buy the fabrics after the selections were made. Since we had been reunited there had been no indication of any understanding whatsoever. But I had to put my sensitivity aside and view Magda as a client. She was my second major account and I would have to view her as such. I could not afford any distractions. I hoped she would bring the necklace.

Magda called to cancel our Monday appointment an hour before she was due. It gave me a chance to remind her to bring the necklace and an advance for the materials. We reset the appointment for Tuesday morning at ten. Magda breezed in at eleven.

I ignored the affront and her fidgeting, and got down to the business of selecting the fabrics and styles and scheduling fittings.

"Would you pay attention to me for a moment now, please," I said. "We have four weeks. That's all. You must promise me you will keep our appointments. It is impossible to get these things right for your big night without doing what I ask. Do you want to look like an overdressed street urchin when you play? We should probably schedule your fittings for the morning before you practice so you won't be too tired to stand."

"Yes, that would be best," she said. "And I am sorry for having to cancel and for being late. There is just so much I have to do."

Magda's eyes wandered off into the middle distance. I made recommendations as to the styles and what materials to use and she neither nodded nor uttered an affirmation. That was all there was to it.

She kept her promise, appearing on time for the fittings of her gowns. She had not fought me over an advance check and she didn't fight me when I asked for a greater amount to cover all the materials. In two weeks the fittings were done and Magda's eyes were red. She came in for the final fitting with her hair dull and unkempt and her blouse in conflict with the suit she wore. We were in the final stages of the gown she would wear for her opening number.

"Magda, did you bring the necklace? We have to cut the neckline to curve under where the necklace falls below your throat."

She fumbled for a cigarette.

"Oh, Alice. I forgot it. Is it really necessary? You should have called to remind me."

We finished the fitting by guessing where the necklace would be.

Carmen and Maria were putting the finishing touches on the other outfits. I decided to try to get Magda's attention by showing her the almost finished products.

Magda suddenly became very demanding.

"Isn't this sleeve a little too constricting?" She hadn't even tried the gown on.

"This neckline looks too high."

"Are you sure we want white buttons with this? How about gold?"

There seemed to be no end to her criticism.

"Magda," I finally said. "Why don't you get some rest? Stop by in a few days, at your leisure, and see if there are any last-minute touches we need before the concert. It is only two weeks away. We need to finish so you can practice changing."

"I'm sure everything will be all right," she said. "I'm sorry, it's just that I am so excited. And everything looks so dreamy. It's going to be a wonderful night."

"Yes, it is."

When she bid me goodbye, our eyes hardly met. She was distracted by something. I had no idea what it might be. Her triumph was only days away. She should have been happy. It was probably just nerves, I conjectured.

One by one, Carmen, Maria, and I completed the work on Magda's gowns. The green taffeta turned out to be her favorite, with its yards and yards of fluffy flounces. She was also pleased with the sleek black silk dress with the slit to mid-thigh. It had been her idea, the slit that is, and I thought it would end up being her favorite. It was not. We changed the buttons on the red chiffon, taking off the white ones and putting gold in their place. Magda never noticed.

Three days later she was back and tried on every outfit. I noticed that she seemed far more relaxed that she had been lately, but I said nothing. Finally, Magda caught me by surprise.

"Alice, darling, I was thinking: We never had a chance to discuss your business. How is it going?"

"Very well, thank you," I said. "It will take awhile before it really gets going, but I already have a couple of accounts that will help in both regular work and recommendations. And my work speaks for itself. The future looks bright."

"I'm so happy for you," she said.

It almost seemed like she meant it and I chided myself for feeling let down by her lack of offers of help. I was on my own but

I was confident. I really needn't blame her, I thought, being preoccupied with her own success. I was truly disappointed, though, in her lack of caring. She no longer had the charm of that young prodigy I had once known in Budapest.

"The wonderful client, my first, got me off to a good start, a busy start at that. And now your orders are certainly going to be a boost. They should be done by the end of the week. That will give you a whole week to get comfortable in them before the concert. Would you like to pick them up this weekend and we can settle our business?"

Magda suddenly turned pale and began glancing around the room.

"Are you all right Magda? You look troubled."

"No, I am fine," she said, a little sharply. "All the rehearsals have made me jumpy. And you . . . you have just reminded me how close we are to the concert."

She forced a smile and I answered in kind.

"Perhaps you just have a small case of stage fright. You will be fine. The audience will love you."

"And the gowns," she said.

After Magda left I sat down to catch my breath. Carmen and Maria glanced at me occasionally. I had noticed their gestures while Magda had visited, and the rolled eyeballs. I couldn't chastise them because I could hardly disagree with them.

The telephone startled me.

"Hello, Miss Dunn," the voice said when I answered.

"Yes? How may I help you?"

"This is Paul Singer. How are you?"

"Why, Mr. Singer! How pleasant of you to call. I have heard a great deal about you from Magda and have wondered when we might meet."

"Well, if I could impose, perhaps today? I am in the area and, if it won't disturb you, I would like to stop over and see Magda's gowns. I understand they are almost finished."

"I'd love for you to come. Of course it would be no bother at all, not for me, anyway. I hope you will excuse my humble little shop."

He laughed a rich, glowing laugh.

"From what I've heard, the humble is what you use to counterbalance the beauty of your designs."

"Thank you. You are very gracious," I said. "Whenever you wish to stop by will be fine with me. Do you have the address?"

He assured me that he did.

"Fine. We will be waiting for you."

"We?"

"Yes. Carmen, Maria, and myself. It is a busy little office. Much of the credit for that goes to you and Magda."

"Very glad to help," he said. "But it was Magda's idea. And I'm certain she made an excellent choice."

"I look forward to your opinion," I said. "See you soon."

"Thank you," he said, and rang off.

"Finally," I said to myself, "I will get a chance to meet this man."

There was no time to look through the paper for notices of the concert. No sooner did I correct my lipstick and brush my hair than the door opened on a medium-sized man wearing a tweed coat and hat, dark slacks, and black shoes. He showed graying hair at the temples and a gray mustache over a strong chin and full lips. His eyes were ice blue. He stepped inside the door and closed it gently behind him as I approached.

"You must be Mr. Paul Singer," I said, extending my hand.

"And you," he said with a perfect smile, "must be Alice Dunn. It is a pleasure to meet you."

"The pleasure is all mine."

"Please forgive the intrusion," he said, "but I simply had to see the gowns before the audience does. I hope you don't mind."

"How could I?" I said.

One by one I brought out the gowns. Mr. Singer sat on the couch and inspected every one dutifully. He had pulled off his coat to reveal a maroon blazer over a gray shirt and tie. His coat and hat sat next to him on the sofa.

He commented on each creation, smiling all the while.

"I admire your taste and your ability," he said, letting the hem of the purple chiffon float like a cloud over his fingertips. The silver and gold brocade shift drew an admiring "mmmmm."

"Perfect for under the strong stage lights," he said of the green silk taffeta.

When I brought out the white satin gown with the shoulders and hemline trimmed in white mink he held a finger against his lips and the twinkle in his eyes brightened. This one he did not comment on. He simply nodded and smiled.

By the time I returned after hanging up the last gown, Mr. Singer was on his feet and his coat was on.

"Magnificent," he said. "Truly magnificent. You are an artist. Tell me: Do you do clothes for men?"

"I'm afraid not," I said. "But then, you already have an excellent tailor."

"Yes," he said. "But not one so imaginative or so gifted."

"Thank you," I said.

"Miss Dunn, it has been a treat. Magda will come in and take care of the bill, herself, if you don't mind."

"That will be fine," I said. "Would you like a copy?"

"No, that won't be necessary. Again, I'm sorry to have disturbed you. Good luck in your future business. After Magda's appearance at the concert in these gowns, I doubt luck will have anything to do with it."

"I hope you are right," I said.

At the door Mr. Singer paused, then he took my hand and kissed it in the old-world style. I had met a perfect gentleman, low key and charming; a man with the assured style and bearing of the affluent. I thought Magda a very lucky young lady indeed.

Chapter XXXIII

TIME-TESTED LOVE AFFAIR

Another man had entered my life. Not a wealthy man by any stretch of the imagination. At least not in material things. Just the same, he was a man worth the wait.

Jerry, as I had come to know him after that brief meeting at Magda's first concert in America, had come into my life slowly. An occasional lunch date, dinner once in a while, perhaps a movie or concert now and then. It was a relationship that grew with time and on my terms and his.

When we first started seeing each other, Jerry had been frank. Just back from the other side of the world and the Japanese war crimes trial, he had little to offer. And he said so.

I had less, and was able to admit that to Jerry, and more.

Yet he was a man who inspired a feeling of confidence almost immediately. So when Mother found out about our budding courtship, she helped things along by finding excuses to invite Jerry for dinner.

The rest was left up to us.

Though candid in some areas, Jerry was guarded in others. He was a quiet man with an expression of complete control on his face at all times. The challenge to me was getting to know the man behind that mask. It turned out to be a most pleasurable experience.

It really began not long after that first concert. Jerry simply appeared at Jay Thorpe—Mother must have told him where to find me—and took me to lunch. It was a short meeting but one that suddenly found me brimming with expectation.

Other lunch invitations were sporadic at first, then grew more regular as the days shortened. I found myself wondering when Jerry would be around to surprise me again—he never made a date, he just appeared—and on the other hand questioned why I was so eager to see him.

Was I too eager? I didn't pursue the matter. That in itself was a kind of relief for me, once I realized it. I had been without a suitor for many months and had denied myself any prospects for the future. Now I had tested my wings in New York and found them capable of sustaining me, at least in the business world. Jerry seemed the right medication for that other part of my life.

It was on a crisp December evening that Jerry nudged me over the edge. Rather, he let me walk to the precipice and see that I had nothing to fear.

He had met me at the end of work at Jay Thorpe and had invited me to dinner. By this time I had become accustomed to his way of showing up out of nowhere, and the idea of a night out with him was more than a little attractive.

We went to Csardas, a well-known Hungarian restaurant where they greeted their patrons with gypsy music and knew Jerry by name. We took a table in a subdued corner of the room where we could see everything, but few could see us.

It turned out to be a very long evening. Jerry, whose sparkling brown eyes never left mine, was a good listener. He spoke very little until I realized that I had told him everything about my life over the years and had learned very little about his. All I knew about Jerry Adler, really, was that he was an attorney, had worked at the war crimes trials in Japan, and that I trusted him implicitly.

"There is little more to tell," Jerry concluded. "I have only been back in the States a few months, only weeks when we first met, and now you have come into my life. I consider myself very fortunate in that regard."

"That's very sweet," I told him. "There must be more, though. Your life didn't begin with your trip to the Orient."

"No," Jerry laughed, "I suppose not. But it is very uneventful compared to yours. The life of Alice Dunn seems, and is, far more interesting than the life of an attorney in his early forties, who is still trying to find his niche in life."

"Just the same, I would like to hear about it."

"Perhaps another time," Jerry said, and I nearly scowled at him. "Right now, though, I believe they are trying to close this restaurant. We'll have to leave."

It wasn't long after that date that I left Jay Thorpe. Jerry had little trouble finding me, though. If he had a question, he could always call Mother. She was more than willing to help nurture the relationship.

Once I opened the studio, Jerry called every day. It is to his credit that he did not interfere with the workings of the business or my decision to go ahead with it. He did volunteer to look over the lease papers and all the contracts I would sign during the life of my business. But he stayed out of it. He offered no unsolicited advice, kept his reservations private, and, I believe, he must have crossed his fingers, hoping it would succeed against the existing odds.

As it happened, my own success preceded Jerry's. Thankfully it had no effect on our relationship.

One day he came by around closing time and picked me up, offering to take me home in a cab. I was delighted.

At Central Park, Jerry stopped the cab and we got out. I could see something was troubling him as we walked around the reservoir.

"I must talk to you," he said. I waited.

Haltingly, in his low-key manner, he related the problem.

"Alice, I don't know how to say this or how to proceed once it is said, so I will just go ahead. What I want to tell you is that I am falling madly in love with you. But at the same time I have no right to take up your time, to prevent you from seeing other people."

I tried to stop him, but was unable to.

"Look, I have nothing to offer you. You know that. I am just now starting to get on my feet. It is going to take some time before I can provide for you the kind of life you once had, and the kind of life you deserve, the kind of life I want to give to you."

It was nothing he had not told me before and it was a great deal more of his feelings than he had ever previously revealed. I wasn't exactly sure what he was alluding to.

I admired Jerry for his intellect, his warm heart, his compassion, and his honesty. There was, and never had been, any pretense between the two of us. I interpreted what he said to mean that he did not want to make a commitment, did not want to tie me down.

I was most afraid that he might be suggesting we break off the relationship completely. Though I did not feel quite ready for anything more serious—even though my feelings for Jerry were approaching what he felt for me—I was horrified at the thought of not being able to see him.

"Jerry," I said softly, "you shouldn't worry. A man of your intellect and ability has the whole world in front of him. Your time is coming."

"Yes," he said. "I do believe that. It is all in the future, not the present. Therein lies the problem."

"Well," I heard myself saying, "I'm here. And I'm not going anywhere. Perhaps I can bring you luck."

I recounted the tale to my mother that night at supper. She could tell that it disturbed me to a greater extent than I was willing to admit. Yet she said little. But I knew what she was thinking. Her time to speak was not far away.

Chapter XXXIV

GROWING SUSPICION

Just as Jerry allowed me to run, or refused to interfere in, my own business, he also left my friends to me. His friends were his and became acquaintances of mine. My friends were mine and became acquaintances of his. Those friends we made together were ours together.

But Magda was mine alone.

On the Thursday before her concert a cab was parked in front of my studio as I arrived for work. It was a typical New York taxi—the bumper dingy with soot from the exhaust, snow tires still mounted in case of a late flurry, scraped fender on the passenger side, paint peeling around the door handles, no hubcaps. Someone had scrawled "WASH ME" across the back windshield, etching the letters in the grime.

Magda got out of the cab as I turned up to my building. I stopped with one foot on the steps.

Magda could have been the driver. As she walked slowly toward me, she fidgeted with the top button of her wrinkled shirt. As she did so my eyes fell on her fingernails. Once long and flashy they were now chewed to the quick. She had pulled her black hair back in a knot and a few strands escaped to hang in front of a face without make-up. Her skirt was creased as though it had been slept in. I took her arm and led her up the few stairs and into my studio.

"Are you all right? Is something the matter?" I asked, as I closed the door to the studio behind us.

"No, no," she said hastily, "I'm just exhausted from all the goings on. And I might have a touch of a virus, a stomach flu of some kind. Maybe it's just nerves. I'll be all right for the concert Saturday."

I shed my scarf and struggled out of my coat. Magda did not move away from the door. She just lit a cigarette.

"I'm sorry I haven't been by to see you, to congratulate you personally, but we have been so busy. Are you happy? You look it."

She gave me a chance to nod.

"The reason I'm really here is I'd like to just pick up the gowns and get back to rehearsing. Do you mind if I come by to pay you for them tomorrow?" she asked.

I looked at her eyes, puffy and a little pink.

"That's fine, Magda," I said, and I went to the work area to get the gowns. Each was wrapped and hung individually. I brought them to her. She still had not moved away from the entrance. She opened the door and then reached out for the dresses. I handed them to her and she took two of the five off my arm. I followed her out the door and together we smoothed the outfits into the back seat of the taxi. The driver was smoking a cigar and watching the meter. I imagined he must have been smiling. Magda closed the door to the back seat and took a step forward.

"Are you sure everything is okay?" I asked again.

"Just fine," she laughed, blowing cigarette smoke into the crisp March air. "I only need to get through this weekend."

I nodded and she leaned over and kissed me quickly on the cheek.

"I'll come by tomorrow with a check," she said as she got into the cab next to the driver. "God bless."

I managed a smile.

I didn't believe that everything was all right. But I did not feel there was anything I could do to help. Magda had chosen not to share with me whatever was bothering her. That was strictly her business. She had her life and I had mine. The extent to which she needed my help now was in providing her with a way to look good for her audience. So be it. It was impossible for me to help if I wasn't privy to what it was that had her at such loose ends.

Perhaps Mr. Singer knew. But it would be presumptuous to impose my worries about Magda on him. And it would be quite deceitful to go behind her back. No, there was really nothing else I could do.

That is not to say that I didn't want to help. Only a few times since the war had I felt in a position to help someone; that I had the capacity to help someone in an emotional way; help to take off the pressure, whatever it might be.

Perhaps Magda just thought she was being noble to suffer in silence. Maybe it was just a case of nerves. If so, then she was carrying it to the extreme. But then, I had never before seen her this close to a major concert. It could well be the way she always behaved under such circumstances. After all, how many times had she been in this position before. Two? Three? Only three that I was aware of. And only this time was I privy to the preparations this close to the final act.

I reassured myself that it was simply a case of stage fright.

"You are okey-dokey?" It was Carmen; I hadn't seen her come in. Her inquiring look told me I must have had a peculiar expression on my face. I smiled.

"I'm fine," I said. "Is Maria with you?"

"*Si*, Maria coming now."

"Good," I said. "We have a new order that came in yesterday after you both left. The sketches and instructions are here on the table. The order involves fabric we already have, so there's no need for delay. We can go to work immediately."

Carmen nodded as she looked over the sketches and instructions I had handed her. They were mostly illustrations of what was to be done. Occasionally she would stop and hold one out for me if she didn't understand, and we would try another explanation. But I had discovered that when she nodded acquiescence, she really did understand. I had complete faith in her.

Maria breezed in a moment later and waved to me. As she peeled off her coat, Carmen began chattering a repetition of the instructions, and the two walked to their work table together. I was left again to my own thoughts and work.

There was plenty to do, plenty to keep my mind occupied. I phoned to pay my respects to the daytime concierge at the Waldorf. He had been responsible for sending me the last order, and I wanted to thank him as soon as possible. I would thank him more properly with a gift later.

When I dialed the number there was no answer. I thought that strange until I realized I had dialed Magda's number by mistake.

I laughed at myself, drawing a snicker from the girls, and flipped through my address book for the number at the Waldorf. This time I got through and was able to thank the concierge, who promised me that there would be more customers in the future.

Throughout the morning I checked my inventory and tried to balance my desire to come up with new creations against the more important balance sheet—what business I could count on. The venture was still new and revenues did not yet match ambition. I would have to wait on a number of things. I even figured Magda's payment into the equation and knew it would allow me some leeway, at least as long as I had new customers coming in. I wasn't yet totally optimistic.

Jerry had offered whatever financial help he could lend. With his new career though, that was minimal. And we had both decided that this was something I should be responsible for on my own.

I considered how little I had told Jerry about Magda. What could possibly be on her mind? Perhaps the same problems that had almost felled me, were finally catching up to her. Perhaps in her case the nightmares had been delayed, and were only now catching up with her.

No, that could not be it. We had both been shipwrecked, victimized, yet she had bounced back long before I had. At last she seemed to need my help and I was disturbed that I felt impotent. Whatever it was, she was internalizing it. That, I knew from experience, was the worst solution.

Carmen and Maria suddenly stopped working. I watched as they walked over to the coat rack and picked up their wraps. Then each fished a small brown bag from a pocket. I looked at my watch. It was noon, time for lunch.

I thought of how hard it had been for me to survive. Not just the Holocaust, but the fear, the wondering, and the questioning that had accompanied my survival. The self-doubt about what I was still doing here. It had been a minor miracle for me, it seemed, to get this far. Now it was time to help someone else. But there was no one to help. Or no one willing to let me try. I did not resent Magda for denying me this chance to complete my recovery. I was simply puzzled as to what she was hiding, and why.

I checked on the orders we had obtained and their various stages of completion. Some needed only a particular style of buttons, already ordered. Others needed this type of backing or that type of lace. Carmen and Maria had done wonderfully and had been an asset to my new business. I felt fortunate to have them working with me rather than for someone else.

Magda was just as fortunate, perhaps more so, I thought. She had the considerable resources of Paul Singer backing her, helping her along. His was the invaluable help of financial as well as emotional support. Then again, perhaps that was what Magda was lacking. Perhaps it was only financial help she was getting from Singer. I knew so little about their relationship. Perhaps she might well be feeling very much on her own. Maybe she needed a little nudge, a little reassurance in the right direction, maybe a little advice. I resolved to call her and try once more.

I never got a chance to make, and subsequently regret, that phone call. Less than two minutes after Carmen and Maria bade me farewell that day, Magda came through the door.

If she had seemed unkempt when I saw her last that morning, she was now a total wreck. Her hair had pulled out of its knot and hung randomly around her face. Her eyes were red slits, swollen and ugly. She wore the same pale yellow blouse and crumpled brown leather skirt as she had that morning. Only this time, the blouse was just barely tucked in and she made no effort to hide her appearance.

Only when she inhaled did I realize that she was crying. Chapped lips pressed together, she sucked in air and exhaled in a low whine, almost a hum, as she stumbled toward me. I was afraid she might collapse in the middle of the studio.

I raced to her, put my arm around her, and led her to a chair by my table. I still had some coffee in a thermos and reached for it.

"What happened?" What is going on, darling?" I said, more stunned than when I had seen her in that hospital. I twisted the cup attached to the thermos and removed it. The contents were still steaming. I poured her a couple of swallows; I didn't want her to spill the coffee I placed in her shaking hands.

Until I moved the cup close to her mouth, Magda seemed frozen in place. She just stared straight ahead, out the window facing the street. It was not as though she was searching for something, she was just in a trance.

Magda took the cup from me and held it in front of her, resting her elbows on the arms of the chair. Tears streamed from her eyes and ran down her cheeks.

I knelt beside her and put my arms around her shoulders.

"What has happened?" I asked softly. "What has happened to you?"

"It's over," she whispered.

"What is over?"

Magda leaped to her feet and threw the coffee cup across the room.

"It's over!" she shrieked at the window. "It . . . is . . . all . . . . over! Don't you understand? Over! *Finis! Végem van* (I am finished)! Kaput! There is nothing more. The concert has been canceled. I am finished. There is nothing left for me!"

"Magda, darling," I said, worried at her strange behavior and appearance as she arose from her chair trembling, her fists clenched. "Magda, it is not over," I tried to reassure her. "There will be more concerts, other concerts. You have come too far to be stopped now. What is happening? Please confide in me."

"There is nothing to tell," she growled, her jaw tight. "The concert has been canceled and my career is at an end. That is all there is to it."

Magda pulled a pack of cigarettes out of the pocket of her skirt and shook one out. She lit it, using a match from an aging matchbook.

I went to the washroom in the hall for a wet cloth and she was still staring out the window when I returned. I took her elbow in one hand and placed my other hand against her back guiding her back into her chair. Then I dabbed at her forehead with the wet cloth.

"Why is it all over? Tell me what has happened. It will do you good to confide in someone. Perhaps it is not as bad as you think."

She snorted. "Do you have an ashtray?"

"Yes, just a minute." I found one.

When I got back, Magda had stopped crying but continued to shake visibly. I dragged a chair from near the work table and sat down in front of her. She just looked past me out the window. Now, it seemed, she was looking for someone. Her eyes were focused again.

Then she looked at me.

"Please don't tell anyone I was here," she said, smiling. "I don't want anyone to know I was here. Or anyone to know that I am here. That is why I waited until your helpers left. I want this visit known only to you and myself."

"Of course, darling. That's fine. Now tell me what is bothering you."

I watched her thinking and saw the tears coming again. I handed her the cloth, and as I did, the phone rang. Magda jumped as though the ring had been a gunshot.

"You promised," she said fiercely as I rose to answer the phone. "No one must know."

"Don't worry," I said. "I will keep my word."

The phone rang a third time before I reached it.

"Alice Dunn, alterations."

"Miss Dunn," I heard, and immediately recognized Paul Singer's voice. "Forgive me for disturbing you. Do you have a moment?"

"Yes," I said, making a mental note of the obvious strain in his voice. "Of course, Mr. Singer, what can I do for you?"

Magda was waving her arms in front of her.

"Well," he said, hesitating, "it is Magda. Is it possible she has been by there today? Have you seen her?"

"Of course," I said, trying to sound reassuring. "She was here earlier to pick up the gowns. This morning, actually. She seemed a little nervous about the concert, now that I think about it, but otherwise she seemed fine."

"So she has been there?"

"Yes. This morning."

"But not since then?"

It was my turn to hesitate.

"Mr. Singer, you sound very troubled. What is wrong?"

"Nothing, I hope," he said. "It is simply that she has vanished. You are the only person I can locate who has seen her today. Other than yourself, she hasn't been seen by anyone, including myself."

"Well, she is a big girl. Perhaps she is just walking off a little early stage fright."

"I'm afraid there may be more to it than that."

Quite by reflex I turned my back on Magda.

"Now, what else could it possibly be? I'm sure it's just a case of nerves."

"I certainly hope you're right."

"Of course I am. Have you tried her apartment?"

"I am there now," he said gently. "It does not look like she has been here for some time. Miss Dunn, I am really worried."

"Mr. Singer, why don't you level with me? Perhaps we can both help her, if there is really something wrong."

"I am not sure there is a real problem at all," he said.

"Then why the concern?"

I heard him take a deep breath.

"Miss Dunn, how well do you know Magda?"

"I have known her since before the war. I designed and made the gown she was to wear for her very first concert for the Archduchess Katherine."

"I see. How much do you know about her experiences in the camps? Were you and she in the same camps? She has never related anything about it to me."

I was reminded of how little I really knew about the time between last seeing her in Budapest and then finding her in the Red Cross hospital.

"I know very little about those times," I admitted. "At least about what she went through. What does that have to do with her problems right now?"

"I believe that something terrible happened to her in one of those camps, and that the recall of those events, as Dr. Lovas is helping her to do, is haunting her. You know, affecting her mentally. I must find out what those ghosts from the past are, so that I can prevent them from annihilating her. But so far she has been unwilling, or unable to confide in me. And of course, Dr. Lovas cannot breach his professional confidence with Magda. I'm very much afraid that unless we can help her deal with those memories, she won't survive them the second time around."

I was stunned by his analysis. To date, I had always envied Magda for the way she had succeeded in dealing with her past through the skillful guidance of her psychiatrist. Now I was hearing something quite different. What could it be, this terrible thing that was haunting her?

"What would you like me to do, Mr. Singer? How can I help Magda?"

"I need to speak with her. I know that Magda trusts you . . . holds you in very high esteem. I'm sure that she'll contact you again before too long. I want you to try and arrange a meeting between the two of us. Or the three of us, if you would like to be included. I think that would be most helpful. Please, when you see her, Miss Dunn, try to convince her to confide in me. Reassure her that I'm her friend as well as her sponsor. If there's anything really awful in her past, I'll understand. I won't let it come between us. I think you know that, don't you? Magda must be made to understand that she need not fear losing me."

He sounded desperate. It was a plea for my assistance. How could I refuse, especially since it concerned Magda's welfare, perhaps her very existence!

"All right, Mr. Singer. I'll do the best I can. I promise to get in touch with you as soon as I hear from her. As you must know, I want to help her as badly as you do."

"Of course. I knew I could count on you. Thank you so very much!"

I took down his phone number before hanging up. But, when I turned to confront my friend, I was amazed to find her gone.

Chapter XXXV

THE REVELATION

I made my way home in the fading glow of New York at dusk. Trying to make sense of it all made my head swim. There simply had to be an explanation! Mr. Singer had alluded to it, but I had to find out for myself. I had to see Magda!

When I got home I found the apartment empty. It was Thursday, I reminded myself, the day Jerry worked late. He would be over later for a snack before going home. And Mother was at the movies with one of her friends. She always discreetly arranged to attend a late show on Thursdays. I was grateful to be by myself for a while. I needed time to sort out my thoughts, and to ponder the cause of Magda's strange behavior. I was somehow tied in to her emotionally, perhaps because of our similar experiences in Europe, but I wasn't sure. All I knew was that she had unsettled me terribly.

I went through the motions of gathering items for a tasty snack, but my mind was elsewhere tonight. I could feel the walls of the kitchen closing in on me. It was a feeling I had experienced before, in my own apartment in Budapest, before I was taken prisoner by the Nazis. I walked into the living room and stared out the window to the east . . . across the Atlantic . . . to Europe . . . and to Auschwitz.

Auschwitz! There was a connection there, somewhere.

Thinking of Magda and her problems somehow reminded me of that ghastly place.

What could it be, this terrible thing that was haunting Magda, ruining her life? I had undergone the most terrifying experiences myself, experiences that I had somehow miraculously survived. But Magda? If she had survived them the first time, they were now about to exact their full toll the second time around. Could I expect a similar fate?

I didn't know the answer, I could only guess. But right now, I needed to clear my head with some fresh air. I called George on the intercom and asked him to have Jerry come up to the roof to find me when he arrived.

The darkness had descended on the city by the time I got upstairs. There was only a tiny layer of orange left on the western horizon. Just as well! The ugliness of the roof with its tarpaper surface would remain hidden from me. I was enchanted by the city lights glowing all around me, the highways shining in the darkness like pearl necklaces.

But my thoughts were not centered on the beauty of the city at night. Very quickly, they turned to my friend and her terrible problems. How strange they made me feel! My conflicting emotions encompassed simultaneous feelings of both sympathy and envy. And, above all, confusion and puzzlement. I had to see Magda again. I had to make her confide in me, and Mr. Singer too, of course. I had to help her overcome those horrible memories. But how? And when?

Suddenly, I found myself hallucinating. Instead of the sounds of car horns, I began hearing the hum of the electrified fences. And the auto exhaust began to take on the odor of smoke, belching from the ovens, as they consumed their consignment of human remains. I felt as though I was about to drop through a trap door, back into that awful past . . . back to the memories I had tried so hard to repress. I became so absorbed in my thoughts that I never heard the door to the roof open. Quite suddenly I noticed a silhouette, only a shade darker than the night, standing off to my right.

"Alice!" I heard a voice call my name. It was Magda. My wish had come true!

"Magda! What are you doing up here? How did you know where to find me?"

"George told me you were up here." I saw a flame from a match flicker. Then a cigarette glowed in the dark. "I don't know what I'm doing here. I really didn't want to burden you with my problems. But I'm desperate. I have no one to go to . . . not Dr. Lovas, not Mr. Singer . . . no one. You're the only one I can really trust to understand. You've been a victim yourself. You can appreciate what I've had to go through. Will you help me?"

"Of course, my dear. I've already asked you to take me into your confidence. You know I want to help you any way I can."

She walked over to me, facing me, her eyes on the ground. "I can't go on like this. What am I to do? I feel my life going up in smoke. My career is demolished. I have nothing left to live for. Please, Alice, help me!"

She turned away, walking to the edge of the roof and glancing down at the street far below. Slowly, I walked over to her. I took her right hand in mine and gradually, but forcefully, pulled her away from the edge.

"Magda, I want to help you. Nothing is ever as bad as it seems at a particular moment. I think I can help you. But you must trust me, and Mr. Singer too. We're your friends. We want to help you work these things out, whatever they are. But we can't do anything unless you take us into your confidence."

She lit another cigarette, using the stub of the first one. Then she discarded the butt over the edge of the roof. She took a long puff, then exhaled into the air, forming a cloud over our heads. When she finally started to speak once more, her voice was filled with desperation. She was pleading for her life.

"You don't understand . . . either of you. I have a problem without a solution. My past is closing in on me . . . choking me. I can't deal with it. Not even with Dr. Lovas's help."

"Magda, dear, tell me. Why is this happening to you now? You seemed to be handling everything so well until just a few days ago. You had everything going your way . . . your career, your association with Mr. Singer, your upcoming concert. What changed it all? What happened?"

"Well, Dr. Lovas . . . he was helping me to recall my experiences at Dachau, so I would be able to deal with them more effectively . . . put them behind me, as he put it. But instead, the memories became more vivid. They started taking over my whole life . . . my piano playing, my eating, my sleep. I began thinking about them constantly. My dreams became nightmares. I haven't had a night's rest in over a week. Dr. Lovas kept saying that I had to expect a reaction. That the memories would go away eventually. But I'm afraid that before that happens, I'll be gone. I can't deal with those awful, horrible nightmares. I'm afraid that the only way to make them go away is to kill myself!"

"Magda, you must listen to me! You must confide in me. You must share those awful memories with me. It's the only way I'll be able to help you."

"All right. I'll do what you ask. But I warn you. You won't think of them any differently than I. You'll hate me just like I hate myself. Just like Mr. Singer will reject me if he finds out. You won't tell him, will you?"

"Not if you don't want me to. But I'm sure that you're mistaken. Neither of us will reject you, no matter what happened . . . no matter what you've done. I promise you. We both love you, you must know that."

"That's easy for you to say. You don't know what I've done. When I'm finished, neither Mr. Singer nor you will ever want anything to do with me again."

"All right. Test me. Tell me what happened . . . the terrible thing that's causing you all that anguish."

She stepped back, lighting another cigarette before the last one had been half-consumed. She closed her eyes and clasped her hands in front of her, opening and closing them as she began speaking, her voice a mere whisper.

"It all happened *in* late November or early December of 1945. It was cold . . . terribly cold. They had us working on the railroad tracks . . . from dawn to dusk, every day. They wouldn't let us rest. If one of us collapsed, they took her away. We would never see her again. I knew that I couldn't last the winter. I wasn't strong . . . like many of the others in our detail. We had been specially selected because of our youth . . . our potential for work. But I was a pianist. My hands had never been asked to hold a pick or shovel. I had used them only for playing the piano . . . for combing my hair . . . for trying on clothes. I had led a very sheltered life. You know what I mean, don't you?"

She looked up at me, waiting for an acknowledgement. I nodded my head.

"Go on, Magda. Please. I know exactly what you mean. I was at one of those camps also, you know. Please, go on with your story."

"Well, one day two Nazi guards were watching us work. I could tell that they were studying me . . . watching my every move. I thought they were going to take me away because I was unable to work as efficiently as the others. Then, one of the guards, as SS officer, beckoned to me with his swagger stick. He was motioning for me to follow him. I thought it was all over. But what could I do? He would have shot me on the spot if I refused or tried to run away. I had witnessed such executions many times before."

She hesitated, drawing in her breath at the memory. I could tell how difficult it was for her to continue. But somehow she managed it.

I followed him reluctantly, several paces behind. He was tall and blond, and had he not been SS, I could have thought him handsome. When we finally got to his office, he just stood there, staring at me with those gray eyes . . . looking right through me. When he spoke it was in measured tones. I understood his clear German pronunciation very well, but I didn't want to let him know that. But that didn't stop him . . ."

There were tears in her eyes. She stopped speaking, as if questioning whether to go on with her story. It was the proper time for me to interject my own feelings. To lend my support.

"Please go on, Magda. I know how awful this must make you feel, but it's important that you continue . . . that you share the horrors of that moment with someone . . . a friend who'll understand."

As she began to speak again, her whole body shook visibly. I stood next to her, taking her hand in mine.

"You can imagine what happened next. First, he carefully locked his office door. Then he walked over to me, and with one forceful grasp he ripped the few clothes I was wearing off my body. Then he threw me to the floor, and in a flash he was on top of me. He raped me again and again, all the while whispering what a beautiful girl I was. The most beautiful in the camp, he said, as if that meant anything to me."

Magda began to sob. I knew that she would be unable to continue. I walked over to her and held her in my arms, hugging her tightly to me. "The pig!" I murmured. "It's not the first time I heard of something like that. It wasn't your fault, Magda! There was nothing you could have done to stop him. And you certainly couldn't help your appearance! You had nothing whatever to do with what happened. Please! Remember that!"

She stopped sobbing as my reassuring words comforted her. She extracted a handkerchief from her pocketbook and wiped her tears.

"That's not all, Alice. You don't know the worst of it! After he had satisfied himself he told me to get dressed. Then he said that he was going to change my work detail. I would have to report to the warehouse from now on. He led me over there and showed me how to sort the clothes and shoes that they took from the new arrivals. I had to admit, finally, that I was able to understand his directions.

"So the next day I went to the warehouse. I was happy to be working indoors, out of the cold. And the treatment at the hands of the *Aufseherinnen* seemed a little more humane. Also, the work itself wasn't nearly as physically demanding as my last detail."

"Well, it sounds as though you were lucky to have been befriended by this officer. After all, he saved you from the worst, didn't he?" I chimed in.

"How can you say such a thing? How can you be so naive? Don't you understand what he had in mind?" Magda looked at me with frustration in her eyes. "He wasn't being altruistic! It was all part of a scheme! At the end of the day he came to me and asked how I liked my new job. I had to admit that I preferred it to my former work. He then winked at me slyly and told me that my hours would have to be extended to make up for my light workload. He wanted me back at the warehouse at night, but I was not to tell anyone where I was going. He made it sound very secretive." She paused momentarily to gather her strength and continue the story.

"Well, that night I slipped out of the barracks unnoticed, and proceeded cautiously to the warehouse. He was waiting there for me with another SS officer, who introduced himself to me. I don't even remember what he looked like. Then the second officer led me to a small room off the warehouse storage area. They must have used it as a day room. It had a sofa, some chairs, and several small tables in it. There were playing cards, ashtrays filled with cigarette butts, and dirty cups scattered all over the place. It was a real mess! I thought that he had brought me there to straighten it up and clean it. But that was not on his mind at all."

I realized how hard it was for her to go on.

"I pleaded with him. I begged him not to make me participate in any more sexual games. I told him that I was just an inexperienced virgin." She heaved a sigh of resignation. "Nothing helped. He just laughed at me. He said that I was hardly a virgin after what he had heard . . . that I would get better with experience . . . that he would teach me all I had to know."

She began sobbing, huge heaving sobs.

"Oh, Magda! You poor darling! No, don't tell me!"

She stifled her crying, nodding affirmatively. "Yes, he did it also. He forced me to have sex with him. But somehow, it didn't seem as bad as my first experience. I don't remember feeling anything. It was as though I had become a zombie . . . a person without any emotions . . . without a conscience.

"For the remainder of my incarceration I did it with all the officers. They took their turns at me every night. I became the camp . . ." Her voice broke. She tried to speak but nothing came out. Finally she whispered it . . . the word she loathed. She enunciated it with all the hatred she could muster.

"Yes. Alice. Can you believe it? I became the camp WHORE!"

"Listen, Magda! Remember the circumstances. You couldn't help yourself! It was either that, or the ovens. You mustn't blame yourself!"

"No, Alice. It was only like that at the beginning. After the first few encounters I actually became a willing accomplice to their lust. It stopped bothering me. I almost began to look forward to receiving some real bread from them. And they gave me chocolate bars . . . and marzipan. Oh, how I loved the marzipan! And I didn't have to work in the bitter cold. After a while they even had a mattress there.

"Naturally, the other inmates knew what I was doing. They rejected me. No one would look at me, much less talk to me.

"Then, after some time I began to get this strange sensation whenever I got up in the morning. At first, I attributed it to a lack of sleep. But then I began to feel dizzy and lightheaded as well. Sometimes I would be overcome by nausea. All I wanted to do was to stay in bed and sleep. I soon realized that something was wrong. Finally, one evening, I received permission to visit the camp infirmary. It was run by a woman doctor, herself an inmate. She told me what I least wanted to hear. That I was pregnant!"

"My first instinct was to kill myself. They, those Nazis, certainly would have done it for me if they had found out. But then I thought of another solution. I asked the doctor if she would perform an abortion on me. But she refused. She said she only had their permission to dispense medication for illnesses and to clean wounds, nothing else. She said that if they found out, she would be shot. What could I do?"

She looked at me as if asking for advice. I cringed, knowing what Magda was about to tell me.

"There was only one way out. I stole a piece of baling wire from the warehouse when no one was watching. That night, while everyone slept, I used the wire to abort that little Nazi monster inside my body."

She began to laugh . . . a low haunting laugh. I stood there, horrified. I could hardly imagine the suffering she had undergone. Suffering that had never ended . . . and perhaps never would.

She continued. "The irony is that we were liberated the very next day. Can you imagine that? If I had waited one more day, I could have been helped by a real doctor. But of course, it was too late. When they found me I was already unconscious. I had lost too much blood. But, unfortunately, I survived somehow. When I finally did regain consciousness some weeks later, I was in a hospital. You remember, Alice. You visited me there. Well, you know the rest."

She paused, as if waiting for a comment from me. Her face was a study in agony and pain. She had done her part by recalling the gruesome details. They really did support her justifiable feelings of guilt. But now it was up to me to offer her the support and the comforting she needed so desperately.

But I could only stand there, unnerved, not knowing what to say.

"You see, Alice, I knew you would react this way. You're as disgusted with my behavior as I am . . . as Mr. Singer will be if he finds out. There is no excuse for it. I'm a whore . . . a collaborator! I did it with the enemy! Those vile Nazis! I satisfied their lust. I deserve to die . . . yes, even to be shot like a traitor! Don't you agree, Alice? Be honest with me! Give me your honest reaction. I'll know if you're lying to make me feel good!" She was shouting. Her eyes were wild, almost popping out of her head.

What could I say? I could hardly approve of her actions. But, then, who was I to judge others? Hadn't I also collaborated by making those clothes for that horrible Margit? But that had not been in the same class as Magda's behavior. I would never have done what she did. But we were so different. Also, neither of us had done anything to harm the other inmates. We were both victims, not perpetrators. We did what we felt had to be done to stay alive under the most dreadful of circumstances. No, I could not indict her for her behavior. I had to make her understand that what she had done was not criminal.

I was about to make my point to her, when Jerry appeared on the rooftop. I ran to him, throwing my arms around his neck. I surprised myself. I had never done that before. It was an almost automatic reaction. But I needed his comforting, and his sound, rational advice very badly. Hearing Magda's story had made me vulnerable all over again. It had aroused those old, bad feelings within me. I wanted him to reassure me . . . to let me know that I was blameless of any wrongdoing. And of course, that Magda was innocent as well.

After a long hug and kiss, I let go of him. I wanted to do for Magda what Jerry was doing for me. But, as I looked to the spot where I had just left her standing a moment ago, I was surprised to find her gone. Only a small pile of cigarette butts remained in her place. She had disappeared once again, and before I had been able to give her the reassurance she so badly wanted!

Jerry and I searched for her on the roof, looking behind every structure, down every stairway. But she was gone. Would I ever be able to assuage her guilt now . . . let her know that her indiscretions required no further punishment? That her agony and remorse had served as sufficient punishment already?

I certainly hoped so. But it would have to wait. I had no idea where to find her.

Chapter XXXVI

THE FUNERAL

When we returned to the apartment, Jerry removed his hat and coat and motioned to me to sit next to him on the sofa. He took me in his arms, and without saying a word, held me close to him. He could see that I was unnerved and badly shaken. After a few minutes I was beginning to feel much better. His presence, his strength and caring, were a salve for my wounds.

"What do you think I should do, Jerry?" I asked, knowing that he would be able to provide the answers that I, myself, felt utterly incapable of supplying.

"First you have to tell me what happened up there. I can't offer any advice unless I know the whole story." He took both my hands in his, and looked straight into my eyes. "Listen, I have an idea. Why don't you make us a pot of tea and then you can tell me all about it."

It was the attorney in him speaking. His impeccable logic was once again taking charge of the situation. I admired him greatly for it.

After making the tea, accompanied by some cheese and crackers, I sat down next to him and began relating the details of my last two encounters with Magda, as well as Mr. Singer's latest phone call. I watched the intent expression on his face as he listened to every detail. He never interrupted my story, and when I had finished, he looked at me with sympathy in his eyes.

"I can see that this poor girl's problems have really gotten to you. Now that she has finally let you in on the gruesome details of her past, you must be feeling a greater responsibility for her. Especially since you were unable to get across your feelings on the matter and assuage some of her guilt. Tell me, babe, what do you think she'll do now?" He hesitated, then added cautiously, "Are you afraid that she might kill herself?"

"Yes, Jerry, I am. But how can I stop her? I don't even know where to find her. Mr. Singer mentioned that he had been unsuccessful in his attempts to locate her over the past few days. She never answered her phone or her doorbell."

"Well, nonetheless, we have to start by trying her at home. We might get lucky. After that, the only other person who may know her whereabouts, according to what you've told me, is her psychiatrist, what's his name?"

"Dr. Lovas. He's the same one I visited. He's Mr. Singer's friend. I think you're right Jerry. If I can't get her at home, I'll call Mr. Singer and ask him to have Lovas contact Magda. I'm sure Mr. Singer will also want to know what took place tonight, up on the roof. Will you excuse me?"

"Sure. Do what you have to do. Don't worry about me. I'll just make myself at home."

With Jerry's reassurance, I proceeded into the kitchen and started dialing the numbers. Just as I expected, there was no answer at Magda's place. Then, when I dialed Mr. Singer's number I was surprised to have him pick up on the first ring. It seemed as though he had been waiting for my call.

"Hello, Miss Dunn!" He sounded more formal and solemn than usual. "I've just been trying to reach you. We must have some mental telepathy between us. Your line was busy, though."

"Yes, I know. I was trying to reach Magda. I wanted to speak to her." There was a momentary awkward silence from his end. When he spoke again, it was in a halting voice.

"I'm sorry to have to tell you this, Miss Dunn, but I'm afraid it's too late for that." I could feel a choking sensation in my throat as I dreaded the words I was about to hear. "I got a phone call from the police not five minutes ago. Magda's dead . . ." His voice began to break. He couldn't go on speaking.

I gasped. I didn't want to believe what I was hearing. I was too late!

"She must have jumped off her roof. They found her on the sidewalk, next to her building . . . I still can't believe it myself. What could have made her do it?"

Jerry was standing next to me now, his arm around my shoulder. He realized something was terribly wrong.

"Magda's dead, Jerry," I whispered to him, holding my hand over the speaker. "She committed suicide." Then I started to sob and shake, the phone dropping from my grasp. Jerry grabbed the instrument and began speaking into it. My knees felt terribly weak. His voice sounded so far away.

"Hello, Mr. Singer! This is Jerry Adler. I'm a close friend of Alice's. Can you give me the details. I'm afraid she's too unnerved to speak to you right now. I'm taking her into the living room to sit down. Please hold the line!"

He helped me into the living room, sitting me down on the couch. "Here, let me pour you some of this tea. Go ahead, drink it. It'll make you feel a little better. Good! . . . I'll finish speaking to Mr. Singer. You stay here."

"Yes, I'm back," I heard him say into the phone. "Please go on."

He was back at my side in just a minute or so. "Mr. Singer said that the funeral will have to be tomorrow. They want to get it in before the Sabbath. He'll call me at my office in the morning with the details. Then I'll get in touch with you. Okay?"

Jerry and I sat on the couch, talking into the night. I had so much I wanted to share with him about Magda. He listened sympathetically to every word, but as the hour grew late, he realized a decision had to be made.

"I don't want to leave you alone tonight. Would you like me to spend the night here with you? I'll be happy to keep you company."

I thanked him for his thoughtfulness, and for listening to me all night long, but I reassured him that Mother would be back momentarily and that I would not be alone. Jerry gave in and kissed me good night, but not before letting me know that he would cancel his appointments so he could attend Magda's funeral with me. I was most grateful. I was just beginning to realize how much I was depending on his moral support.

After Jerry had left I found myself too exhausted to wait up for Mother. I knew that I lacked the strength to tell her all that had happened. I would speak to her in the morning.

But as tired as I was, I didn't get much sleep that night. I kept waking up in a cold sweat every time I drowsed off. Then, when my eyes closed, I would start to relive again some of my Auschwitz experiences: the line-ups, the barracks, the electrified fence . . . It was all too real . . . too terrifying. I began thinking about Magda. I still found it hard to believe that she was gone . . . that I would never see her or speak to her again. I began to wonder about my part in her suicide. Could I have prevented it, I asked myself over and over again.

It soon became apparent that my mind would not let me sleep in peace that night. Finally, I got up, dressed, and made my way in the elevator down to the street. The early morning air was chilly, but it felt good. It helped to clear my head of all the night monsters. After a brief walk around the block, I went back upstairs and made myself breakfast. The phone rang promptly at 7 AM I hoped it hadn't wakened Mother. It was Jerry.

"Hi, how are you doing? Want to have breakfast with me? We can go to the Waldorf . . . or the Plaza. Or would you prefer the atmosphere of Chock-Full-o-Nuts?"

It was Jerry's way of trying to cheer me up. He knew how badly last night's experiences had affected me.

"Oh, Jerry! I'm so glad you called. But why not come up here? Mother's still sleeping, but I'll be glad to make you a Hungarian omelette and a cup of real coffee. Please come over. I need to speak with you."

"I'll be over in half an hour. Don't let the water burn."

There was a knock on the door at precisely 7:35. It was Jerry. I let him in and we sat and talked in the kitchen for an hour. He was a great listener, and I was happy to have someone other than my poor mother to pour my heart out to. Before he left, we decided to have him call me at my shop as soon as he heard from Mr. Singer about the funeral.

When I got to work that morning, I found it very hard to concentrate on what I was doing. Suddenly I realized that I still hadn't told Mother about Magda. Strange, I mused. Since my arrival in America, Mother had always been the first one I had gone to with my problems. Now, Jerry had taken on that role. I pondered the significance of that change before dialing my home.

Mother was naturally quite shocked by the news. She wanted to accompany us to the funeral parlor, and I told her that Jerry was going to pick us up at home later in the day. She promised to wait for me.

Jerry, Mother, and I arrived at Magda's funeral some time that afternoon. I couldn't remember where it was or when we got there. There were wreaths and other flowers around the casket; Mr. Singer had seen to that. But there were only two other people in attendance besides Mr. Singer and the three of us. The rabbi mentioned that Magda's mother, and the rest of her family, had been killed in the Holocaust. Mr. Singer gave the eulogy. He spoke of Magda's courage throughout her captivity, and how she had never given up on her hope to become a fine concert pianist. It was an eloquent speech, but somehow it left me frustrated and dissatisfied. There was not one mention made of the role the Nazis had played in her death. In my mind, they had killed her as surely as if she had been gassed and thrown in an oven, like so many millions of other innocents. I wanted to say something, but quickly realized that her memory would not be well served if her reason for suicide were revealed. Right now, Jerry, Mother, and I, and Dr. Lovas, of course, were the only ones who knew. We would let the ugly details die with her. Her honor would be preserved.

After the services, Jerry took Mother home. She had declined his thoughtful invitation to take both of us out to dinner to cheer us up. Naturally, I accepted.

I don't even remember where we went that evening, or what we had to eat. I only remember Jerry's gentle and sympathetic handling of my fragile state of mind. He knew what losing Magda had meant to me . . . how my life had become so intertwined with hers. He gave me the time to grieve, but he also made sure that I would not think that my own life might some day come to a similar end. And he let me know that he cared very deeply for me and my future. Then, from out of nowhere, he sprung a surprise.

"Alice, do you know what day this is?"

I looked at him blankly. "What do you mean, Jerry?"

"It's the 750th day since we met. Haven't you been keeping count? And, I would like to celebrate the occasion by inviting you to accompany me on a trip to Albany this weekend. I promise you, you won't be disappointed!"

Chapter XXXVII

A PROPHECY FULFILLED

Jerry and I sat next to each other in the half-empty train, watching the shabby tenements of the South Bronx whiz past the dirty train windows. It was Thursday morning and we were on our way to Albany, which I knew to be the state capital. Jerry had asked me to accompany him on some seemingly mysterious mission, which he was loathe to explain. Naturally, I had agreed to go along. As we sat there, holding hands, I could feel the tension in his body. He hadn't uttered a word since our boarding the train at Grand Central Station a half-hour earlier, and I felt reluctant to press him. I decided to let him divulge the reason for our excursion whenever he was ready to do so. In the meantime, my own private thoughts reflected back on other train rides . . . many eons ago. How different this one seemed! I was feeling so secure and protected and filled with anticipation.

Jerry was the first one to break the silence. "You're probably wondering why we're taking this trip, aren't you?"

"Yes, to tell the truth, I'm dying of curiosity. But I'm perfectly content to wait for your explanation. You know that you have my implicit trust in these matters. On the other hand, I must admit that you've made things a little difficult for me. I was at a total loss in attempting to answer Mother's questions this morning, and also, I didn't quite know how to dress for whatever it is we're doing. Do I look all right to you?"

"You look great! You always do. I promise I'll let you in on my little secret as soon as I get some inkling of how things go up there. But I guarantee you won't be disappointed, no matter what." He squeezed my hand reassuringly, then continued looking out the window.

The passing scenery was quite lovely now, with rolling farmland and distant mountains replacing the ugly tenements and crowded streets of the inner city. I had never had the opportunity to venture beyond the city limits since my arrival in the United States and I was surprised to find such a great contrast in landscape so close by. I promised myself to get Jerry to take me on another trip into the country this summer . . . just for pleasure. But before I had a chance to contemplate any additional trips, I became conscious of the train slowing down as it pulled into the Albany station. The excitement within me was aroused once more as I speculated on when Jerry would reveal his little secret. I still had not the slightest idea as to why we had come to Albany.

Upon debarking from the train, Jerry hailed a taxi and asked the driver to take us to 39 Columbia Street. It took less than ten minutes to get there. I was somewhat disappointed to find our destination to be an unimpressive, fairly old office building in the downtown area. Once inside, Jerry consulted the building directory and we took the elevator up to the second floor. As the elevator door opened, we found ourselves facing a sign on the wall which read: "N.Y. State Alcoholic Beverage Control Board." As we entered the reception room, the secretary at the desk looked up from her book and inquired, "May I help you, please?"

"Yes, I'm Jerry Adler. I have an appointment with the commissioner for 11:30." It was the lawyer speaking again, brief and self-assured.

"Oh yes, Mr. Adler. The Commissioner is waiting for you." With that, she picked up the phone, and after dialing a number, said to the person on the other end, "Mr. Adler is here to see you, Commissioner." Then, she directed Jerry to a door marked with gold lettering: "John F. O'Connell, Commissioner." "Please go in, Mr. Adler," she directed Jerry. Now she turned her attention to me. "You can take a seat over there, Mrs. Adler. I think you'll find some magazines on that table that might interest you."

Strangely, Jerry, who was still within earshot, did not correct her. And neither did I. It was the first time I had heard that name being used, and quite frankly, I liked the sound of it.

Before Jerry disappeared into the commissioner's office he turned toward me and announced, "I don't think this will take too long. Please wait for me out here. I'll explain later." Then he was gone from view, as the door closed behind him.

The whole affair was really beginning to challenge my logic. What business did Jerry have to conduct with the commissioner of the N.Y. State Alcoholic Beverage Control Board? Could it have to do with some case he was working on? And why hadn't he corrected the secretary when she had falsely assumed that I was his wife? "Very strange," I thought to myself. But I knew I would soon have all the answers. Jerry had promised that. I assumed that he had good reasons for his actions. But still, I could hardly keep my attention focused on the magazine I had selected, as I waited for the door to open once more.

After about a half-hour or so, Jerry and a tall, distinguished-looking man emerged from the commissioner's office. Jerry was the first to speak as he saw me rise from my seat. "I want you to meet Commissioner O'Connell, my new boss." Then he turned to the commissioner. "Commissioner, this is my fiancée, Alice Dunn."

"Did I hear correctly? Was Jerry introducing me as his fiancée?" My head started to spin as I contemplated the meaning of his choice of words.

The commissioner walked toward me with a broad grin on his handsome Irish face. "I'm real pleased to meet you, Alice. You don't mind my calling you by your first name, do you?"

For one of the few times in my life, I was speechless. I nodded my head in agreement, and took the man's hand. It was a huge paw that completely enveloped my hand in its firm grip.

"I've heard a lot about you from Jerry," the commissioner continued. "I can readily see why Jerry is so enamored with you. Would you mind letting me hear some of that charming Hungarian accent?"

I was at a loss for words. I hated making a complete fool of myself, so I managed to utter something innocuous about hoping that he and Jerry would have a good working relationship. The commissioner then shook hands with both of us, and wished us a safe return to the city.

"Don't forget the swearing-in ceremony on February 17th!" he shouted after us, as we walked down the corridor toward the elevators. "I'm sure the Governor will have no problem getting Senate confirmation for your candidacy." Jerry waved to him as the doors closed behind us.

By now my patience was rapidly approaching its limit. I needed some explanations from Jerry, and the privacy of the elevator seemed as good a place as any.

"Jerry, why did you introduce me as your fiancée? You surprised . . ."

"I'm sorry, babe," Jerry interrupted, taking me into his arms and holding me tightly. "I should have said something on the way up. But I wanted to surprise you." He paused meaningfully, looking into my eyes with a devilish grin on his face. "Unfortunately, I'm going to have to ask you to bear with me for another few minutes. We have just enough time to catch the 12:30 train back to New York, if we hurry. Let me hail a cab and I promise to tell you everything as soon as we're on the train. Okay?"

I nodded my head in agreement and followed him out into the street. What other choice did I have?

As soon as we were seated on the train, Jerry began telling his story, his face flushed with excitement. It seems that Melvin Osterman, chairman of the Westside Republican Club, of which Jerry was an active member, had made several phone calls to Governor Thomas E. Dewey's office in Albany, recommending Jerry for a vacancy caused by the resignation of one of the assistant commissioners on the N.Y. State Alcoholic Beverage Control Board. Jerry had received a call from the commission office, asking him to come up to the Albany headquarters for an interview.

"Naturally, I was happy to comply. It was the opportunity I'd been waiting for. You know what the security of a job like that means for us, don't you?"

I nodded my head. I remembered Jerry telling me only recently why he was afraid of a serious relationship.

"Jerry, I'm truly thrilled for you. But does this mean that

you'll be moving to Albany? I don't think you're planning to commute there."

"Of course not. The Authority has an office in downtown New York at 270 Broadway. That's where I'll be working. Isn't that great?"

"It sure is! I'm so happy for you! But let me get back to another subject. Why did you introduce me as your fiancée? You really gave me quite a shock, you know. You left me almost speechless."

"I'm sorry, babe. I know I should have said something on the way up, but I was a little concerned about the interview. You know, I was the last of eight candidates to be seen by the commissioner. And I understand they were all well qualified. I guess my experience with litigation from the war crimes trials helped me get the job. Gee, I hope I didn't upset you too much!"

"Upset me? Of course not! But you certainly surprised me. Was that your idea of a marriage proposal?"

Jerry fumbled in his coat pocket and pulled out a tiny, velvet-covered box. He placed the box in my lap. "I guess this is a little more conventional. I hope you'll like the contents."

I opened the box to discover a beautiful diamond ring. For the second time on the same day I was dumbfounded. I threw my arms around Jerry's neck, kissing him and crying at the same time.

Just then, the conductor entered the car to punch our tickets. "Hey, you lovebirds! Cut that out! You're making me jealous." As he took the tickets from Jerry, he noticed the small open box in my lap. "Hey, are you two engaged? Congratulations!" As he walked away from us through the empty car, he began whistling a familiar tune. I recognized it immediately. It was Gershwin's "Love Walked Right In."

"Isn't that lovely?" I commented. "That song sure echoes my feelings. What a nice man."

That night, Jerry and I had dinner at Csardas again. The setting was most romantic, with champagne and candlelight accompanying a superb meal. We found ourselves discussing many details of our upcoming nuptials, including a possible date.

"How would you like to be married by the same judge who's going to officiate at my swearing-in ceremony? His name is Brisaque.

He was one of my favorite professors at law school. I know he'd be delighted to marry us. If you like, I'll call him on Monday and arrange a date," Jerry offered enthusiastically.

The idea suited me perfectly. I hardly wanted a formal wedding, since Jerry had mentioned that it would make him uncomfortable. Also, I realized that Mother would want to pay for it and I certainly didn't wish to cause her any financial hardships. As it was, she had graciously offered us her apartment to live in until we were able to find something suitable. She casually said that she had been promising to visit her cousin in Florida for a long time, and this seemed the perfect opportunity. I could not possibly turn down her most generous offer.

Thus it came to pass that on December 10th, 1950, Jerry and I became husband and wife in Judge Brisaque's impressive chambers in the courthouse on Foley Square. It was a day I would remember forever. I couldn't have been happier or more proud than I was on the day I became Mrs. Jerome Adler, and a citizen of the United States of America. To be permanently united with both the man and the country I loved was the achievement of a lifelong dream.

As Judge Brisaque declared us man and wife, I glanced at the family members who had gathered to honor us on our day. There, in their midst, I thought I spotted a familiar face. Was I imagining it, or was that really Silbiger Boriska, her craggy features creased in a broad smile? She seemed to be nodding her head at us in approval. It was then that I realized yet another, and by far the happiest of her predictions for me, had come to pass.

EPILOGUE

In spite of the world going up in flames, our whole family reunited in America, which is quite a miracle. "Thank you Boriska!"

Happy events followed one another. The man in my life asked me to marry him. It all happened so fast. Getting married, to build a new life, represented a wonderful challenge. I liked challenges. Born a perfectionist, my total devotion was centered on becoming the best wife I could be.

My husband's steadily growing professional success gave me time to create a home, pursue studies in the Art Students League, attend lectures, collect antique dolls and furniture and work as a volunteer in the Lighthouse for the Blind.

Jerry and I were always grateful to God, that we could make my dear Mother's few remaining years joyful, involving her in all our activities. How much I count my blessings, that after my purgatory, I can pray at my Mother's graveside; she doesn't have to share it with thousands!

Growing professional demands took their toll, and we never regretted our move to Sarasota, Florida, in exchange for New York's vibrant life. A wide range of civic and charitable activities, as well as social commitments took much of my time. The never ending amazement of nature took the rest.

Jerry passed away in 1988. His razor-sharp mind and recall, his sense of humor to the end, made him the special person loved by all who knew him. And life goes on.

✱ *"When I speak to children, I tell them they are looking at a survivor. I tell them they are America's future and they must never say to themselves, 'I can't do it!'" Today Alice Dunn Adler is a healer of souls as she shares her moving story with all who, like her, are "young" enough to fight for freedom from prejudice. hyprocracy and discrimination.*

Alice Dunn Adler

.